SUMMONING THE GODS

ESSAYS ON PAGANISM IN A GOD-FORSAKEN WORLD

BY

COLLIN CLEARY

EDITED BY GREG JOHNSON

Counter-Currents Publishing Ltd.
San Francisco
2011

Copyright © 2011 by Counter-Currents Publishing Ltd.
All rights reserved

Cover image:
Arthur Rackham, "Wotan's Farewell"

Cover design by
Kevin I. Slaughter

Published in the United States by
COUNTER-CURRENTS PUBLISHING LTD.
P.O. Box 22638
San Francisco, CA 94122
USA
http://www.counter-currents.com/

Hardcover Edition:
ISBN: 978-1-935965-21-3

Paperback Edition:
ISBN: 978-1-935965-22-0

COLLIN CLEARY

(Courtesy Max Ribaric/*Occidental Congress*)

"Larvatus prodeo." — René Descartes

Contents

Editor's Introduction ♦ iii

Author's Acknowledgements ♦ xi

Neo-Paganism

1. Knowing the Gods ♦ 1
2. Summoning the Gods:
The Phenomenology of Divine Presence ♦ 21
3. Paganism without Gods:
Alain de Benoist's *On Being a Pagan* ♦ 62

Nordic Paganism

4. What God Did Odin Worship? ♦ 81
5. Philosophical Notes on the Runes ♦ 93
6. The Missing Man in Norse Cosmogony ♦ 121
7. Karl Maria Wiligut's Commandments of Gôt ♦ 132

Among the Ruins

8. Patrick McGoohan's *The Prisoner* ♦ 148
9. The Spiritual Journey of Alejandro Jodorowsky ♦ 172

Index ♦ 193

About the Author ♦ 198

Editor's Introduction

Collin Cleary—the enigmatic sage of Sandpoint, Idaho—burst onto the intellectual scene almost ten years ago, with the publication of the first volume of the journal *TYR*. Along with Joshua Buckley and Michael Moynihan, Cleary was one of the founding editors of *TYR*, having a hand in all aspects of the first volume and contributing three substantial articles and several reviews. (Although he is now no longer involved in editing *TYR*, he continues to contribute to it.)

Who is Collin Cleary? He could accurately be described as a theologian of neo-paganism, specifically of the Nordic variety. He is also a Traditionalist with a capital T, meaning that he falls within the same school of thought as René Guénon and Julius Evola. He is a *Tantrika* (no mean feat for a Nordic pagan). And he is an anti-modern thinker. Cleary is a polymath who has read widely in philosophy, religion, mysticism, mythology, and literature. His principal influences are a surprising combination of figures: Martin Heidegger, D. H. Lawrence, G. W. F. Hegel, Lao Tzu, Evola (but not Guénon, interestingly), the Indologist Alain Daniélou, and the Nordic pagan theorist Edred Thorsson. All of Cleary's interests and influences are on display in the remarkable essays collected in this volume.

The *Leitmotiv* of these essays is the hypothesis that our ancestors possessed a special kind of "openness" which made them aware of the gods—something that we have now lost. In other words, Cleary does not believe that our ancestors "invented" their gods; instead, they were literally aware of aspects of reality now closed to us. Cleary believes that this openness is closely bound up with openness to the natural world (though they are not, strictly speaking, the same thing), and that the loss of this state of mind is the root of most of our modern problems: environmental abuse, the collapse of communities, the breakdown of relations between the sexes, the folly of social engineering, moral relativism, scientism, and much else. In

Cleary's view, therefore, the recovery of this openness would not just be simply a return to belief in the gods, but also an antidote to modern decadence and dissolution.

How exactly can openness be recovered? This is the difficult problem Cleary poses for himself. In one way or another, he deals with it in every essay in this volume. What we find in Cleary's body of work is not the same ideas repeated over and over, applied in cookie-cutter fashion to a succession of issues, but an approach that develops over time. From the first essay ("Knowing the Gods") to the last (on the autobiography of Alejandro Jodorowsky), we find Cleary continually elaborating and refining his answer to how we might recover the lost openness enjoyed by our ancestors.

"Knowing the Gods" is Cleary's first major essay, published in the flagship volume of *TYR*. The central feature of the piece is an insistence that we must eschew all attempts to "explain" the gods or our ancestors' experience of them. Why? Quite simply because trying to "explain" the gods—trying to say, for example that "Thor is just x" (or "the experience of Thor is *really* the experience of x")—reflects the standpoint of modern rationalism and scientism. To approach the gods in such a fashion is therefore to adopt a mindset that guarantees we will be unable to recover the perspective of our ancestors—who most certainly did not reflect on what the gods *really* were (or what the experience of them *really* was).

In effect, Cleary proposes a strategy for coming to knowledge of the gods: assume that the gods are a brute fact and that we have lost our ability to know them. Then address the issue of reconstructing or restoring the state of mind that made possible our ancestors' experience of the gods. He takes this position, in part, simply because of the gross psychological implausibility of the claim that our ancestors simply "made up" their gods and then chose to believe in them. As he makes clear in a subsequent essay, Cleary is not insisting that we should believe that Thor wields a literal hammer, or that the gods of the Greeks are literally to be found atop Olympus (a claim the ancients, who had been to the top of Olympus, all knew to be literally false). But he believes that in speaking of the gods, our ancestors were speaking of, again, some aspect of reality of which we seemingly can no longer even conceive. To recover this, Clearly makes a Heideggerian proposal: that we adopt the standpoint of "openness to being."

Cleary tells us that openness to the gods begins with openness to the being of things as such. He argues that the "flight of the gods" begins not specifically with our disbelieving in them, but in the adoption of a more general attitude—what Heidegger calls *das Gestell* (translated into English, rather imperfectly, as "enframing"). This is the attitude of regarding all that exists as essentially raw material that waits upon human beings to rework or "perfect" it. This mindset is, in fact, the essence of modernity.

In a real sense modern people do not regard the things of this world as possessing any intrinsic being or nature. They are all pure potential, waiting for us to put our stamp upon them. Trees are potential pencils, a mighty river (to use Heidegger's famous example) is a potential power source, and the men of today are, with proper re-education, the new and improved men of tomorrow. For modern people, therefore, things have no real nature of their own—their nature is always something that has yet to emerge, with our assistance. And so modernity always orients itself toward the future, toward a promise of perfection to come. For Cleary, what causes the flight of the gods is just this attitude, which recognizes no limits on human power and rejects the idea of things having any definite, intrinsic being.

Cleary's essay "Summoning the Gods" (written for the second volume of *TYR*) provides a more expansive answer as to why he thinks this is the case. In this essay, Cleary argues that the experience of the gods *just is* an experience of wonder in the face of the being of things. Thus, openness to the gods presupposes openness to being-as-such. The experience of a god is man's wonder in the face of some aspect of reality he has not created, which awes him with its beauty, or power, or dreadfulness. We are struck by the sheer *facticity* of things; we wonder that certain things should be at all, or be the way that they are. It is like the Zen experience of *satori*, in which one is suddenly struck with awe before the simple fact that the rose bush *is*, or that the storm *is*. For Cleary, this experience is in fact the "intuition" a god. The gods thus might be described (and Cleary toys with this expression) as "regions of being," which have been personified and assigned iconographies and mythologies.

Clearly has not violated the strictures he laid down in "Knowing the Gods": the subsequent essay does not attempt to "explain away" the gods at all. In other words it does not reduce the experience of the gods to something else, thereby deflating and invalidating it. Like Rudolf Otto, Cleary is attempting a phenomenological description of divine presence: how the divine shows up to us; how we become aware of it. Cleary's ideas about how our ancestors encountered their gods are based partly upon the study of classical texts and upon philosophical speculation, guided by a sense of what is psychologically and culturally plausible. They are also partly inspired by Cleary's own personal experience: the result of following the recommendations he lays out in the original "appendix" to "Knowing the Gods" (published here for the first time).

Though Cleary believes it is impossible to "think" one's way back into the mindset of our pagan ancestors, he has drawn certain reasonable theoretical boundaries around what would constitute a cogent understanding of divine presence. For instance, Cleary insists, reasonably, that it is condescending and naïve to think that our ancestors took their myths and the symbolism and iconography of the gods literally. (Those who think that Cleary's phenomenological account of divine presence is, in fact, deflationary are probably those who have somehow assumed erroneously that a "genuine" experience of a god would be, for example, actually seeing a tall, one-eyed, humanoid Odin leaning on an enormous spear.) Cleary argues that myth and symbol are used to explicate or to "fix," imaginatively, the being of a god—or the nature of a region of being. Such myths and symbols sprang from the imagination spontaneously. There was, further, a "logic" to these imaginative offerings: once established, they allowed man to elaborate his knowledge of the regions of being, and to draw profound connections between one region and another. For Cleary, this imaginative reflection—occasioned by wonder in the presence of the being of things—is the basis for the Tradition extolled by Guénon, Evola, and others.

"Summoning the Gods" is a long and rich essay—the most substantial and important of Cleary's writings. Cleary supports the points he makes by reference to Traditional sources and even the etymology of words used to refer to the divine. He also draws interesting parallels between his ideas and those of authors like Ernst Cassirer and Hermann Usener. The essay includes a lengthy and fascinating discussion of how Cleary's phenomenology of divine presence can shed light on Plato's theory of forms—arguing, strikingly, that Platonism is "polytheism for atheists." (First time readers primarily interested in neo-paganism could be forgiven for skipping this section—though it contains profound reflections on ancient philosophy.)

"Knowing the Gods" and "Summoning the Gods" can safely be said to be Cleary's major theoretical works. His other essays fall into the following categories: those that deal narrowly with Germanic paganism, essays dealing with works concerning paganism, and essays dealing with popular culture.

Cleary's critical but respectful review of Alain de Benoist's *On Being a Pagan* is significant in that it reiterates his insistence in "Knowing the Gods" that those who would be pagans must reject anything that buys into modern Promethean anthropocentrism. Here, Cleary also goes on the attack against relativism (which appears in Benoist's book as Nietzschean "perspectivism"). Relativism is an ubiquitous feature of our modern world, and is certainly prevalent in the "neo-pagan" movement and in all aspects of the "new age." (Ironically, some of those who profess to be "radical Traditionalists" also espouse a kind of relativism.) Cleary argues, however, that relativism is not only an untenable position but a thoroughly modern one, incompatible with the perspective of our ancestors. As Heidegger taught us, openness to being is simultaneously openness to *truth*. If openness to the gods requires openness to being, then would-be pagans cannot recover belief in the gods if they imagine that truth is simply theirs to invent. The essay concludes with Cleary drawing again from Heidegger, and this time also from Lao Tzu. He suggests that what we need is not the Prometheanism of Benoist's quasi-Nietzschean paganism, but *Gelassenheit* ("letting being be") or *wu wei* ("non-action"). Openness to the gods requires that we relinquish the modern desire to control and manipulate—including the desire to manipulate ourselves into belief in the gods—and make a kind of "space" within ourselves, in which the divine might show itself again.

Cleary's essays on Nordic paganism are grounded in original source materials and in philology, but they also contain a great deal of speculation. In these essays, Cleary displays a remarkable knowledge of myth and the secondary literature surrounding it, as well as a wide knowledge of the philosophical and mystical traditions, both East and West. Cleary's essay on Karl Maria Wiligut is daring just in that it attempts to make sense out of the ideas of a man who was not only a member of Himmler's SS, but also thought by many to be insane. The essay does a remarkable job of making sense out of what often seems like nonsense. This piece and Cleary's "Philosophical Notes on the Runes" both show his deep immersion in the German philosophical tradition. Cleary originally wrote "Philosophical Notes on the Runes" purely as a personal exercise (it was first published in *Rûna* long after it was written). When Cleary sent a copy of the essay to Edred Thorsson shortly after completing it, he was promptly promoted in the Rune-Gild from "Learner" to "Fellow."

Cleary's essays "What God did Odin Worship?" and "The Missing Man in Norse Cosmogony" also display his fascination with Indian philosophy. "What God did Odin Worship?" is really an attempt to synthesize Asatru with Shaivism, and it is his most daring and speculative essay. Cleary has had a long-standing interest in Tantra and Shaivism, but was troubled by their apparent incompatibility with the Nordic pagan tradition. Feeling a strong affinity for both, for many years he studied the two along parallel tracks. Those finally intersect in "What God Did Odin Worship?" (which appears here for the first time in print). In this essay, Cleary argues that in order to understand the story of Odin's "self-sacrifice" in the *Poetic Edda*, we must recognize that the god has dual aspects, which correspond to the Indian gods Rudra and Shiva. Cleary does not stop there, however. He goes on to suggest that Odin's sacrifice of himself to himself represents a path of self-transformation similar to that outlined by Julius Evola in several of his writings. (In fact, it is this essay more than any of the others which demonstrates Cleary's careful study of Evola.)

The volume concludes with two essays on "popular culture." The first deals with *The Prisoner* television series. This is genuinely one of the great series, and worthy of the attention it has garnered over the years. Nevertheless, a tremendous amount of pretentious nonsense has been written about it. Cleary's essay is, without question, the most profound and penetrating analysis of *The Prisoner* that has ever been published. Cleary shows why the series is not really about "individualism" at all, as is frequently asserted. He interprets it as a religious critique of individualism, and as fundamentally anti-modern.

The final essay in the volume concerns the intellectual autobiography of Alejandro Jodorowsky, the creator of the cult films *El Topo* (1970) and *The Holy Mountain* (1973). This essay was written for the projected fourth volume of *TYR* (which, as of this writing, has not yet appeared), and it also reflects Cleary's profound interest in Tantra. Here he comes full circle, back to the concerns of "Knowing the Gods," arguing that Tantra (understood in a certain way) can be seen as a path to the recovery of Tradition. The conclusion to this essay makes a perfect conclusion to the volume itself and is some of Cleary's best writing.

The neo-pagan movement has its share of New Age charlatans, half-educated cranks, and books and websites so bad they invite ridicule. The great virtue of Collin Cleary's writings on paganism is that they achieve a remarkably high level of philosophical sophistication and profundity. This means that they will appeal only to the most serious-minded individuals interested in neo-paganism. In other words, they will appeal only to the few. (Many of those who identify as neo-pagans today have been infected by the modern pathologies Cleary brilliantly skewers in the pages of this collection.)

Savitri Devi divided individuals into "men in time" (those who "go with the flow" of time and are entirely ruled by mundane concerns), "men above time" (those, like mystics, detached not just from their age but from any), and "men against time." Collin Cleary is most definitely a "man against time," setting himself not against this modern problem or that, but against modernity itself. Whatever one may think of him, he is without question the most dangerous man in Sandpoint.

Greg Johnson
San Francisco
May 27, 2011

Author's Acknowledgements

I would like to thank Josh Buckley, Michael Moynihan, Ian Read, and Greg Johnson for previously editing and publishing eight of the nine essays in this volume. I wish to thank Edred Thorsson for his comments on some of these pieces, and Alain de Benoist, Stephen Flowers, Stephen McNallen, Michael Moynihan, Juleigh Howard-Hobson, and Christopher Plaisance for their kind words.

I also wish to thank Greg Johnson and Michael Polignano of Counter-Currents Publishing. Greg deserves special thanks for suggesting the idea for this volume to me, and for his splendid editorial work and Introduction. I must also thank Kevin Slaughter for his attractive cover design and Matthew Peters for his careful proofreading.

My intellectual debts include a long list of philosophers and mystics—too long to print here, though Greg Johnson offers an abbreviated list in his Introduction.

For the most part, these essays appear in their original form. Although my thinking has evolved since "Knowing the Gods" was first published, I made no major changes to the ideas contained in these essays. I have not, however, been able to resist the temptation here and there to try and improve upon how I expressed them.

Collin Cleary
Sandpoint, Idaho
June 5, 2011

Knowing the Gods*

1. A False Knowing

There are those today who wish to return humanity (or a portion of humanity) to an older, pre-Christian faith. Almost all of these religious radicals hold that the gods exist, but that human beings have somehow become "closed" to them. The most common explanation for this "closedness" is the development of the intellect: man's big brain has shut him off from an experience of the divine. This explanation is dangerous, for it leads to anti-intellectualism (see, for example, the works of Jack London, D. H. Lawrence, and others). It is a theory that erroneously brands all use of reason as "rationalism," then posits that the only cure is the polar opposite error, irrationalism.

If one asks the proponents of this view what openness to the gods consists in, one is usually told that it means openness to certain natural "forces" which are recognized or intuited by human beings in the form of "archetypes." One finds something like this view, for example, in Julius Evola:

> Before the high and snowy peaks, the silence of the woods, the flowing of the rivers, mysterious caves, and so on, traditional man did not have poetic and subjective impressions typical of a [modern] romantic soul, but rather real sensations—even though at times confused—of the supernatural, of the powers (*numina*) that permeated those places; these sensations were translated into various images (spirits and gods of the elements, waterfalls, woods, and so on) often determined by the imagination, yet not arbitrarily and subjectively, but according to a necessary process.... [The power of imagination in traditional man] was so disposed as to be able to perceive and translate into plastic forms subtler impressions of the en-

---

* First published in *TYR: Myth – Culture – Tradition*, vol. 1, ed. Joshua Buckley, Collin Cleary, and Michael Moynihan (Atlanta: Ultra, 2002), 23–40.

vironment, which nonetheless were not arbitrary and subjective.[1]

Certain forces of nature are simply perceived by man *as* Thor, or *as* Indra, in the same way that a certain molecular configuration of the surface of objects is perceived *as* red, and another *as* green. Red is not "subjective" in the sense that it is "invented" by the subject. I have no choice when I open my eyes but to experience a cardinal's wings as red. But "red" would not exist without eyes capable of registering light waves refracted off of those wings, and a brain capable of processing the data in a certain manner. (The intrinsic structure of the object would exist with or without a perceiver, but the sense datum of "red" would not.) Thus, red is not subjective in the strong sense—but in a weaker sense it clearly is subjective, since without perceivers redness would not exist.

Let us apply this reasoning to the experience of the gods. The forces in nature registered by imagination (according to set processes) would exist with or without a subject. But the registration of those processes as sensuously-given "gods" would not. *Ergo, without human beings there would be no gods.* This conclusion was drawn by the German philosopher G. W. F. Hegel in the nineteenth century. His follower Ludwig Feuerbach took it one further, logical step and declared that Man is God. Feuerbach's contemporary Karl Marx then took the final step of declaring that if this is the case we may dispense with talking about God altogether.

The theory of "openness to the gods" outlined above is part and parcel of the modern perspective, which is rationalist, reductionist, and man-centered. It takes the experience of the gods as something to be "explained" rationally. It analyzes it as an "imaginative intuition" of natural forces, processed according to laws which are presumably physiological. It reduces the

---

[1] Julius Evola, *Revolt Against the Modern World*, trans. Guido Stucco (Rochester, Vt.: Inner Traditions, 1995), 150–51. Evola would, of course, reject my use of the term "archetype," as he was a strong critic of Jung.

experience of the divine to a neural epiphenomenon. And it thereby implicitly declares that without human brains "gods" would exist no more than would "red." If the proponents of this theory are even partially correct in thinking that modern rationalism has eradicated man's openness to the gods, how in heaven's name do they think their theory could help to restore it?

2. OPENNESS TO BEING

The first step in recovering the openness I have described is to reject the idea that we must "explain" the gods, or the experience of them claimed by our ancestors. Such an approach implicitly rejects belief in the gods; it assumes that the gods may be "reduced" to something else. In short, it attempts to explain the gods *away*. We must abandon all talk of archetypes and Innate Releasing Mechanisms, of Bicameral Minds and the powers of mushrooms — if we wish to again open ourselves to the gods. Openness must be openness to the gods . . . and nothing else.

We must open ourselves to the possibility that we live in a world which may contain unfathomable mysteries, and that amongst these may be the gods. We must entertain the idea that genuine rationality may involve the recognition that some things may be truly inexplicable, and so must simply be accepted as such.

This suggestion might be misinterpreted as the idea that we should somehow talk ourselves into believing in the gods in an impossibly *literal* way. In other words, believing, for example, that to encounter Freya means to encounter a literal blonde beauty in a literal chariot drawn by literal cats. However, not only am I not suggesting this, I do not even think that this is how our "primitive" ancestors believed in their gods. The standpoint I am proposing we adopt is one that could be described as *naïve* — but only in the sense that it rejects all preconceptions about the gods (and how our ancestors experienced them). It rejects all attempts to somehow show that the gods are *really* something else (i.e., all attempts to show that the sacred *really is* the profane!).

However — and now I come to a point of crucial importance—openness to the divine is made possible by a more basic standpoint: openness to the being of things as such. Here I am drawing upon Heidegger, who saw that our age is one in which we are closed to the being of things, and always forcing some form or some design upon them (a point I will treat at length later in this essay). As an antidote, Heidegger recommends the standpoint of *Gelassenheit* (a term he draws from the German mystical tradition), which is often translated "letting beings be." This refers to a state of openness in which we allow things to unfold their being for us without interference; to reveal to us their true nature.

My hypothesis is that this openness is *natural* to humankind, and hence, I believe, recoverable. It is our current state of "closedness" that is unnatural. In order to return to openness, however, it is not enough just to understand the concept. What is required is a radical shift in our way of orienting ourselves toward beings, and this must begin with a radical, unsparing critique of every aspect of our modern world.

3. WILL

An old Scandinavian legend from Christian times tells how when the gods ceased being worshipped in the Northlands, the dwarves abandoned that country, hiring a ferryman to take them across the river one night and away from the land of men. On reaching the other side, the ferryman was informed that the dwarves "were leaving the country forever in consequence of the unbelief of the people."[2]

This tale tells of closedness from its other side: when we cease to believe in them, the gods depart; they close themselves off from us. But in truth, the action of closing is performed by man. We close ourselves to the gods. The gods *do* nothing (nor should we expect them to, for they are gods). Human beings have a remarkable capacity for closing themselves off to the truth. Human nature is actual only in this relationship to the supernatural, but this relationship is a channel that must be kept open.

---

[2] H. A. Guerber, *Myths of the Norsemen* (Mineola, N.Y.: Dover Publications, 1992), 243.

Human nature, as actual living in the presence of what is "higher" (the supernatural, the divine, the transcendent, the ideal) exists in a constant tension between twin impulses: the impulse to open to the higher, and the impulse to close to it. One is the impulse to reach out to something greater than ourselves, letting it direct us and (literally) inspire us. The other is the impulse to close ourselves to this and to raise ourselves above all else. For lack of a better word, I will refer to this latter tendency as *Will*. Both tendencies—openness and Will—are present in all men. They explain the greatness of men, as well as their evil.

Will is an impulse to "close off" to the not-self. It is a shutting-off that is at the same time an elevation and exalting of the self to absolute status. Will manifests itself in its most basic form as a lashing out against whatever frustrates the self's desires. In human life, this begins in infancy merely as *screaming*, but once the organism has attained a certain strength and dexterity, it graduates to acts of destruction directed at the frustrating other. It devours or destroys that which opposes it. In consistently removing or rebelling against the other which limits its desires, the organism wills the principle that it exist without limit. This is why Will is an exalting of the self to absolute status. The (unrealizable) *telos* of Will would be a condition in which the organism would exist unopposed—and this could only be, of course, if the organism were the only thing in existence. The lashing-out of Will is also a closing to the other, for to seek the annihilation of otherness is to deny it ultimate reality.

Based on this description, it can easily be seen that all organisms, not just man, exhibit Will. Only man, however, can complement Will with the openness to the higher. Also, it is clear that all men *begin* life purely as an embodiment of Will, and growth and maturation involve a tempering of Will. If pure Will—the absolute shutting-off to all otherness, including the divine—is the nature of evil, then human beings begin life as purely evil. The infant recognizes nothing higher than himself. He wails and beats his fists against the world as soon as his desires are frustrated. The parents are "loved" (at first) only as conduits for the satisfaction of his desires (and even long after birth, the psychic boundary between the infant and the mother remains blurry—it is the father who is the problematic other). What we call "selfishness" is just Will, and this is why we regard it as evil.

Throughout the course of a human life, Will comes to manifest itself in different and more refined forms. In its higher forms, Will manifests itself not in destruction but in (1) the transformation of the given world according to human designs, and (2) the yearning to penetrate and master the world through the instrument of the human mind—through exploration, analysis, dissection, categorization, observation, and theory. In its most refined form, Will becomes what might be called a "Titanic Humanism": a seeking to make man the measure, to exalt man as the be-all and end-all of existence, to bend all things to human desires. It is no accident that all the grand schemes and contrivances of modernity (the technological mastery of nature, the global marketplace, socialism, universal health care, etc.) have as their end exactly what the infant seeks: the satisfaction of desires, and the maintenance of comfort and security. The modern age is the Age of Will, the age of Titanic Humanism. Modernity is unique in human history in that at no other time has Will so thoroughly triumphed over openness.

This description may make it seem that much of what we consider to be human is to be attributed to Will. This leads to troubling questions. For example, if scientific curiosity is a manifestation of Will, does that make science "evil"? The answer is a qualified *no*. Only an unbounded and unchecked Will is evil—and so only an unbounded and unchecked scientific curiosity would be evil. Will is natural and necessary to human nature. Like anything else, however, it must be held within the bonds of a limit. Human nature happens in the tension between Will and openness, between closing and opening. We open to receive truth—to receive the *logos*, to receive the will of the gods—then we take possession of such truth as our own and project it on the world, transforming the world, propagating the truth we have won from openness to what is beyond the human. In acting thus man fulfills his role as *steward* of the divine creation: assisting nature in achieving perfection. Will becomes destructive only when it is completely disconnected from what is beyond the human. There is then, in the properly human being, an oscillation between opening out to receive truth and closing and taking that truth in, making the truth one's own, and willing that this should be the truth for all.

If human beings begin in Will, how did man ever become open to what lies outside him? Children are forced to open by a power stronger than themselves which puts them in awe: their parents, teachers, and (formerly) clergy. If ancient man was more open, it was because he was put in awe by his surroundings, by nature, by the hardships of existence. Modern man is insulated from the awe-full by (1) technology, which allows him to manipulate the natural world and thus to avoid confronting the natural in its pure form, (2) by impregnable dwellings that shelter him from nature, (3) by cities that create a whole human world apart from nature, and (4) by science, the story we tell about nature, which leaves us with the impression that its mysteries have been fully penetrated and cancelled.

It is by the forces of nature shocking us into awareness that we are thrown into a world of *facts*: of beings and forces we did not devise and are mostly powerless to control. Openness to the world of nature, appreciated in just this sobering way, makes possible openness to another world of forces and powers—one that contains, yet transcends nature. This is the world of the gods. Shutting ourselves off from the natural world inevitably means shutting ourselves off from the divine. In fact, not only will we be shut off from belief in the gods, but also from our own nature, since human nature (as I will discuss shortly) is openness to the divine. But there is more: it is in this same openness that we receive the ideals and standards that have traditionally guided us. In closing ourselves to the natural world, and the supernatural world that encompasses it, we have closed ourselves off from Tradition.

4. THE AGE OF WILL

As mentioned earlier, it is in the modern period that Will has been loosed from its bonds and has torn us away from the gods. The form taken by Will in the modern period is the ideal of humanism, which is the man-centered, scientific, materialist, rationalist project of transforming the world and human beings in order to progress towards a state in which all resistance to desire is cancelled and all frustrations are ameliorated.

The modern humanist project, as an expression of infantile Will, is an attempt to cancel the otherness of nature. This is expressed quite nicely in the opening passages of Ayn Rand's *The Fountainhead*:

> He looked at the granite. To be cut, he thought, and made into walls. He looked at a tree. To be split and made into rafters. He looked at a streak of rust on the stone and thought of iron ore under the ground. To be melted and to emerge as girders against the sky. These rocks, he thought, are here for me; waiting for the drill, the dynamite and my voice; waiting to be split, ripped, pounded, reborn; waiting for the shape my hands will give them.[3]

In regarding nature only as raw material to be made over according to our designs, modern people take the position that, for all intents and purposes, nature *has no being*. Instead, it waits for us to confer being (or form, or meaning) upon it. We recognize no limits on our power to manipulate and to control. (When we do encounter what appear to be limits, we insist that *eventually* they will all be overcome, as Progress marches on.) It can easily be seen that this desire to remake, reorder, and perfect everything—this desire to place our stamp upon all—amounts to a kind of nihilistic desire to negate all otherness and to make the self (or the human) absolute.

Such an approach is a recipe for madness. Sanity depends upon the subject's being in touch with the outer, objective world, which acts as a check upon our ideas and aspirations. Indeed, it is only through interaction with an objective world—that which is *not* us—that human self-identity develops; it is through interacting with an other that we delineate the limits of the self. It should not surprise us that modern people lack a

---

[3] Ayn Rand, *The Fountainhead* (New York: Bobbs-Merrill, 1968), 4.

strong sense of self—that they are narcissistic, prone to constantly "reinventing" themselves and flitting from one fashion to another. We recognize no natural boundaries, nothing that may not be somehow, someday refined or reformed or improved.

And when we are "left alone" with ourselves in the universe, when the universe is no longer other at all, and the self has become absolute, what then? For Hegel, history is ended, and human beings find themselves at their zenith. Hegel thought that for man to learn his true nature was for him to achieve self-actualization. It would lead to an experience of exaltation. The truth is rather different, as we have discovered since this mighty Prometheus was struck down by cholera in 1831.[4] The truth, in fact, is closer to what Nietzsche's "Madman" tells us in *The Gay Science*. The Madman comes to the market place in the bright morning with a lantern, telling the people that they have killed God:

> *We have killed him*—you and I. All of us are his murderers. But how have we done this? How were we able to drink up the sea? Who gave us the sponge to wipe away the entire horizon? What did we do when we unchained this earth from its sun? Whither is it moving now? Whither are we moving now? Away from all suns? Are we not plunging continually? Backward, sideward, forward, in all directions? Is there any up or down left? Are we not straying as through an infinite nothing? Do we not feel the breath of empty space? Has it not become colder?[5]

---

[4] This was the official story, but the evidence indicates Hegel may actually have died of an acute gastrointestinal ailment.

[5] *The Portable Nietzsche*, ed. and trans. Walter Kaufmann (New York: Viking, 1968), 95–96. It must be added that Nietzsche's answer to the modern predicament is a more radical dose of humanism. Speaking of the murder of God, he writes, "Must not we ourselves become gods simply to seem worthy of it?" Nietzsche's belief is that the ideals we have abandoned are empty ideals, and that "God" never really existed at all. Having discovered this, we must "invent" new ideals. Nietzsche's "overmen" have the strength to do this—and to

The modern humanist project of the penetration, mastery, and control of nature is the sponge that has wiped away the entire horizon. It has refused to allow beings to be anything other than what we want them to be, and so they have hidden themselves from us—and the gods have hidden themselves from us too. Nietzsche's reference to the sun calls to mind the sun of Plato's *Republic*, which represents the "Idea of the Good," the ultimate source of all, the highest ideal, the being of beings. We have "unchained this earth from its sun," Nietzsche says. We have disconnected ourselves from the ideal, from Tradition. There is no "up or down" anymore because we no longer recognize anything objective with which we can orient ourselves in this universe. Having lost this sun, it has become colder.

But Nietzsche's "death of God" was no mere accident, brought about when people stopped going to church. Given the logic of Christian monotheism, God had to die—and to give way to the new god of humanism, which Freud called "our God *Logos*."[6]

5. Modernism & Monotheism

In order for the gods to appear to us again, we must create a "space" or, in Heidegger's words, a "clearing" in which that appearance can happen. We take the first step toward this when we recognize inherent limits on our power to understand and alter the world. Again, the modern world is built upon the rejection of such limits. Once we abandon this standpoint and surrender to the fact that ultimately this universe is a dark mystery, openness becomes possible again.

Acknowledging that there are such limits means, in fact, re-

---

test their mettle by doing battle over these ideals. But is it psychologically realistic to think that anyone could fight and die for ideals he has simply "made up," and does not honestly believe to be objectively true? (For more information, see my essay "Paganism without Gods: Alain de Benoist's *On Being a Pagan*," chapter 3 below.)

[6] See Sigmund Freud, *The Future of an Illusion*, trans. James Strachey (New York: W. W. Norton, 1961). By *Logos* Freud means simply logic or reason. He does not mean "the *logos*" in Heraclitus's sense of the term—a use of *logos* I alluded to earlier.

cognizing and affirming the being of beings. We must affirm that the world confronts us with *natures* that we did not choose and that we try to alter at our peril. That this world is, and is the way that it is, confronts us then as a sublime and impenetrable mystery. This is the beginning of wisdom (and the first step in invoking the gods).

Monotheists could agree with everything said above, but they will, of course, attribute the mystery to the one God. However, this is an abstract, theoretical conclusion (actually, a *non sequitur*) that is actually quite removed from the experience of openness I have described. If we somehow find the divine in openness to the multiplicity of natural forms that surrounds us, it is actually polytheism that suggests itself. It is a short step from the affirmation of those forms to glimpsing each as the manifestation of a divinity.[7] Further, those forms are on this earth, not in some heaven beyond.

Monotheism is moved not by openness to being, but by Will in its guise as "philosophy." Monotheism essentially seeks to go *behind the phenomena*, and beyond the gods, and asks, "but what *accounts for* these brute facts? It is no explanation simply to chalk these things up to gods. What explains these 'gods'?" In a sense, monotheists have a point. There is no genuine metaphysical explanation in polytheism. There is no answer to the question "why is there something rather than nothing?"[8] But polytheists essentially believe that there can be no answer to this question, and that none is needed. Existence needs no explanation — or justification — outside itself.

The "explanation" of the world provided by monotheism is vacuous: behind the gods, there lies . . . GOD. This may seem a peculiar way to describe the transition from polytheism to monotheism, but this is in fact exactly how it occurs. Through one agency or another, one God becomes supreme. Others become less important, until their worship finally dies out, or is actively killed.

---

[7] See chapter 2, "Summoning the Gods: The Phenomenology of Divine Presence," for an elaboration of this very point.

[8] Polytheist creation myths never begin with a literal *nothing*.

God is a supreme deity, existing outside the world, who created everything in the world. The schoolboy question, "If everything needs a maker, who made God?" forces the monotheist toward more and more abstruse, philosophical, and remote descriptions of this God. In the hands of Christian theologians like St. Thomas Aquinas, God essentially becomes a kind of "principle" which we must *think* if we are to think the world. For Aquinas, God is "the act of existing" itself . . . and so He becomes indistinguishable from that brute facticity He was intended to explain. In short, He becomes . . . a mystery!

Meanwhile, what has become of man's relationship to nature? Monotheism sucks all the mystery out of nature and injects it into God, who is the "explanation" for nature. While polytheism, through the worship of many gods, affirms the life and mystery of the world in all its complexity, monotheism declares the world to be a mere artifact, the product of God's making, and thus about as living and mysterious as a thumbtack. The transition from polytheism to monotheism is the "degodding" of the different aspects of the world.

Monotheists therefore progressively cede the complexity of creation to the natural scientist. And what happens to their God as a result of this? The natural scientist need make no reference to God in any of his investigations of nature. The entire material world is (so he supposes) understandable by science on its own terms. Eventually, scientists and others realize that this is the case and God essentially becomes a *deus otiosus*. God becomes a dispensable "hypothesis" that does no work in explaining the world. The scientist then steps in to take God's place.

The scientist recognizes that the world exhibits an intelligible order, but without God to underwrite creation, the natures of things no longer seem so "fixed." John Locke founded his doctrine of individual rights (life, liberty, and property) on the idea that man's nature is created by God. Remove belief in God and the status of man's nature—and his rights—becomes highly questionable. Less than two hundred years later the followers of Marx (e.g. Trotsky) explicitly declared their intention to change human nature through "scientific socialism." The result to the supposed "rights" of men is well-known.

Thus, in the absence of God (or the gods) the scientists come to believe that they can radically, infinitely alter what they study. Since there is no God, there is no reason to believe in the soul, or in any non-physical reality. Human beings are therefore simply a highly complex form of meat, which can be studied and manipulated using the same methods we use to study and manipulate other meat.

Since there is no non-physical reality, there are no objective or eternal ideals. Truth is "posited" by human beings.[9] This must mean, then, that moral idealism is a delusion. Men who exhibit the quality Plato called "spiritedness," men who are ready to fight for ideals, are simply sick or deluded. This position was explicitly put forward in the twentieth century by the so-called Frankfurt School of sociology.[10] Modern "humanism"—modern science and psychology—considers a person "normal" if his concerns do not rise above the level of what Plato called "appetite": concern with the satisfaction of desires and the maintenance or attainment of security and comfort. Hence the almost complete disappearance of terms like "honor," "nobility," and "self-sacrifice" from modern discourse.[11]

Here again, we see Will manifested: the closing off to anything "higher" than the self and the setting up of personal desire-fulfillment as the end of existence. But human beings cannot live entirely without ideals, and so a new ideal is created: the achievement of a society in which *everyone's* desires are satisfied, in which physical security, comfort and health are perfectly realized. Having cut themselves off from any higher as-

---

[9] Eventually, of course, in the hands of thinkers like Nietzsche, this logical consequence of scientific humanism is turned as a weapon on science itself.

[10] Actually, it is implicit in the works of the founder of modern political theory, Thomas Hobbes.

[11] "Courage" is a term one still encounters, but it is rarely applied to the man who risks his life in service to an ideal. It is applied to people desperately hanging onto life in the face of a debilitating, terminal disease, or to homosexuals coming out of the closet, or to Supreme Court justices who have made a leftward turn in their old age.

piration, scientists rush to place themselves in the service of this ideal.

And so, to come back to the beginning, what is the ultimate result of monotheism? Atheism, the violation of nature, the destruction of ideals, the destruction of morals, the barbarization of men, the eradication of human dignity, and the general debasement of human life (what is called "materialism").

6. THE ACHIEVEMENT OF OPENNESS

Only by overcoming that which has robbed us of openness can we hope ever to restore it. It follows that it is necessary to critique modernity—to critique all of our modern ideals, values, ways of thinking, and ways of orienting ourselves in the world. And we must know where these have come from—how modernity has come into being. This requires a knowledge of history and, especially, intellectual history. Someone might point out that this "critical" standpoint is quintessentially modern. This is true—but here we must learn from Julius Evola and "ride the tiger." In the *Kali Yuga*, in the end-time, it is permissible to utilize even forms of decadence as means to transcend modern decadence itself.

All of our efforts to explain what the gods "really" are, or what our ancestors "really" experienced, are thoroughly modern. It is part of the modern mindset to insist that *everything* can be explained, that everything is penetrable and knowable. The gods show up for us, however, in our experience of the brute facticity of existence itself—in our wonder that this world, and all that is in it, exists and is the way that it is. No "explanation" of why something is the way that it is can remove our wonder in the simple fact that it should be at all. (Scientists, for example, tell us that it is chlorophyll that makes the forest green—but that there is such a substance, which produces such incomparable beauty, is an occasion for wonder, and the intuition of a god.) The gods stand at the outer limits of our perception of reality, defining the real for us. Explanation only takes place within those limits.

Our ancestors believed in their gods, but had no "explanation" for what the gods were, or for their experience of the gods. Therefore, if we adopt the modern standpoint and insist upon explanation, we have removed ourselves even further from the standpoint of our ancestors. Indeed, we have negated it, and guaranteed that our desire to return to the gods will go unrealized.

Not only must we give up all attempts to explain the gods, we must also cease trying to explain what the "purpose" or "function" of religion is. Such an approach reflects, again, our modern critical distance from the standpoint of our ancestors. The modern approach to understanding religion consists in treating it as one of many activities men participate in—in addition to founding cities, making music, doing science, etc. In other words, the modern approach treats religion as merely one human characteristic among many. The truth, however, is that one finds the very *being* of man in religion itself.

For thousands of years philosophers have tried to identify what it is that makes us essentially different from other animals. Aristotle said it is that we "desire to know" (specifically to know the most fundamental and important things); Hegel said that it consists in our capacity for self-consciousness. These proposals are true, but they do not delve deeply enough. What is that makes possible our quest for knowledge of the most fundamental things, and for knowledge of ourselves and our place in the universe? It is the openness I have described—the openness which, in its highest and most sublime form, makes possible knowledge of the gods. Unlike all other creatures, we are not just Will, we are this openness. If knowledge of the gods is truly the consummation of this openness, then we may say that we are defined by our relation to the divine. In other words, we are defined by religion, and we are only truly human in lives lived in relation to the divine. In negating the openness that makes religion possible, modernity therefore negates our very nature.

Our nature is openness to being and, through that, openness to the gods. However, we can only be open to the presence of the gods if there is a concomitant absence in us. Again, we must have within us a "space" or "clearing" in which, or through which, the divine can presence itself. In a sense, this means that we are forever incomplete, forever yearning. We live in an abiding orientation toward the gods, but we can never consummate the desire to possess or to understand the divine. Yearning does not always have to frustrate or embitter us, however. Sometimes it may lift us up and give our lives strength and meaning. The real predicament of modern life is that our yearning is now exclusively directed toward profane objects which have no possibility of ever making us whole.

At this point, an objection might occur to some. Isn't this description of openness to the divine as "incompleteness" and "yearning" a rather Christianized, monotheist treatment? This does not seem to describe the religious experience of, for example, the Norse or the Greeks.

Yearning is, admittedly, an inadequate term for a very difficult concept. But one finds the sort of thing I am talking about in Greek descriptions of the "awe" with which men regard the divine (see especially Homer). The "yearning" I have described is not really a desire to become a god or, certainly, to physically possess a god. Rather, to describe it from the other end, it is a "pull" exerted by the divine on the human. What the divine provides is a frame of reference, an order, a structure to existence, which *fascinates*—and the nature of the fascination is not reducible just to these terms. Human nature just is this directedness toward, pulling toward, or fascination with the divine.

Will destroys religion in two related ways. The first is the way I have already described: man can spurn the beloved, declare that he has no need of it. "I can stand alone. I don't need you," man declares. This is modern rationalism and scientism. The second way is to try and devise some special method of bridging the gap between human and divine, without denying the reality of the latter. This way is called mysticism. Mystics think that they are raising themselves to at-one-ment with the divine. They fail to see that this process could equally well be described from the other end: as the lowering of God to the level of man. The divinization of man and the anthropomorphization of God are the same. The rise of mysticism has always signaled the corruption or degeneration of a religion. The *Upanishads* were the undoing of the *Vedas*—the destruction of the religion of the warrior and the exalting of the priest as supreme even over the gods. The result of this Titanic humanism for India requires no comment.

7. CONCLUSION, WITH SOME PRACTICAL SUGGESTIONS

I have argued that in order to restore openness to the divine, we must root out and negate all that which has brought about closedness. This means that we must engage in an all-encompassing critique of modernity itself, and of the ways in which we have been shaped by it. Opening to the gods happens only through openness to the being of things as such. Our ancestors possessed this openness, and if we are able to recover it, we may again encounter the gods.

I mentioned earlier that modern man cuts himself off from the being of nature through four basic things: (1) technology (which manipulates what is), (2) self-contained, self-sufficient and impregnable dwellings, (3) cities (whole "human worlds"), and (4) science (the story of how we have supposedly cancelled the hiddenness of nature). A reasonable formula for beginning to recover openness would thus be to:

(1) eliminate technology as much as possible from one's life. To live as simply as possible. To eliminate technologically-created "needs" (which are really unnecessary wants). To live from nature directly (e.g., to grow or to kill one's own food).
(2) to leave one's dwelling and encounter nature, as often as possible.
(3) to live, ideally, in such a way that nature can be encountered directly simply by stepping outside of one's home; i.e., not to live in a city.
(4) to develop a healthy skepticism about the claims of science. (An excellent place to begin would be with a critical examination of the theory of evolution, which is more problematic than we have been led to believe, and which enjoys the status of a religion-substitute among scientists.)

Through such a physical and mental separation from modernity, it is hoped that a meditation may begin, and that this meditation will lead to a rediscovery of that space within us which is the precondition of openness. In an oscillation between, on the one hand, self-examination and critique of modernity and Will, and, on the other hand, an encounter with being, openness becomes possible again.

A familiarity with the polytheistic traditions of our ancestors would also be helpful, as a kind of roadmap to guide us in understanding that which will enter in, once we are open.

APPENDIX:
SOME NOTES ON A FORM
OF "THERAPY" FOR MODERNS[12]

I have given suggestions above on how one might begin to re-establish an openness to the Gods, and to being as such. If my readers have found the argument of this paper on the whole convincing, they will undoubtedly want more concrete and detailed suggestions. This appendix attempts to provide some.

I understand this work as a kind of therapy — not just for a few unhappy or "disturbed" people, but for all modern people. Because we are closed to being, we are, as I have argued, closed to ourselves. We all suffer from an identity crisis and a crisis of meaning. We compulsively "act out" in various ways to compensate for this, and so it follows that we are all essentially neurotic, and in need some form of therapy.

I propose two sets of activities which can be (and should be) entered into simultaneously: Ego-Displacing Activities, and what I will call "Primal" Activities. Some Ego-Displacing activities are also Primal Activities.

Ego-Displacing activities are intended to momentarily "lift away" the individual ego with all of its history, concerns, idiosyncrasies, "problems," obsessions, fears, and preferences. This

---

[12] This appendix appears in print for the first time here. It was omitted when "Knowing the Gods" was printed in *TYR*, vol. 1.

allows influences to enter in, which might otherwise be blocked, and allows contact with parts of the self which lie "beneath" the personal ego.

Ego-Displacing Activities fall into roughly three categories:

1. Inducing "peak experiences" through physical *risk* or through a relentless "pushing" of oneself (physically or mentally) to go beyond one's known boundaries. Such activities include, for example, climbing a mountain, fighting, making war, skydiving, running a marathon, engaging in a sexual marathon, swimming the English Channel, etc.
2. Meditation or other forms of mental exercise in which normal or mundane thoughts are "stopped."
3. The use of mind-altering drugs which cause one to have a sense of transcending the personal ego.

Primal Activities are called such for three reasons. They (a) involve contact with the non-human; or (b) involve contact with a more primal and basic (non-reflective, non-intellectual) sides of ourselves; or (c) they are activities engaged in by our simpler and more "authentic" ancestors. Such activities include:

1. Activities carried out in nature: hiking and camping, fishing, gardening, raising animals, etc.
2. Hunting, slaughtering animals, field dressing game, etc.
3. Sport or other competitive (physical) activities. For example, fighting.
4. Sex.

Ideally, one should engage in a variety of these activities—both Ego-Displacing and Primal. *In particular, one should engage in those activities which one is predisposed to avoid.* One should engage in activities which one fears (e.g. skydiving, if one fears heights). Needless to say, simple prudence is called for here. But the idea is to push and challenge oneself. This breaks down the sense of who we are—but in a positive way, for it leads to this sense being "built back up" in a stronger, more authentic form. It makes new realizations, new revelations more likely. It opens one up to new influences.

While engaging in a regular program of these activities, one should immerse oneself in the study of the religion, culture, and traditions of one's ancestors. This involves, ideally, the following components:

1. Reading original texts containing myths or rituals.
2. Reading scholarly (but accessible) accounts of religion, myth, and culture.
3. Listening to traditional music.
4. Learning the language or languages of one's ancestors.
5. Making pilgrimages to the land of one's ancestors.

One should develop a regular program of self-study, and daily "rituals" or activities designed to orient one each day toward the world of one's ancestors. It is important to do something on awakening, and just before bed (such as reading a few pages of the *Poetic Edda*). If the Ego-Displacing and Primal Activities are successful in their aim, this makes it more likely that what we will experience when we have gotten beyond our personal, modern ego is that which our ancestors experienced. This is what was meant by my remark above, that familiarity with the traditions of our ancestors would serve "as a kind of roadmap to guide us in understanding that which will enter in, once we are open."

Summoning the Gods:
The Phenomenology of Divine Presence[*]

1. Introduction

The problem with our modern, Western pagans is that they do not genuinely believe in their gods, they merely believe in believing in them.

My ancestors believed, but I do not know how they believed. I confess that I do not know what it is like to live in a world in which there are gods. Occasionally I will catch some glimpse of what it might be like, but on a day-to-day basis I live in a world that seems thoroughly human, and thoroughly profane. It is no use telling myself that the world seems this way to me because I have been imprinted by modern scientism and materialism. *Knowing* that this is the case does not automatically open the world up for me in a different way. It is also no use telling myself how much healthier I would be (and the world would be) if we still believed in the gods. This is a purely intellectual, even ideological approach that will simply not do the trick.

So why, it might be asked, am I at all bothered with the "problem" of not believing in the gods? Because I know that it is utterly implausible to think that my ancestors simply sat around and "invented" their gods.[1] The thought nags me that

---

[*] First published in *TYR: Myth – Culture – Tradition*, vol. 2, ed. Joshua Buckley and Michael Moynihan (Atlanta: Ultra, 2004), 25–64.

[1] I am assuming that my readers do not need me to convince them of the naïveté of the nineteenth-century view that myths are primitive attempts at scientific explanation. Lawrence J. Hatab handles this quite well: "Explanation answers the question *why* or *how* something is by discovering a prior cause, tracing the cause of a thing back to (another) profane thing. Myths, on the other hand, should be seen to disclose *that* something is, the *first* meaningful form a world takes, the background of which is hidden. Myth is therefore not explanation but *presentation* of the arrival/withdrawal of existential meaning. The shift from mythical disclosure to rational and scientific thinking can-

they possessed a different sort of consciousness, or some special sense that has now atrophied in us, which allowed the gods to show up for them. And then there is also my conviction that something very important has been lost to us in the "Post-Pagan" world. I have tried to *think* my way back into belief in the gods; to convince myself, intellectually, of their existence. I know that this does not work, nor do I think it will work for anyone else. So what are our other options?

In my essay "Knowing the Gods," I argued something along the following lines. I rejected the modern approach of trying to "explain" what the gods are by reducing them to something else (e.g., "forces"). I argued that "openness to the gods" involves an openness to Being as such. In saying this I am, of course, drawing on the thought of Heidegger. For Heidegger, what makes the difference between the ancients and moderns is that the moderns see nature simply as "raw material" to be transformed according to human projects and human ideals. In other words, for the moderns, nature essentially has no Being: it waits on humans to confer identity upon it. According to Heidegger, the attitude of the ancients was quite different. It would probably be a distortion to describe the ancients as facing nature (*phusis*, in Greek) with "reverence." This sounds too much like the attitude of city-dwellers coming upon nature after a long absence from it; it is not the attitude of those who live with nature day-to-day. To use the language of Kant, what may be said is that the ancients regarded natural objects as ends-in-themselves, not merely as means to human ends.

To explain this idea, I will make use of a very simple analogy. It is not uncommon to see marriages in which the husband

---

not be seen as a correction of myth because it was a shift to a *new* intention—the reduction of beings to the explanatory capacities of the human mind or verifiable natural causes. To see myth as an error (a wrong explanation) is an anachronistic misunderstanding of the function of myth." See Lawrence J. Hatab, *Myth and Philosophy: A Contest of Truths* (LaSalle, Illinois: Open Court, 1990), 23. See also (especially) p. 26. Later in the same work, Hatab writes of Hesiod's *Theogony*, noting that it is not, properly speaking a story of "creation." The first gods "simply *appear*; we are not told from where" (p. 64).

is the dominant figure — so much so that the wife seems hardly to have a presence at all. He sounds off on some issue, in the company of friends, and shoots a sidelong glance at the wife: "You think so too, don't you dear?" And before she can answer he's off on something else. Even if she were given time to answer, she would never dare oppose him. Such a man is apt to be very surprised when, years down the road, he discovers somehow that his wife is quite dissatisfied with this arrangement. He is in for a shock when he finds out that she has an inner life all her own, and that by forbidding this inner life to ever come to expression, he has made a very unhappy marriage for himself. This situation is exactly analogous to the relationship of modern man to nature. Nature, treated merely as something on which man imposes his will, clams up. She falls silent and ceases to reveal her inner life, her secrets to man. All the while, of course, man thinks that he has plumbed nature's depths, and that she has few secrets left to reveal. But, as Heraclitus said, "nature loves to hide."

Western, Christian man had once believed that the world was an artifact created by an omnipotent God. Modern man has jettisoned God, but retained the idea that the earth is an artifact. Our scientists strive to find out how natural objects are "constructed" or "put together." They break things down into their "parts" or "components." With an artifact one can, of course, tear it down and use its "matter" to build something else — perhaps something better than was originally built. This is how modern man views nature: simply as stuff to be made over into other, better stuff. And the stuff we make just keeps on getting better and better. Or so we imagine. In the face of a humanity which no longer confronts nature as anything at all, any being in its own right, the gods, it seems, have left us. As Heidegger has said, "on the earth, all over it, a darkening of the world is happening. The essential happenings in this darkening are: the flight of the gods, the destruction of the earth, the reduction of human beings to a mass, the pre-eminence of the mediocre."[2]

---

[2] Martin Heidegger, *Introduction to Metaphysics*, trans. Gregory Fried and Richard Polt (New Haven: Yale University Press, 2000), 47.

In closing ourselves to the being of nature, we simultaneously close ourselves to the being of the gods. This is a major part of what I argued in "Knowing the Gods." The gods and what we call nature belong to the same realm: the realm of the "of itself so." In Chinese, "Nature" is *tzu-jan*. It is written using two pictographs, one of which can be translated as "of itself," and the other "so." What does this mean? The "of itself so" is that which is, or has happened, independently of conscious, human action or intervention.[3] It has approximately the same meaning as the Greek *phusis*.

I was once at a conference, and had occasion to speak to an academic about "nature." She demanded to know what I meant by this word. I expressed surprise that she did not know, whereupon she informed me that nature is a "social construct." We were seated at a table and I asked if she would extend her arm and bare her wrist. I took her wrist in my hand, and when I had found her pulse I instructed her to put her other hand there and feel it. "There," I said. "That's nature. Society didn't construct that. Nor has it come about of your own choice or design. It just happens, whether you like it or not." This is the "of itself so."

Human beings have the choice of opening to the "of itself so" or closing to it. Modern man has chosen to close. But although the "of itself so" is translated "nature," it is a much broader category. In closing to the "of itself so," man has closed to otherness as such: to what we call nature, and to anything else that *is* in its own right, apart from humanity — including whatever might be "super-natural."

The purpose of this essay, which I think of as a sequel to "Knowing the Gods," is to ask specifically how we can restore openness to the "of itself so." This was the question that the other essay left largely unanswered. In case it is not clear, let me state again what I take openness to the "of itself so" to entail. I take it to mean an awareness and acceptance of that which has being in its own right. I take "nature" to be part of

---

[3] See Alan W. Watts, *Nature, Man and Woman* (New York: Vintage Books, 1970), 10.

this "of itself so," along with that which has been designated the "supernatural": the gods, as well as god-knows-what.

First of all, it must be understood that what is "of itself so," is also a part of us. The pulse that beats in our wrists is an example of this. So is the hunger that one feels when a meal is a long time in coming, or the sexual desire that wells up, quite without the intellect's permission. When I say that modern man has closed himself to otherness, I do not mean that he has closed himself to all that is outside his skin. Modern man has identified himself with his conscious intellect alone. He treats his body in the way that he treats every other natural object: as something that "belongs" to him, and that must be mastered, and even, as we often say today, "made over." We do not have to go "outside ourselves" to encounter nature or the "of itself so," provided we have a conception of self that encompasses more than conscious intellect.

Openness must therefore involve rejecting the idea that the mind is all there is to one's identity. It must involve the recognition that much of one's "self" is not consciously chosen or controlled. Openness then becomes not so much the opening of a space that then gets filled, but rather a kind of communing with an other that is now, in a way, no longer so other.

In an essay on, of all people, Benjamin Franklin, D. H. Lawrence offers his own "creed," in opposition to the "sensible," Enlightenment creed of Franklin. He writes that he believes

> 'That I am I.'
> 'That my soul is a dark forest.'
> 'That my known self will never be more than a little clearing in the forest.'
> 'That gods, strange gods, come forth from the forest into the clearing of my known self, and then go back.'
> 'That I must have the courage to let them come and go.'
> 'That I will never let mankind put anything over me, but that I will try always to recognize and submit to the gods in me and the gods in other men and women.'[4]

---

[4] D. H. Lawrence, *Studies in Classic American Literature* (New York:

The soul is indeed a dark forest. As Heraclitus said, "You would not discover the limits of the soul although you traveled every road: it has so deep a *logos*."[5] But modern man has identified himself with the little clearing of the known self. Outside that clearing is a great dark forest, and beyond lies the greater wilderness that is the world itself. Man shines his flashlight into it and imagines that outside the corona of his beam there is only void. And "lumber" is the clever word he uses to describe the tiny bit he illuminates.

2. How to Summon the Gods

Let's stop and examine when it is—on what occasions—we experience a sense of the reality of otherness. The best examples are when things break down or somehow frustrate our expectations. This is how Heidegger approaches the issue. We get in the car to set off on a busy day of doing business and running errands—and find that it won't start. My experience in such situations is that there is at first almost a feeling of "unreality." We want to say (and often do), "I can't believe this is happening." And suddenly the being of this two-ton concatenation of metal and plastic confronts us in all its frustrating *facticity*. A still worse situation is when the body becomes ill, when it suddenly does not work as we expect it to. The body then seems to us to be a brute other. Both these situations, and all others like them, are occasions when something that has been taken for granted, suddenly seems to assert itself. What had been regarded merely as a tool, as an extension of human will, becomes a being in its own right. The result is frustration, amazement, fury, and something like awe.

But, in religious terms, what we want is not to be put in awe of this or that, but somehow to come to find the world itself awe-ful in its otherness. Must the world "break down," like a car, for us to experience this? Of course, the answer is that it

---

Penguin, 1991), 22. Italics omitted.

[5] Heraclitus, Fragment 104, trans. Richard D. McKirahan, in *A Presocratics Reader*, ed. Patricia Curd (Indianapolis, Indiana: Hackett Publishing, 1996), 40.

cannot. What very often happens instead is that *we* break down and the world confronts us as something that may be lost to us forever. I have in mind situations where human beings have a brush with death or insanity, or come face to face with their own mortality or fragility. And I've often thought that some men deliberately take risks—deliberately precipitate a brush with death—just so that they may feel a renewed sense of awe or wonder in the face of existence. Such men very often develop a "sense" not only of the world's strange otherness, but also a "mystical" intuition of something like divine providence working behind the scenes.[6]

Fortunately, we need not jump out of airplanes or climb mountains in order to achieve openness of the kind I am concerned with. We need only ask and ponder a single question: *why are there beings at all, rather than nothing?* Here, again, I am borrowing from Heidegger, but in order to take things in a direction Heidegger did not really explore.[7]

In India, there is a very simple meditation exercise often performed by seekers of wisdom. It consists in taking any object no matter how mundane—it could be a rock, or a cigarette butt—placing it on the earth, and drawing a ring around it in the dirt. The effect is to take an object that normally is taken for granted, that figures in life merely as a tool or as something barely noticed, and to make us aware of its being. Say that it is a cigarette butt. When we place a ring around it, it becomes a suitable object of meditation. What we meditate on is not its gross cigarette-butt-nature, but the *fact* of its being—the very fact that it has being at all. It is a way of becoming attuned to the wonder of being.

To ask the question *why are there beings at all, rather than nothing?* is to put a ring around that which is, *as such*. It is a way in

---

[6] Which is essentially why the way of the warrior is also a path to wisdom.

[7] I should point out that although I owe a great deal to Heidegger, I am not a Heideggerian, nor is this an essay in Heideggerian philosophy. In particular, I must warn the reader that my use of the terms "being," "beings," and "existence" does not strictly accord with Heidegger's use.

which, in the twinkling of an eye, the entire world in which we find ourselves can become an object of meditation—and of awe and wonder.

When we confront being-as-such as a miracle it is natural (and inevitable) that we should ask where it comes from. The childish version of this question is "who made it?" The more sophisticated version asks not about the physical coming-into-being of the universe considered as a totality, but about the *source* of the abundance that confronts us in the universe. We wonder at the inexhaustible richness of the universe, at the infinite multiplicity of types of things, and variations on these types, and at the infinite complexity of each thing, no matter how mundane. We wonder at the continual replenishment of beings—the continual parade of types giving rise to others like themselves, and the resilience of beings in regenerating and healing themselves. It is natural to wonder at the source of all of this. It is the "source of being" that this fundamental question, *why are there beings at all, rather than nothing?*, makes thematic.

Think for a moment of the source of a spring. Where does the spring end and the source begin (or vice versa)? At its source, the spring disappears into the ground. Is the source the hole in the ground? Obviously not. Is the source a body of water distinct from the spring? Again, obviously not. The spring and its source blend together. The origin of the stream is invisible. But we understand that the spring flows out from this invisible source. This is exactly how the Greeks conceived *phusis*, as surging forth continually out of an ultimate source—*archē*, in Greek. This realization is the meaning of such ancient symbols as the horn or cauldron of plenty, and the Holy Grail. The *archē* is the groundless ground of all abundance.

The root problem with human beings is that they want to, in effect, make themselves the *archē*, the source of all things. All of our attempts to understand something involve coming to see how the being of the thing flows from certain principles we have discovered. Our attempts at understanding are attempts at *under-standing*. We strive, in effect, to cut away an object's grounding and to make ourselves the ground by coming to see how the object's being flows from *our* ideas. When the scientist, for example, understands phenomena, he insists that the phenomena flow from principles he legislates.[8] But when we turn our minds to the ultimate *archē* — from which we ourselves flow — in spite of all our claims to have conquered nature, being shows up as a mysterious, miraculous given. The *archē* is the ground against which the figure of being-as-such shows up.

However, as the example of the ring around the cigarette butt indicates, one can find wonder in a single being, as well as in being-as-such. And when we turn, with this attitude of wonder, toward the individual phenomena *within* existence, another fundamental question arises. We may ask of anything, *why should this particular thing be, and be the way that it is?* Take the phenomenon of sex. When the mind attempts to think dispassionately about sex it comes off seeming like a rather absurd and grotesque activity. Why should *this* be so fascinating? Why should *this* absorb so much of our time and be so important to us? And yet there it is. And the more one tries to think about it this way the more one worries one might wind up ruining the whole thing! The result is that, awed by the sheer, inexplicable reality of sex, we continue to wonder at it and pursue it as before. In fact, this may be the only area, in the lives of many, in which wonder still happens.[9]

---

[8] Hatab says the following: "The path of philosophy turns away from the sacred imagery of myth toward empirical and conceptual models of thought. This entails a turn from the existential lived world toward abstract representations of the world. Now the world is measured according to principles of unity, universality, and constancy, and the mind aims for empirical and conceptual foundations which permit a kind of certainty. Thus disclosure of the world moves from a process of unconcealment toward a kind of foundationalism, where thought is reduced to a knowable, fixed form and structure" (Hatab, *Myth and Philosophy*, 13).

[9] Most of what qualifies as "pornography" constitutes a concerted effort to demystify sex and to deny or destroy its wonder. The pervasive irony and irreverence of pornography and its packaging (which is not in the least "sexy") are an attempt to, in effect, "laugh off" the awesome mystery that is sex, and make it non-threatening to modern

But everything else may be approached with this attitude of wonder. A beautiful animal is to be wondered at. *Why should this particular thing be, and be the way that it is?* The fact of the wind and the rain, the sun and the stars, all may occasion wonder, and the asking of this question. And it need not be a physical or perceptible entity: it might be the fact of birth, or of death, or of natural cycles, etc.

Now, when we do ask this question, it may sound like we are asking for some sort of official, scientific explanation, but we are not. No lecture on natural selection will have the effect of removing my wonder at the being of my cat—my wonder that such a thing is, and is the way it is. I do not have any quarrel with scientific explanation. But scientific explanation cannot remove this ultimate, metaphysical wonder at the sheer existence of things. I am perfectly willing to accept the scientist's explanation of how cats came into being—but I still look at my cat and say, "Isn't it incredible that we live in a world where such marvelous things would come about?"

My thesis is this: *our wonder at the being of particular things is an intuition of a god, or divine being.*

Am I saying that when I look at my cat and experience this sense of wonder I am intuiting that my cat is a god? Yes and no. The wonder I experience is *that things such as this exist at all*. I can just as well have this experience when contemplating the sun, the wind, the rain, the ocean, the mountains, etc. My wonder at the being of these things *just is* an experience of their divinity. Thus, there are gods of the sun, the wind, the rain, the ocean, the mountains, and, yes, of cats (the Egyptians saw this

---

men, whose goal is the destruction of mystery, and the achievement of complete control and knowledge of reality. What is perceived by feminists as the "misogyny" of porn also has its root in this: woman, as the source of the mystery, is brutalized and mocked precisely in order to deny her mystery. Much of what counts as "science," qualifies as pornography. A scientist who tells young people "It's silly to think there's anything mysterious about lightning: it's just atmospheric electrical discharge," is no less a pornographer than a Larry Flynt, who tells the same young people "It's silly to think there's anything mysterious about the vagina: it's just a cunt."

quite well). In truth, all things shine with divinity; all things are God. And there is no contradiction between this statement and the statement that there are *gods*. These are just two different ways of looking at the same thing. In so far as the divinity of cats shines through my cat, it *is* the god of cats.

There is a further aspect to this experience. When we confront things in their being, and wonder that such things are at all, our perception of time and space changes. When a thing is regarded with wonder, in the sense I have described, we simultaneously experience its being as stretched beyond the temporal present. The object is there before us, in the present, but simultaneously we intuit an aspect of eternity in the thing. When I wonder that such things as my cat exist at all, what I am wondering at is, in a sense, the "fact of catness" in the world. As Alan Watts would probably have put it, we wonder at the fact that there is *catting*, and *dogging*, and *peopling*, and *flowering*, and *fruiting* in this world. This is the aspect of divinity that shines through the thing, regarded in a certain way.

We might think of the gods as "regions" within being. There are as many gods as there are regions of being.[10] Our awareness of regions of being does not come through philosophical analysis or speculative system-building. It comes through experience and intuition. There are as many regions as there are experiences of wonder at the fact that "things such as X" exist

---

[10] I have borrowed the term "region" from the phenomenology of Husserl, but my idea of a region has little in common with Husserl's. Actually, the term Husserl uses is "regional essences." These represent fundamental divisions in reality itself. Their fundamentality is demonstrated by the fact that the differences between them are qualitative, as opposed to quantitative (i.e., they differ in kind, rather than in degree). Two vegetables—a lettuce and a cucumber, let us say—do not differ in kind, and thus they belong to the same "region." But a dog and a cucumber are not just *very* different, they are fundamentally different in kind. As are a cucumber and a quartz crystal. Thus, we can easily identify three regions corresponding to a traditional, commonsensical division: animal, vegetable, and mineral. My regions are also "divisions" within reality, but my concept of a region is more open-ended, as will shortly become apparent.

at all. And there are regions within regions. It was thus with supreme good sense that the Indians left things very vague with respect to the number of their gods. Hindu accounts differ. Some say that there are 330,000,000 gods. Such a huge number is not meant to be an exact figure. It is meant to suggest, in fact, the infinity of gods, an infinity grounded in the fact that there are infinite possible experiences of wonder at things. In just the same way, ancient Chinese authors speak of "the ten thousand things," not to give an exact figure, but to suggest the incomprehensible vastness of existence.

3. Objections and Replies

The position outlined above is simple, but likely to produce a great deal of skepticism. And the skeptics will come from almost every established "camp": rationalists, empiricists, theologians, and even pagans. In order to try and answer some of their complaints in advance, I present the following set of objections and replies, in the style of St. Thomas Aquinas.

Objection One: I have said that the question *why are there beings at all, rather than nothing?* allows us to "set off" all of existence and to regard it with wonder. I said, further, that the question *why should this particular thing exist, and be the way that it is?* allows us to experience objects within the world with wonder, and that this wonder at the sheer being of things is an experience of the divine. But are we to believe that our ancestors gamboled about the forest (or elsewhere) looking at things and thinking, in whatever language was theirs, *"why should this particular thing exist, and be the way that it is?"*

Reply: Of course not. In fact, one of my claims is that our ancestors had a natural and spontaneous capacity for wonder, a childlike capacity that we moderns (even modern children) have mostly lost. The questions I present here are attempts to formulate in words the tacit mental attitude necessary to make divinity come to presence. Nevertheless, they are not merely descriptive, but prescriptive also. For those of us who have lost the capacity for spontaneous wonder, the conscious asking of these questions may be a way back into the mentality of our ancestors.

Objection Two: A related objection might go as follows: the mental attitude of regarding things with wonder is a kind of "second order" achievement of consciousness. Most of us go through the day with a purely "worldly" focus: i.e., we are involved with things themselves, not with the wonder of their "sheer being." From this, two problems follow. First, it stands to reason that the farther we go back in time, the more "worldly" the focus of our ancestors had to have been, given the harshness of the conditions under which they lived. They would have had little occasion for "reflection." And from this problem flows a second one: if I am merely describing the "tacit mental attitude necessary to make divinity come to presence," and the turn to wonder is not conscious or deliberate, then it must be *occasioned* by certain events. In other words, something had to "happen" in order for man to turn from a "worldly" focus, to an attitude of wonder. What was it?

Reply: As to the first problem, it may be that the capacity to turn from a worldly focus to an attitude of wonder is what makes human beings unique in the animal kingdom. At some point in our evolution, it became possible to "switch attitudes" toward the world in this fashion. As to what occasioned this extraordinary leap in mental capacities, I have no theories of my own to offer. Obviously, it has nothing to do with the establishment of agriculture, or technology, or cities, or an increase in leisure time, since we find experiences of the divine in both planting and hunting cultures, in those with technology and in those without, in those located in villages and in those located in cities. But a word about leisure: modern people tend to exaggerate the degree to which "hardship" made the lives of ancient men chaotic and perilous, with little time for rest, let alone religion. The fact of the matter is that ancient men, particularly in hunter-gatherer cultures, had a tremendous amount of time for reflection, since hunting *mainly* involves sitting quietly and waiting. (I tend to think, also, that far from freeing us and providing us with more leisure, technology has made life more complicated, busy, and burdensome.) So, if we assume that the capacity to experience wonder came into being at a certain point, it is safe to assume that there was ample "free time" in which to actualize it.

As to the second objection—what occasioned the experience of wonder?—I immediately think of Vico, who claimed in *The New Science* (1730/1744) that awareness of divinity began at the first clap of thunder, when our primitive ancestors scattered back to their caves with cries of "Jove!" (the first God name). There is something to this theory, in spite of its naïveté. As I discussed earlier, what moves us from worldly involvement with things to reflection on their Being must be some kind of arresting experience. Things have to surprise us, frustrate us, overcome us, in some fashion. (And it need not be a "negative" sense of "overcoming" or "surprise.") In my own experience, I sometimes have a spontaneous sense of wonder at things, and very often I can't put my finger on what occasioned it.

Objection Three: Let's return for a moment to the cigarette butt mentioned earlier. I said that one could draw a ring (literal or figurative) around any object and come to wonder at its being, including a rock or a cigarette butt. Is there a god of cigarette butts? Are there gods of trash bags, coffee cups, toy trucks, and TV sets? This, certainly, seems absurd. And if my position compels us to declare, for consistency's sake, that there are such gods, then that surely qualifies as a *reductio* of it.

Reply: Fortunately, my position does not require this. First of all, what I said earlier still stands: it is perfectly possible to wonder at the sheer existence of cigarette butts and TV sets. These are artifacts: objects created by human beings. When one wonders at *natural objects*, the root of the wonder, the sense of mystery which cannot be eradicated, lies in the mysteriousness of the ultimate source of their being. In the case of artifacts, there is no mystery at all about their source: human beings created them.[11] Thus, when we wonder at the facticity of an artifact, what we are actually wondering at is the being of man himself, the *archē* (or architect) of the artifact. Is man himself a god? Of course. But there are no gods of his creations, no god

---

[11] Of course, the *materials* we create artifacts out of are, ultimately, natural. But when we contemplate an artifact *as* artifact, this is not the dimension of their being that is given to us.

of the machine.[12] This is why the very idea of a god of cigarette butts is immediately absurd to us, whereas it does not seem absurd at all to wonder at the being of the animal capable of creating such things and, especially, much grander things like supersonic jets, symphonies, computers, epic poems, suspension bridges, space shuttles, and cathedrals. One may argue that some of these things—perhaps even man himself—are a cancer on the planet, but one must still be awestruck by what man can do, by the fact that there is a being who wields such remarkable powers.

But if man is a god, he is only one god among infinitely many. If people today seem to behave as if they think man is the only god, this is perfectly explicable. We live in a world in which it is artifacts, *not natural objects*, which are most ready-to-hand. We live in immediate contact with cigarette butts, trash bags, coffee cups, TV sets, supersonic jets, computers, suspension bridges, and space shuttles. For most of us, our contact with such things as the wind, the rain, the ocean, the mountains, and "nature" in general is mediated through artifacts. Our houses and buildings shield us from the sun, the wind, and the rain. Most of us, remarkably enough, have *seen* the entire world: but only through photography books, over our TV sets, and online. Our climate control systems shield us even from the seasons: we are pleasingly warm in winter and pleasingly cool in summer. Some people live by the ocean, but very few live *by means of it*. And their dwellings shield them from its

---

[12] However, it is the case that, traditionally, there are gods of human activities, e.g. of human crafts. One need only think of the various divinities associated with the smith and with metalworking, such as the Irish Goibniu, Welsh Gofann, Latin Vulcan, and Greek Hephaistos. In Indian mythology we encounter Tvástr and Visvakaram (the "all accomplishing"). Very often such divinities not only play a role in creation, but are the teachers of skill to mankind. Probably the best example of such a figure would be the Greek Hermes. The "source" of these deities seems thus to be, at least in part, intuition of the marvelous character of the crafts by which we transform nature. They are thought to require a transhuman origin in order to be explicable.

violence (most of the time).

If artifacts are what we come into contact with on a regular basis, and if through and by means of artifacts the only god we intuit is ourselves, is it any wonder that such "isms" as "humanism," "scientism," and "atheism" reign? Is it any wonder that modern people live their lives on the assumption that they are the highest beings of all, and master of all? Cut off from direct contact with nature, they are cut off from the experience of its wonder, which is the experience of the infinity of gods. *This is the "flight of the gods."* The gods have not, to be exact, flown. We have merely blinded ourselves to them, by erecting a fabricated world that has obstructed the real world.

Objection Four: Now, it might be charged that the above attempt to account for the experience of the divine constitutes an abuse of language. I have said that our wonder at the being of things is an intuition of divinity. Thus, wonder that there is such a thing as the wind *just is* the experience of the "God of wind." But, the critic may charge, this is not what we have in mind by what a god is. I have merely substituted an entirely different understanding of divinity, one that has little to do with the traditional understanding (or so the objection would go). The god of wind is a *personality*. In India, he is Vâyu. He is depicted as white, riding a deer, and carrying a bow and arrows. The myths involve the feelings, thoughts, speeches, and actions of such gods. The gods, in short, are supposed to be conscious beings who run around and do things.

Reply: The trouble with this way of understanding things is that it confuses symbols with their referents. The god of wind is a personality because human beings have consciously and deliberated personified him. And separating the personified symbol from its referent is very difficult. Note that I said that "human beings have consciously and deliberately personified *him*." I should, perhaps, have said "it." But that somehow doesn't sound right. We personify because we have a drive to personify in order to hold the god in mind. Really, what this means is that we personify in order to hold in mind the wind, taken not as a "natural phenomenon" (as a scientist would take it) but as a *noumenon*, as a being awakening wonder. The drive to personify is natural, and it may be the case that some of the concrete ways in which we personify are also "built into" our consciousness. The researches of C. G. Jung and his students seem to confirm this. But it is hard to know where to draw the line. That Ganesha is depicted as having the head of an elephant is obviously attributable entirely to the historical accident that his symbolism was developed in India.

The symbolism of a god, the god's sex (male or female), the god's attributes, and associated myths, all serve to tell us something about the nature of some phenomenon taken in its numinous aspect. There is no better symbolism with which to illustrate this than that of Hinduism. Hindu iconography is extremely complex, and each element is symbolic of some power or aspect of a god.

Within any religion there are levels of understanding. There are undoubtedly Hindus whose piety consists in a lifelong confusion of symbol and referent. In other words, there are undoubtedly Hindus who think that truly believing in Vâyu means believing that there actually is an all-white being who rides a deer and carries a bow and arrows. We tend to assume that such "low level," or literal-minded understanding is a characteristic of the "common people," but that the higher-ups (the priests, the Brahmins) understand better. Assuming this is a dangerous business, however. In the West, for example, particularly in America, confusing the symbol with the referent is by no means confined to simple folk. It is a feature of the belief of most Christians, regardless of their level of education. Western atheists also confuse the symbol with the referent, and on that basis declare that religion is manifestly absurd. Seminarians understand that a symbol is a symbol, but find it very difficult to believe in that which it is a symbol of. Hence, they declare that we can keep religion, if we understand that it is really all about the "religious community," or about moral instruction, or social activism.

Some time ago I watched a British documentary about Hinduism, which included footage of a week-long festival in honor of a goddess (I think it was Sarasvati). The celebration involved the molding and painting of an elaborate clay figure of the goddess. A new one was created each year, and at the conclusion of the festival it was joyously dumped into the river. The British host asked a Brahmin if the people were worshipping the statue. The Brahmin smiled and said that he very much doubted that any of the celebrants, no matter how simple-minded, thought that the clay statue actually was Sarasvati. After all, they had to notice that each year it was a new statue! In truth, it was the Western journalist here who was simple-minded. Indeed, the typical way we Westerners understand polytheism (or so-called "primitive" religion) is, to put it mildly, psychologically naïve.

Objection Five: Referring back to my earlier essay, "Knowing the Gods," I can imagine someone objecting to the present essay by saying, "Look, in the other piece you begin by rejecting any attempt to explain what the gods are, or to explain the experience of the gods. To take such a reflective standpoint, you said, is to immediately distance ourselves from the phenomenon; to cut ourselves off from it even more decisively. But in this piece you do precisely what you say shouldn't be done: you've offered an explanation of the gods by claiming that 'the gods' are what show up when we are struck by the mysterious being of a being."

Reply: In fact, I have not *explained* the gods, or the experience of the gods, at all. To explain a phenomenon is to take it as an effect of some cause, and then to ferret out the cause (e.g., the explanation of why the water boiled is that it was heated to the temperature of 212 degrees Fahrenheit). But this is not what I have done. What I have given is not an explanation, but a phenomenological description. In other words, I have merely described how the divine "shows up" or "appears" to us. I have described the circumstances in which the divine shows up, the attitude of mind necessary for man to "notice" the divine, and how he responds to the divine once it shows up. This may seem like an oversimplification of what I have done in the preceding, rather lengthy text, but it is not. It is just that in this case, with a matter as mysterious as this one, phenomenological description is a bit more difficult than say, the phenomenological description of how a mailbox shows up for us. If the reader will go back and think over what has been said, he will find that the theory I have given of how the divine shows up is actually fairly simple. Unfortunately, we have been conditioned to think of the divine in such a wrongheaded way, that getting to the right description involves a great deal of explanation, examples, definition of terms, etymology (as we shall see), and, in general, *unlearning*.

Finally, *Objection Six*: This is perhaps the most serious objection of all. Doesn't my account completely "subjectivize" the gods? Aren't I saying that the gods are somehow functions of the way we regard things, and that without us, there would be no divine? The whole phenomenological, neo-Kantian approach described above seems to suggest this very clearly.

Reply: I can certainly see why someone might react this way — especially given my appeal to phenomenology, but, in fact, the objection represents a misunderstanding of my position (as well as a misunderstanding of phenomenology and of Kantianism, but I can't go into those points here). I have not said anything even approaching the idea that "the divine" is a subjective, mental category and that without human perceivers there would be no gods. I would certainly contend that without a certain cognitive "structure" (whatever it might be) we could not be aware of the gods, but this does not commit me to subjectivism. We need ears in order to notice sound waves, but nobody thinks that this means that ears "create" sound waves.[13] To repeat, I have given a phenomenological descrip-

---

[13] However, as I suggested earlier, in mentioning Jung, there may be certain innate structures that determine, to some degree, the manner in which we personify or depict the gods. *N.B.*: In actual fact we can "notice" sound waves without hearing them. Their vibrations can be felt indistinctly by the tactile sense. If there is something like a "sense" through which we become aware of the divine, might the presence of the divine also be registered by other senses, though indistinctly? I think this is a possibility and, again, the tactile sense seems to be involved. I am thinking of such phenomena as feeling one's flesh "crawl," or feeling the hair stand up on the back of the head. Such things happen when individuals have a brush with the "uncanny," and they often happen even in the absence of any *cogni-*

tion of, to quote my earlier formulation, "the attitude of mind necessary for man to 'notice' the divine." I did not say "create" the divine, I said *notice* it. I have spoken of the divine coming to presence, not of being invented or "posited" by humans.

However, someone might say at this point, "all right, but apart from the *appearance* of the gods to us, are there really any gods out there?" Put in Kantian language, this says: aside from the phenomenal appearance of gods, do gods exist *in themselves*? The best I can do to answer this is to paraphrase Kant himself: even though we can never perceive things as they are in themselves (i.e., apart from our perceptions of them) we must at least be able to *think* the same objects as things in themselves, lest we be landed in the absurd consequence of supposing that *there can be appearance without anything that appears*.[14]

4. Precedents: Usener and Cassirer

The foregoing theory shares some features in common with the views of Hermann Usener, as expounded and developed by Ernst Cassirer. In Cassirer's *Language and Myth*, he explains how Usener believed that the oldest (and, I would say, purest) stage of religious experience, was marked by the "production" of what he called *momentary deities*.[15] Cassirer writes:

---

tive awareness of supernatural presence.

[14] Cf. Immanuel Kant, *Critique of Pure Reason,* trans. Werner S. Pluhar (Indianapolis, Indiana: Hackett Publishing, 1996), 28 (Bxxvi-Bxxvii). My appeal to Kant is not intended to imply that he would have been sympathetic to my phenomenology of the gods. He would most certainly not have been. Kant divides human knowing into sensibility (perception) and understanding (thought), and claims that "phenomena" are objects as perceived by the five senses. However, the experience of the divine described here seems to belong neither to sensibility nor to the understanding, but, in a way, to straddle the two. Thus, my "phenomenal appearances" of the gods should not be understood in the Kantian sense of sensory perceptions (what Kant calls *Anschauungen*).

[15] The work by Usener that Cassirer is principally relying on is *Götternamen. Versuch einer Lehre von der religiösen Begriffsbildung* (Bonn, 1896).

These beings do not personify any force of nature, nor do they represent some special aspect of human life; no recurrent trait or value is retained in them and transformed into a mythico-religious image; it is something purely instantaneous, a fleeting, emerging and vanishing mental content, whose objectification and outward discharge produces the image of the "momentary deity." Every impression that man receives, every wish that stirs in him, every hope that lures him, every danger that threatens him can affect him thus religiously. Just let spontaneous feeling invest the object before him, or his own personal condition, or some display of power that surprises him, with an air of holiness, and the momentary god has been experienced and created.[16]

Now, as I said, this theory shares *some* features in common with my own. What is vague in the Usener-Cassirer account is what it means to have "spontaneous feeling" invest an object. And what is "an air of holiness"? My own theory attempts to account for *specifically how* some object (or state of affairs) could be taken in so unusual a way as to produce in us an intuition of a god. In other words, I attempt to describe specifically what it means to take something as *holy*.

Furthermore, I maintain that while the experience of the "momentary deity" is not immediately that of a personified god, it can develop into that later (on this point, I doubt Usener-Cassirer would disagree). Cassirer continues, "Usener has shown through examples of Greek literature how real this primitive religious feeling was even in the Greeks of the classical period, and how it activated them again and again."[17] And then he quotes Usener:

By reason of this vivacity and responsiveness of their religious sentiment, any idea or object which commands,

---

[16] Ernst Cassirer, *Language and Myth*, trans. Susanne K. Langer (New York: Dover Books, 1953), 17–18.

[17] Cassirer, *Language and Myth*, 18.

for the moment, their undivided interest, may be exalted to divine status: Reason and Understanding, Wealth, Chance, Climax, Wine, Feasting, or the body of the Beloved. . . . Whatever comes to us suddenly like a sending from heaven, whatever rejoices or grieves or oppresses us, seems to the religious consciousness like a divine being. As far back as we can trace the Greeks, they subsume such experiences under the generic name of *daimon*.[18]

According to Usener, after the stage of "momentary gods" comes the stage of "special gods." Although what Usener seems to have in mind here, narrowly, is deities associated with human activities (see my footnote #12 on page 35). Nevertheless, as reported by Cassirer, Usener's ideas are thought-provoking, and intersect with my own:

> Every department of human activity gives rise to a particular deity that represents it. These deities too, which Usener calls "special gods" (*Sondergötter*), have as yet no general function and significance; they do not permeate existence in its whole depth and scope, but are limited to a mere section of it, a narrowly circumscribed department. But within their respective spheres they have attained to permanence and definite character, and therewith to a certain generality. The patron god of harrowing, for instance, the god Occator, rules not only this year's harrowing, or the cultivation of a particular field, but is the god of harrowing in general, who is annually invoked by the whole community as its helper and protector upon the recurrence of this agricultural practice. So he

---

[18] Usener, 290f. Quoted in Cassirer, *Language and Myth*, 18. The translation is presumably Langer's. Note the very problematic language here: "Whatever comes to us suddenly *like* a sending from heaven . . . seems to the religious consciousness *like* a divine being" (my italics). My contention is that whatever came to man in this way *was*, for him, a divine being, a sending from heaven. Usener is speaking as if he thinks man operates with a determinate *idea* of divine being, and regards certain objects as divine because they resemble it.

represents a special and perhaps humble rustic activity, *but he represents it in its generality.*[19]

Building upon the work of Usener, Cassirer goes on to argue in *Language and Myth* that language originated essentially as a means to *fix* in mind these momentary deities (recall that he characterizes them as a "fleeting, emerging and vanishing mental content"). Thus are born words used to communicate and retain these experiences. (On this point, there is an interesting parallel between Cassirer's link between "deities" and words, and my link, described later, between deities and Platonic Forms; see Section 6 below). "Special gods" are deities invested with special names. Eventually, these names become disengaged from the divinity and stand alone as "terms" denoting the activity governed by the original divinity (so, if in some language Word X means "harrowing," X may originally have been the *proper name* for the god of that activity).

Usener gives a multitude of examples of "special" and "functional" gods, a great many of which are drawn from ancient Roman religion. The highest religious achievement, according to Usener, is the development of "personal gods." Cassirer writes: "The many divine names which originally denoted a corresponding number of sharply distinguished special gods now fuse in *one* personality, which has thus emerged; they become the several appellations of this Being, expressing various aspects of his nature, power, and range."[20] It is not very hard to discern a Judeo-Christian bias in such a theory, which construes monotheism not only as the *telos* of all religious development, but also as its apex.

In truth, it is possible, as I suggested earlier, to be both monotheist and polytheist. We can certainly look at the world as an expression of a multiplicity of individual gods. If we see these divinities as, in a sense, "regions of being," we can also see them as different manifestations or expressions of an underlying unity. These are simply two ways of looking at the

---

[19] Cassirer, *Language and Myth*, 19.
[20] Cassirer, *Language and Myth*, 21.

same thing. There is no contradiction in saying that the true God is Brahman, and in saying simultaneously that there are 330,000,000 gods. Most religions have totalized one or the other of these approaches, and the historical trend, it seems, is from polytheism to monotheism, and not the other way around. Why this should be the case is not a question I can address here.[21]

5. THE LANGUAGE OF THE DIVINE

If we look at the etymology of the words we use to speak and think about the divine, we will find further support for my position. This is important, for it is deeply engrained in us that we take the word "god" simply to mean a personal superbeing. (In fact, I think this is what the earlier objection—that I am not talking about what people have meant by "gods" at all—really is based upon.)

The reconstructed Proto-Indo-European term for divinity is *deiwos, and here are some of its forms:

Old Irish *dîa*
Old Welsh *duiu-tit*
Latin *deus*
Old Norse *Týr* (pl. *tívar*, "gods")
Old English *Tîw*
Old High German *Zîo*
Lithuanian *dievas*
Latvian *dìevs*
Avestan *daéva*
Old Indic *devá*

One source says of *deiwos, "In origin a thematic derivative of *dyeu- 'sky, day, sun (god)' meaning '± luminous one, god (in general)."[22]

Now, if *deiwos or God means something like "luminous

---

[21] It was addressed, to some extent, in "Knowing the Gods."
[22] *Encyclopedia of Indo-European Culture*, ed. J. P. Mallory and D. Q. Adams (London: Fitzroy Dearborn Publishers, 1997), 230.

one," there are at least a couple of very different ways to take this. Since the word is derived from *dyeu-, "sky, day, sun," it is generally assumed that the original Indo-European gods (or, at least, the upper echelon of gods, e.g. the Norse *aesir*) are gods of the heavens. Nor is this phenomenon of looking to heaven for divinity confined to the Indo-Europeans, as we all know from Sunday school. But I wonder if there is not, perhaps, a deeper meaning to the idea of God as "the luminous one." As I have discussed above, when we come to awareness of the wonderful being of individual things, it is as if they are suddenly "lit up." And I do not mean this in an exclusively figurative way. Very often the experience literally seems to be one in which things shine with a new light. Descriptions of mystical experiences abound with such language. We speak of ourselves, and things, as being "illuminated." To go back to an earlier example, when I experience the wonder that such things as my cat exist at all, my cat is "lit up" for me in a new way, and the light that shines through my cat is the divinity, the luminous one.

It was only natural that our ancestors should have associated the physical experience of the awesome brightness of the sun, with the psychical experience of the awesome brightness of Being shining through beings. Thus, *deiwos* as "luminous one" is, in effect, an abstraction derived from all that is *dyeu-*, or all that "shines," with "sky," "day," and "sun" being exemplars of shining.

Looking outside the Indo-European tradition, among the Chinese we find what seems to be a similar conception. The oldest Chinese terms for divinity date back to the Shang Dynasty (ca. 1751–1028 B.C.). The supreme god is conceived as celestial. Oddly enough, he is called *Ti* (which simply means Lord) or *Shang Ti* (Lord on High).[23] According to Mircea Eliade,

---

[23] A further oddity is that the Aztec word for god was *Teo*. These linguistic similarities are treated by most reputable scholars as pure coincidence, since Aztec and Chinese belong to language groups which developed quite independently of Indo-European. Nevertheless, the coincidence is striking.

"Ti commands the cosmic rhythms and natural phenomena (rain, wind, drought, etc.); he grants the king victory and insures the abundance of crops or, on the contrary, brings on disasters and sends sicknesses and death."[24] There are other gods (and the Chinese worshipped their ancestors as well), but these are subordinated to Ti. As with Tyr in the Germanic tradition, however, Ti remains somewhat remote from the lives of ordinary believers, and eventually became, in effect, a *deus otiosus*. It would be fascinating to trace out the etymology of "Ti," but I do not know Chinese at all, and I can find few sources in English which deal with this topic.

Returning to the Indo-Europeans, let us consider some other terms for the divine. In an article originally published in *Rúna*, Edred Thorsson analyzes the Germanic terms for "the holy."[25] In Proto-Germanic, these are **wîhaz* and **hailagaz*, in Old English *wîh* and *hâlig*, in Old High German *wîh* and *heilig*, in Gothic *weihs* and *hailags*, in Old Norse *vé* and *heilagr*. Modern German preserves both terms, in *weihen* (to consecrate) and *heilig*. Modern English preserves only the second, in "holy."

As Thorsson points out, **wîhaz* derives from the Proto-Indo-European root **vîk*, which means "to separate." The sense of separation involves a religious or ritual context. From **vîk* comes Latin *victima*, sacrificial animal.[26] Thus, what derives from **vîk* has the sense of being something "separate in some way from the every-day."[27] The **wîhaz* is what has been

---

[24] Mircea Eliade, *A History of Religious Ideas*, Vol. II, trans. William R. Trask (Chicago: University of Chicago Press, 1982), 7.

[25] Edred Thorsson, "The Holy," in *Green Rúna* (Smithville, Tex.: Rûna-Raven Press, 1996), 41–45. All references are to the anthologized text.

[26] Also, Old Norse *vîgja*, "to consecrate," and Old English *wicca*, "witch."

[27] Thorsson, 41. Thorsson goes on to say that this means it is "completely other," and draws on Rudolf Otto's discussion of the *mysterium tremendum* as that which is totally other from mundane or everyday human existence. I'm not sure I can go along with this identification, however, if I have adequately understood Thorsson's point. Otto's analysis of religious experience tends to be heavily prejudiced

"drawn out," as it were, from that which is ready-to-hand, and invested with significance of a very special sort.

What Thorsson does not mention, however, is that *vîk (sometimes given as *wîk) can also mean "appear," as well as separate (or "consecrate"). We thus have Old English wîg ~ wîh ~ wêoh, "image, idol." Lithuanian į-výkti, meaning "happen, occur; come true, be fulfilled" originally seems to have meant "come into sight."[28] Greek eikōn, meaning "image, likeness," is derived from this same root. Plato opposes the eikōn to the eidos, the Form (see Section 6 below). But how can the same linguistic form convey "to separate," "to consecrate," and to "appear," simultaneously? The answer is that something appears in its own right only when it is separated. All appearance involves an opposition of "figure" to "ground." To appear, an object must be somehow "marked off" from its background. "Sacred" objects are objects that have been marked off from profane space (set apart from mundane activities and objects) and profane time (linked to what is eternal).

Thorsson gives the following meanings for the basic Germanic *wîh-:

1. "a site for cultic activity, sacred ground"
2. "a grave mound"
3. "a site where court is held"
4. "an idol, or divine image"
5. "a standard or flag"[29]

What all of these have in common is that they are, ordinarily, "mundane": a patch of ground, a mound of dirt, a clearing, a carved piece of wood, a piece of cloth. But all of these are capable of being regarded in a special way and invested, by asso-

---

in favor of Judeo-Christian experience, in which the divine is indeed something "wholly other" in the sense of absolutely transcendent of the world.

[28] Encyclopedia of Indo-European Culture, 25. This one should be especially exciting to Heideggerians.

[29] Thorsson, Green Rûna, 42.

ciation, with significance (with something like that which anthropologists call "mana").[30] When the mundanity of things is negated in this fashion, they are made "sacred," and then a split in the world comes into being between that which is sacred and that which is profane.[31] As Thorsson discusses, there is even a verb in Old Norse which designates the action of drawing objects out of the realm of the profane and making them sacred: *wîhian*. From that which is **wîh-* comes one of the most significant Norse names for divinity: Vé, who is one of the three divine brothers described in the Norse cosmogony, Óðinn, Vili, and Vé. The term *veár*, from Vé, also is used to mean the plural "gods" in general.[32]

As to the Proto-Germanic root **hail-*, an analysis of the words derived from it in the various Germanic tongues indicates the following set of meanings:

1. "holy"
2. "whole, healthy" (e.g., English "hale and hearty")
3. "health, happiness" (e.g., English "health")
4. "luck, omen"
5. "to heal" (e.g., English "heal")
6. "to greet" (e.g., English "hail!" and German "heil!")
7. "to observe signs and omens"
8. "to invoke spirits, enchant"[33]

---

[30] How objects *associated* with divinities take on this mana-like property is not something I have dealt with here. My analysis has been concerned solely with how the divine is "noticed" in the world to begin with. I hesitate to use the term "mana" because of its association with thoroughly secular and reductive anthropological theory, but I know of no better term.

[31] The Latin *profanum* means literally "before the sanctuary." It designated the ordinary ground outside the enclosure of a sacred place. Hatab writes, "To the mythical mind . . . the profane is that which is meaningless, the sacred is that which is meaningful." Hatab, 23.

[32] Thorsson, *Green Rûna*, 42.

[33] Thorsson, *Green Rûna*, 43.

Thorsson writes that *hail- "is that which takes part in the numinous quality which is blessed and whole, and which evokes the feeling of 'wholeness' or 'oneness' in the religious subject."[34]

Essentially, *hail- involves the participation of the human subject in the divine, whereas *wîh- refers to the divine presence itself. The man who is "whole, healthy" is the man who is permeated by a state of *rightness* or *harmony* which is thought of as connected with divine being. This is very close to the original Greek sense of *eudaimonia* (poorly rendered, in translations of Aristotle, as "happiness"), which literally means something like "well-demoned (daimoned)."[35] "Luck" is divine favor dwelling within a man. "To heal" means to restore that divine-oriented "rightness" to the body or mind. Today, it's pretty uncommon to hear someone greeted with "hail!" and unheard of (post-World War II) to hear a "heil!" When people said that to one another, were they greeting or recognizing the divine within the other person? Was "hail!" in short, similar to the Indian greeting (still in use today) *namastē*?[36] The observation of signs and omens means being watchful for the manifestation of the divine within daily life. Finally, to "enchant" means to place someone under the influence of some kind of divine power.

Finally, turning to Classical Greek, it might be mentioned that the Greek word for piety or religion, *eusebeia*, comes from the verb *sebein*, meaning "to step back from something in awe."

6. PLATO: *EIDOS* VS. *THEOS*

The foregoing analysis of the experience of the divine sheds special light on Greek philosophy, in particular on the relation of Plato's "doctrine of Forms" to traditional Indo-European religion. Looking at this connection also seems to lend further support to the plausibility of my analysis. Indeed, readers may

---

[34] Thorsson, *Green Rûna*, 43.

[35] From the Proto-Indo-European root *sakros (e.g., "sacred") comes Tocharian A *sâkär* meaning "blissful, happy, auspicious." Tocharian B *sâkre* means "blissful, happy, blessed, auspicious."

[36] And, I might add, does today's rather trite "hi!" derive from hail/heil?

have noticed something vaguely "Platonic" in my description of the human experience of divinity. I will argue, in fact, that Plato's philosophy constituted a transformation of Greek religious experience. If I am right, then we may be able to learn a good deal about the nature of that experience from Plato.

I'm sure my readers have some acquaintance with Plato's Forms. Plato believed that the world of experience is, in a sense, unreal, and that what is truly real (or, one could say, what truly *is*) are the "Forms" or "natures" things exhibit. These forms are nonphysical and, unlike the individuals that exemplify them, they last. The Greek word translated "Form" is *eidos* (plural: *eidē*), which is why, somewhat less often, the term is translated "idea."[37] But the literal meaning of *eidos* is "look" in the sense of "appearance." The *eidos* is the "look" of a thing. In German, the same concept is rendered by *Schein*, which is related, of course, to our "shine."

At first glance, there seems to have been a complete transformation in the sense of the Greek *eidos*. What originally meant the "look" of a thing comes to mean, in Plato, its intelligible nature, which presents itself not to the eyes but to the mind. But on closer examination, a subtle connection between the two reveals itself. Let us consider first how Plato describes the way in which we come to be aware of Forms. A classic example is to be found in the *Symposium* (210e). In a "flashback," Socrates recalls how he was instructed in the nature of the beautiful by the wisewoman Diotima. She describes a "ladder of beauty," and tells Socrates that he will come to awareness of Beauty itself (the Form of Beauty) by examining different things said to be "beautiful":

> You see, the man who has been thus far guided in matters of Love, who has beheld beautiful things in the right order and correctly, is coming now to the goal of Loving:

---

[37] The reason *eidos* is translated Form rather than the more natural "Idea" is simple. "Idea" suggests something subjective, whereas Plato's Forms are objective entities existing in a separate, non-spatiotemporal dimension.

all of a sudden he will catch sight of something wonderfully beautiful in its nature [the "Beautiful itself"]; that, Socrates, is the reason for all his earlier labors.[38]

A second, less familiar example occurs in the late dialogue the *Parmenides*. Here, Socrates, depicted as a young man, is conversing with another of his early gurus, the philosopher Parmenides. At 132a, the older man puts Socrates's theory of Forms (then in its earliest and crudest form) to the test:

I suppose you think each form is one on the following ground: whenever some number of things seems to you to be large, perhaps there seems to be some one character, the same as you look at them all, and from that you conclude that the large is one.[39]

These two phenomenological descriptions of how Forms show up for us depict them as *appearing* to the thinker as he contemplates sensible objects. To be sure, it is not as if the Form pops out of things and presents itself as a separate, sensible object. One could say that it appears to "intellect," but this oversimplifies things. What seems to happen in our coming-to-awareness of Forms is that sense and intellect cooperate in some peculiar, ineffable manner. There seems to be a literal transformation of the sensible experience when the Form "appears." We are still seeing the same sensible thing, but we are now seeing a new dimension of it. What I am saying is that if I come to awareness of "Catness" looking at my cat, it seems right to say that the literal "appearance" of the cat doesn't change—but, in another sense, the appearance *does* change. I am now seeing the atemporal aspect of the cat (its nature, its Catness) *through* it, and the sensible experience does *feel* as if it

---

[38] Plato, *Symposium*, trans. Alexander Nehemas and Paul Woodruff, in *Plato: Complete Works*, ed. John M. Cooper (Indianapolis, Indiana: Hackett Publishing, 1997), 493.

[39] Plato, *Parmenides*, trans. Mary Louise Gill and Paul Ryan, in *Plato: Complete Works*, 366.

has been transformed. It is important to note that the verb *eidenai* (to know), which is related to *eidos*, originally meant "to see" or to "catch a glimpse of."

I think this is why Parmenides seems to be forcing Socrates, in the latter part of the dialogue, to go beyond a conception of Forms as things "separate" from sensibles, and toward the idea that the sensible *just is* the Form considered in its unchanging aspect.[40] In earlier dialogues, sensibles are treated as "images" or "likenesses" of the Forms. This is metaphorical, and not meant to be taken literally. Seeing a painting of someone I have seen in person is very different from seeing a painting of someone I have never laid eyes on. In the former case, there is an additional dimension to the experience. I see the real person *in*, or *through* the painting. In the same way, for Plato, we see the true nature of something (e.g., Catness) shining through individual things (e.g., cats).

Now, the same idea seems to be conveyed, in a more sophisticated form, in the latter part of the *Parmenides*, in the peculiar series of "deductions" presented there. Sensibles are said to be "appearances" of Forms. The Greek translated as "appearances" is *phainomena*, which does not have the sense of "mere semblance" or "seeming" that our word "appearance" usually has. In *Being and Time*, Heidegger attempts to recover the originary Greek sense of *phainomenon*, which survives in our language, of course, as "phenomenon." Heidegger writes that *phainomenon* means "that which shows itself, the manifest. . . . [T]*hat which shows itself in itself*, the manifest. Accordingly, the phainomena or 'phenomena' are the totality of what lies in the light of day or can be brought to the light—what the Greeks sometimes identified simply with *ta onta (beings)*."[41] Heidegger goes on to distinguish "phenomenon" from "semblance." By semblance he means something like "image." A semblance

---

[40] See Mitchell H. Miller's *Plato's Parmenides: The Conversion of the Soul* (University Park, Pennsylvania: Pennsylvania State University Press, 1991), in which this thesis is developed masterfully.

[41] Martin Heidegger, *Being and Time*, trans. John Macquarrie and Edward Robinson (New York: Harper and Row, 1961), 51.

could be an illusion, a hallucination, or a representation, such as a painting. None of these are *phenomena*, in the original Greek sense. A phenomenon is not an image of something (least of all a misleading "semblance"), it is the something showing itself. Even our word "appearance" can mean this. If someone tells me that the Queen "made an appearance" in Scotland, I don't take that to mean that somebody saw a picture of her there. I take it to mean that she showed up there herself.[42]

Now, I think it can readily be seen that there is a parallel between how I have described the experience of the gods, and how Plato describes the experience of the Forms. Both the gods and Forms are phenomena: they themselves shine forth from the things in our experience. When Catness shines forth from the cat, in a way it is as if *something else* shines forth from the cat, and in a way it is not. Clearly, in seeing the Catness of the cat we have, in a certain sense, "seen beyond" this particular cat, but in another way we have seen what is fundamental about *this* cat.[43] Both are correct, and they illustrate the dual aspect of Forms as *simultaneously transcendent and immanent*. Seeing the divinity in the cat, as I have described the experience, is practically identical to this. In an attitude of wonder, struck by the fact that beings such as cats exist at all, a hitherto

---

[42] The very recent usage of "phenomenon" to mean "big deal" (as in "the hula hoop phenomenon") obviously has little to do with the meaning I am discussing here.

[43] There are basically four ways in which Plato describes the relation of Forms and sensibles: (a) *mimesis* or imitation (sensibles are "imitations" of Forms), (b) *methexis* or "participation" (sensibles "partake of" Forms), (c) *koinonia* or community, and (d) *parousia* or presence. A and B represent rather naïve, literal-minded construals of the relation which prove inadequate on analysis (the *Parmenides* is devoted, in part, to demonstrating this). But *koinonia* and *parousia* are far more interesting, and defensible. *Koinonia* means that the sensible "communes with" or is "in communion with" the Form. *Parousia* indicates that we encounter the Form as "present in" the sensible; or, in phenomenological jargon, the Form "presences itself" in the sensible *if the sensible is regarded in a certain way*.

concealed aspect of the cat shows up for us: the miraculous being of the cat. And simultaneously, we have the sense of this wonder as having emerged from an equally miraculous source, what I have called the *archē*. The "divinity" of the cat, as I said earlier, both is the cat itself, and is something that transcends this particular cat.

In the *Republic*'s famous "allegory of the cave," the ascent from ignorance to wisdom is likened to the ascent out of a cave and into the sunlight, in which we find the true natures of things "illuminated" (cf. 516a–b). In the *Parmenides*, the young Socrates uses a simile to explain the relation of sensibles to their Form. The Form, he says, is "like one and the same day. That is in many places at the same time and is none the less not separate from itself. If it's like that, each of the forms might be, at the same time, one and the same in all" (131b).[44]

Despite the similarities, there is, in fact, a huge difference between awareness of divinity and awareness of Plato's Forms. What has been banished from Plato's account is wonder and mystery. The divinity of the cat that shines in it is no longer divinity, it is merely the "intelligible nature" of the thing. The sense in which awareness of the *eidos*, the "look" of the thing straddles the sensible and the intellectual, the sense in which awareness of the *eidos* transforms the actual sensuous experience of the thing, has been, for the most part, lost. To be sure, this *eidos* is still "supernatural," it is "above" nature, and outside space and time. But it is treated as a pattern or *paradeigma* (see *Parmenides*, 132d) and it is mathematicized. Under the influence of Pythagoreanism, Plato developed a complex secret teaching which is only hinted at in the dialogues, involving a mathematical conception of reality, flowing from two ultimate "principles," the "One" and the "Indefinite Dyad."[45] It was the

---

[44] Plato, *Parmenides*, p. 365.

[45] The primary testimonies to this come from Aristotle. See *Physics* (209b13-6) and *Metaphysics* (I.6). There are also a number of recent books by Plato scholars dealing with this topic. See Hans Joachim Kramer, *Plato and the Foundations of Metaphysics*, trans. John R. Catan (Albany: State University of New York Press, 1990); and Giovanni Reale, *Toward a New Interpretation of Plato*, trans. John R. Catan (Wash-

ongoing project of Plato and his students to understand the Forms in terms of this mathematical system. The Forms may be "mysterious" in being quite unlike mundane, sensible objects, but they stand in relation to those things as a blueprint stands in relation to a house, and there is nothing inherently mysterious (let alone religious) about that.[46]

My thesis is that Plato is taking up the experience of the divine, and the concept of divinity, and recasting them in a philosophical, even "scientific" form. Religious or mystical experience becomes philosophical or scientific "insight," and the gods become "Forms" or patterns in nature. Plato develops this approach using the mathematical philosophy of the Pythagoreans, while retaining certain "mystical" aspects of Pythagoreanism (especially the doctrine of reincarnation; see the *Phaedo*). Plato makes it possible for a man to be religious, and to take great care with his soul, while disbelieving in "gods."[47] Christianity, as Nietzsche said, may have been Platonism for the people, but Platonism itself was polytheism for atheists. And even Plato's doctrine of reincarnation in the *Phaedo* is defended *on pragmatic grounds* (see *Phaedo*, 114d–e). Platonism is mysticism without mystery.[48]

Plato is open to metaphorical descriptions of the Being of things, but anything like the sort of religious iconography dis-

---

ington, D.C.: Catholic University of America Press, 1997).

[46] The "divine figure" of the Demiurge in the *Timaeus*, who creates the world according to the eternal Forms, was recognized even by the members of Plato's Academy as merely a poetic device.

[47] While also, it must be added, seeming religious enough to avoid the fate of Socrates. Socrates was charged with two crimes: corrupting the youth, and not worshipping the gods of the city.

[48] Nevertheless, it is not without myth, as any student of the dialogues knows. Plato very often interrupts the discussion in a dialogue to have Socrates, or some other character, present a *muthos*. But Plato's myths all fit the nineteenth-century conception of what a myth was: i.e., they are all "likely accounts" which serve an explanatory function. They are essentially substitutes for scientific explanation. This is not to say that they do not very often convey profound truths, but Plato employs myth when no "rational" answer is available.

cussed earlier is rejected entirely. Such imagery, as I have said, helps one to fix in mind and contemplate the mystery and wonder of beings. But Plato's purpose is *understanding*: i.e., the analysis of beings. Thus, in spite of his recognition of the supernatural status of the Being of beings, his Forms are "mundanizations" of being. With Aristotle, the mundanization is pushed even further. Aristotle declares that all philosophy "begins in wonder," but that philosophy has as its task the removal or cancellation of wonder through scientific explanation. He takes over the doctrine of Forms but alters it, and opposes Form to "matter" (an opposition Plato does not really employ). All reality is conceived by Aristotle on the model of human artifacts: a combination of some stuff, and a plan or pattern.

Now, it might be objected that I have been unfair to Plato in claiming that he wants to take the supernatural that shines through things and denude it of wonder and mystery. After all, doesn't Plato very clearly suggest (most famously in the *Republic*) that we can never know the Forms as they are in themselves, that they always transcend our powers to grasp them?[49] This is true, but this doctrine is not presented as an occasion for wonder, or as bringing us back around to religion, but as a regulative ideal *à la* Kant's Ideas of Reason. While total or pure knowledge of the forms is impossible, the goal of total knowledge is one which we approach asymptotically. Knowing the Forms thus becomes an infinite task, and motivates our (scientific) inquiries into the nature of things.

7. Conclusion

A significant problem remains. How exactly do we recapture the ability to make the divine manifest, to *invoke* the gods? To go back to the beginning, it seems like our ancestors did this

---

[49] Actually, Socrates in the *Republic* explicitly states that Forms *are* knowable. But this is an example of Socratic irony. At 516b he has his escapee from the cave stare directly at the Sun, but this is impossible for any length of time without blindness resulting. The implication is that the Form of the Good (symbolized by the Sun), is also not knowable directly or fully. Presumably, this applies to other Forms, as is suggested by some of the other dialogues.

effortlessly, but that in us the power has atrophied. Why this is the case is the main focus of "Knowing the Gods." But what can we do about our situation?

In "Knowing the Gods," I made some concrete suggestions, which essentially amounted to saying "get back to nature, get rid of all your gadgets, and don't trust modern science." Some readers found this unsatisfying—and so, I might add, did the author. It's not much, but it seemed to me to be, unquestionably, a good way to start. (One reader accused me of hypocrisy, since I live in an apartment and write articles on a computer! To this, I plead *nolo contendere*). I stand by these suggestions, and eventually I do intend to follow them myself. However, I think I can now offer more.

The reader may have noticed that the experience of the divine described herein attributes to ancient man something very much like a child's capacity for wonder. This is nothing new, but in the past the "childlike wonder" of ancient man was held to be a mark of his "primitive" nature. It is impossible, however, to recover the capacity to respond to the divinity of the world without reawakening this capacity for wonder.

In discussing this subject, I am reminded of three texts. I will surprise my readers first by quoting the New Testament (Matthew, Chapter 18, Verse 3): "Verily, I say unto you, if you should not turn and become as little children, you may not enter the kingdom of heaven." The second text could well be regarded by some as the antithesis of the first: it comes from Nietzsche's *Thus Spoke Zarathustra*. In "On the Three Metamorphoses," Zarathustra tells us "how the spirit becomes a camel; and the camel, a lion; and the lion, finally, a child."[50] As camel, the spirit is beast of burden, loaded down with "thou shalts." "In the loneliest desert" (a place of spiritual transformation, as Moses, Jesus, and Mohammed knew) the spirit throws off the "thou shalts" and becomes a lion. But the lion is purely reactive: he smashes the thou shalts and lives a life in rebellion against them. He cannot create new values. This must be left to

---

[50] Friedrich Nietzsche, *Thus Spoke Zarathustra*, trans. Walter Kaufmann (New York: Penguin Books, 1978), 25.

the third metamorphosis, the child. "The child is innocence and forgetting, a new beginning, a game, a self-propelled wheel, a first movement, a sacred 'Yes.'"[51]

The third text is seldom, if ever, quoted. It comes from a marvelous letter D. H. Lawrence wrote to Bertrand Russell from Cornwall on February 19, 1916. Lawrence writes:

> One must be an outlaw these days, not a teacher or preacher. One must retire out of the herd & then fire bombs into it. . . . Do cut it—cut your will and leave your old self behind. Even your mathematics are only *dead* truth: and no matter how fine you grind the dead meat, you'll not bring it to life again. Do stop working & writing altogether and become a creature instead of a mechanical instrument. Do clear out of the whole social ship. Do for your very pride's sake become a mere nothing, a mole, a creature that feels its way & doesn't think. Do for heavens sake be a baby, & not a savant any more. Don't *do* anything any more—but for heavens sake begin to *be*—start at the very beginning and be a perfect baby: in the name of courage.[52]

Someone might say that it's easy for a child to experience wonder, since the world is all new to him. But once one gets used to the world, it's natural for wonder to cease, and even for cynicism and weariness to set in. We must reject this. The child's wonder ceases not just because things become familiar to him, but because the adults around him gleefully trample on his wonder, "explaining" everything reductively in the form of "Oh, X? Why, you silly boy, that's only Y" (see my earlier comments on science and pornography).

The recovery of wonder involves a change in the subject. No change in the object is required. There are essentially two "paths" one may follow in seeking change, and these corres-

---

[51] Nietzsche, *Thus Spoke Zarathustra*, 27.
[52] *The Selected Letters of D. H. Lawrence*, ed. Diana Trilling (New York: Farrar, Straus and Cudahy, 1958), 129.

pond to the old Taoist distinction between "internal" and "external" alchemy (or *neidan* and *waidan*, respectively). (I hasten to add that the two paths are not mutually exclusive and can, and should, blend.)

External alchemy, for the Taoists, involved the use of specially-prepared elixirs designed to produce some transformation in the subject (e.g., making him immortal). What we need is an elixir that would alter our awareness of the world and make everything, including what had seemed thoroughly mundane, new and wonderful. Such an elixir would make the profane sacred. I am referring, of course, to psychedelic drugs, which are a useful adjunct to spiritual reawakening, if used wisely and with the utmost seriousness. I use the phrase "spiritual reawakening" because what must always be kept in mind is that we are not attempting to acquire some new ability, but to reawaken an ability that has been slumbering.

The following is an interesting analogy, which may help us to understand our situation better, and what is required of us. In the 1880s and '90s the railroads were being laid from coast to coast, across the great plains of America. Two obstacles stood in the way: the buffalo, and the Indians who hunted them. By dispatching men to slaughter the buffalo, the government and industry were killing two birds with one stone. With the buffalo depleted, the plains Indians were deprived of their major food source, and pressured into submitting to life on government reservations. But the loss of the buffalo meant much more to the Indians than the loss of their food source. The buffalo was the central figure in their religion. Their mythology was based upon the relation of men to the buffalo, who (it was believed) willingly gave themselves to be hunted and eaten. The devastating result of the mass buffalo slaughter, therefore, was the destruction of the religion of the plains Indians within a few short years. The response to this disaster, however, quickly came in the form of small, edible buttons which made their way up from Mexico and into the hands of the Indians. The plains Indians began taking peyote. With great solemnity and ritual, they would gather in lodges and take the peyote, looking within themselves for new myths to fill the void left by the

White man's destruction of the buffalo cult. Ironically, this is much the same situation the White man finds himself in today.[53] And taking peyote buttons (or some such) may be part of the answer for us as well.

Psychedelic drugs awaken wonder immediately and dramatically. They do not produce "hallucinations"; they open a channel through which we may view the world in an entirely new way. But to approach such drug experiences casually is a sacrilege and may backfire on the user. Approached properly, the drugs themselves may produce immediate and lasting personal transformation (as in the cases of alcoholics who were spontaneously, and completely cured, after one dose of LSD). However, I think that they are largely valueless unless one can retain what one has learned on the "trip," and translate that into a new way of looking at things and, in general, *being* in everyday life.

As to that everyday life—by which I essentially mean the long gaps between psychedelic experiences—this is when "internal alchemy" takes place. Internal alchemy embraces all activities the self engages in (without benefit of elixirs) which have as their end the transformation of consciousness. Reading this article is an act of internal alchemy for you, just as writing it was for me. Self-study, where enlightenment is the goal, is internal alchemy. Yoga, with, again, the transformation of consciousness in mind, is internal alchemy. Initiatic paths, such as that offered by the Rune-Gild and other organizations, are a form of internal alchemy. Sitting *zazen* is internal alchemy.

The problem here is selecting a particular form of internal alchemy, since one cannot do everything. A first step is to actually ask the questions I gave earlier, as attempts to articulate the pre-reflective attitude of our ancestors: *why are there beings at all, rather than nothing?* and, *why should this particular thing be, and be the way that it is?* In other words, the first step is to begin

---

[53] I owe this analogy to Joseph Campbell, who presented it in a public lecture in the early 1970s. To my knowledge, the lecture has only been released as a CD: "Confrontation of East and West in Religion" (Joseph Campbell Foundation, 1996).

to experience wonder in life.

But let me say something briefly about meditation and yogic practices. The description I have given of religious experience bears a great deal in common with descriptions of the Zen experience of *satori*. *Satori* is commonly described as an experience of "awakening," or "enlightenment." Describing it is tricky, as no description can actually convey what it is like to *experience satori*, but it seems to involve at least two components. The first is an intuition that what is is *right*. When one experiences *satori*, one feels that everything, just as it is now, is fundamentally right, and that it must be the way it is. Second, time and space seem to be annulled. The experience happens in what is felt to be a kind of "eternal now." And the sense of separation between oneself and the object is also removed. This is not because (as is often stated) one feels that the self and the object are the same. Rather, it is because in the experience of *satori*, the ego drops out, and one is completely overtaken by the experience of the other. But, again, it is a very special experience of what is "other." It is the other experienced in a timeless mode, in which we acquiesce to it, surrender ourselves to it, and affirm it unconditionally.

Given the close relationship between *satori* and my account of the experience of the gods, it stands to reason that the entire Eastern tradition of practices dedicated to effecting *satori, nirvana*, or what have you, ought to be of great interest to us. This does not exactly narrow things down, however, for the East provides us with as many ways to Enlightenment as there are types of individual persons. To each, there is his own yoga. What all these methods have in common, however, is that they are ways to overcome a profane attitude toward things. The best of them teach us to recognize the sacred in the profane, and thus to transform the world before our eyes.

PAGANISM WITHOUT GODS:
ALAIN DE BENOIST'S *ON BEING A PAGAN*[*]

1. INTRODUCTION

Alain de Benoist's *On Being a Pagan*,[1] as its title suggests, is a call for a return to paganism. Much more accurately, it is a call for a *new* paganism. "Paganism" is a term invented by Christians to refer to the religions they wished to supplant. "Neo-paganism" is the attempt to return to these indigenous pre-Christian religions. Although logically neo-paganism could be the return to *any* pre-Christian religion, such as the indigenous religions of the Americas and the Near East, neo-paganism in fact is almost exclusively a European phenomenon, meaning an attempt by people of European descent, wherever they may be, to return to the religions of their ancestors.

Neo-pagans have generated a vast literature, ranging from the scholarly to the cranky, most of it focused on history, comparative mythology, and cultural issues. But so far pagans have shied away from the philosophical and theological questions their project raises: What does it mean to believe in gods? Is it even possible to recover the sort of belief our ancestors had? What are the fundamental differences between monotheism and polytheism? In what ways do modern, neo-pagans unwittingly buy into monotheistic, and even specifically biblical paradigms in attempting to reconstitute paganism? In what ways, if any, has the encounter with the biblical tradition been positive, and what might neo-pagans want to preserve from this encounter, even as they seek to go beyond it? In short, what neo-paganism seems desperately to need is a theology.

On Being a Pagan addresses just such questions and is the closest thing yet to a pagan theology. Inevitably, while its vir-

---

[*] First published in *TYR: Myth – Culture – Tradition*, vol. 3, ed. Joshua Buckley and Michael Moynihan (Atlanta: Ultra, 2007), 429–48.

[1] Alain de Benoist, *On Being a Pagan*, ed. Greg Johnson, trans. Jon Graham (Atlanta: Ultra, 2004).

tues are great, so too are its shortcomings. But the book is so filled with brilliant insights that one is inclined to overlook its flaws. It should be noted that Benoist's philosophy has evolved since *On Being a Pagan* was originally published. I shall discuss some of the ways in which he has altered his position in my conclusion. However, for the bulk of this essay I intend to deal with *On Being a Pagan* on its own, as a self-contained work.

Benoist develops his account of paganism by systematically contrasting it with Biblical monotheism:

> Whatever some may maintain, it is not polytheism that is "old hat," but Judeo-Christian monotheism that now finds itself questioned and creaking all over, while paganism is again manifesting its attraction, although it may appear in forms that are often clumsy and sometimes aberrant.[2]

Much of the book consists in a polemic against Biblical monotheism. Indeed, so penetrating is this polemic that *On Being a Pagan* would be valuable because of it alone, independent of the positive points Benoist makes concerning paganism.

Benoist sees Biblical monotheism as inherently dualistic, in the sense that it makes a sharp division between God and the world. According to orthodox (i.e., non-mystical) Christian theology, God entirely transcends the world and in no way depends upon creation. By contrast, paganism holds that the divine is present in the world, though not immanent in all things, as pantheists would maintain. Pagans find the sacred on earth, but as a result of its rigid separation of God and world, monotheism renders the entire world profane. God has given man dominion over the earth, the monotheists claim, and man may do with it as he pleases.

Dualism, however, proves to be the seed of destruction at the core of monotheism. Since the transcendent God is beyond experience, his existence must somehow be inferred logically. But the arguments for God's existence can all be refuted using

---

[2] Benoist, *On Being a Pagan*, 5.

the same logic: more than two thousand years of philosophical theology have not produced a single sound argument proving the existence of the one God. Recognizing this, atheists reject God and, in effect, elevate logic itself to the throne of heaven (Freud's "our God *Logos*"). Then they turn to the world. Do they question monotheism's profanation of the earth, or the idea that the earth is man's to do with as he likes? No. Instead, they accept these tenets and then get to work on the world using logic, in the form of scientific rationalism, to remake it according to their designs. From Biblical monotheism they also typically adopt a linear view of history, which sees time as moving toward some final state of perfection. Thus is born the secular humanist ideal of "progress," including all the horrors of imperialism, colonialism, and totalitarian social engineering that have plagued much of the world since the Enlightenment.

Some of these points have been made by other authors, but I know of no better synthesis and elaboration than in Benoist's book. To the foregoing criticisms of monotheism I would add the following: along with the ideal of progress usually goes a Promethean image of man as a godlike being. Atheistic humanism, the bastard child of monotheism, exalts man as the measure of all things and glories in his ability to transcend nature, even his own nature, and impose his ideal upon all. I would argue that this tenet is central to modernism and that it stands fundamentally at odds with the pagan worldview. Surprisingly, however, Benoist strongly endorses this radical humanism and, indeed, argues that it is of the essence of being a pagan. Here lies the grave problem with his account of paganism.

2. A Nietzschean Paganism?

Benoist's approach in *On Being a Pagan* is, from start to finish, Nietzschean. He makes no attempt to conceal this: Nietzsche is quoted again and again throughout the book. Indeed, an uncharitable gloss on Benoist's standpoint in this work would be to say that it is a Nietzschean humanism masquerading as paganism. This would indeed be uncharitable, given the book's wealth of insights, but it is not altogether inaccurate.

Benoist quotes at length a passage from Nietzsche's *Gay Science* entitled "The greatest advantage of polytheism":

> There was only one norm, *man*, and every people thought that it possessed this one ultimate norm. But above and outside, in some distant overworld, one was permitted to behold a plurality of norms; one god was not considered a denial of another god nor a blasphemy against him. It was here that the luxury of individuals was first permitted; it was here that one first honored the rights of individuals. The invention of gods, heroes, and superhumans of all kinds, as well as near-humans and subhumans, dwarfs, fairies, centaurs, satyrs, demons, and devils was the inestimable preliminary exercise for the justification of the egoism and sovereignty of the individual: the freedom that one conceded to a god in his relation to other gods — one eventually also granted to oneself in relation to laws, customs, and neighbors. Monotheism on the other hand, this rigid consequence of the doctrine of one human type — the faith in one normal god beside whom there are only pseudo-gods — was perhaps the greatest danger that has yet confronted humanity.[3]

This passage contains much of the inspiration for *On Being a Pagan*. First, there is the thesis that paganism is radically *man-centered*. By this I do not mean the claim that paganism is somehow especially conducive to human flourishing, a proposition for which good arguments have been offered elsewhere. Instead I mean something much more radical: the idea that the human serves as a supreme standard in terms of which the world is measured and the gods *created*. This last is the second major point in the passage which seems to have influenced Benoist: the claim that the gods and other beings of pagan myth are an invention. Further, the only justification for believing in these inventions is a kind of utility: belief in them leads to the "justification of the egoism and sovereignty of the individual."

---

[3] Quoted in Benoist, *On Being a Pagan*, 114.

The influence of Nietzsche on Benoist is, I believe, both positive and negative. Benoist is rightly critical of contemporary neo-pagans who believe naïvely that we can simply jump over more than a thousand years of Christianity and "go back" to believing as our ancestors did. He writes: "Post-Christianity cannot be an *ad integrum* return; it cannot be the simple 'restoration' of what once was. . . . A new paganism must be truly new. To *surpass* Christianity demands both the reactualization of its 'before' and the appropriation of its 'after.'" In other words, today's would-be pagans must hold their noses and ask whether anything about humanity and the world may have been *learned* through the encounter with Christianity.

Benoist continues: "It is [on the occasion of their conversion to Christianity] that Europeans were able to acquire a clear awareness that they did not specifically belong to 'nature'—that they possessed a constitutive 'super-nature' and could acquire another by making the transition from human to super-human." In short, if I understand him correctly, Benoist claims that through Christianity it was revealed to men that their being transcends the merely natural, and that it was possible for human nature to become, as it were, "divinized." I take it that this latter message was imparted to them through the figure of Christ. Certainly, the German mystics are full of the idea that the Incarnation is not a once-only event, but something that may come to pass in every human soul. However, Benoist notes, the Church erected terrific barriers to prevent individuals from realizing this "inner truth" of Christianity. The new paganism, Benoist insists, must be a paganism that has appropriated the truths about man that were won through the encounter with Christianity: specifically, the thesis that man is a super-natural being whose dignity consists in his autonomy and capacity for self-creation. Benoist concludes this passage by claiming, dramatically, that "The paganism of the future will be a Faustian paganism."[4]

In the foregoing, Benoist is very much in line with Nietzsche. In *Twilight of the Idols*, in a passage entitled "Whis-

---

[4] Benoist, *On Being a Pagan*, 168.

pered to the Conservatives," Nietzsche writes, "What was not known formerly, what is known, or might be known, today: a reversion, a return in any sense or degree is simply not possible."[5] It is impossible to "go back." In the *Genealogy of Morals*, Nietzsche presents a portrait of our pre-Christian ancestors, whom he refers to as the "master" types. Theirs is a natural system of values: strength, health, and courage are celebrated, whereas weakness, debility, and cowardice are scorned. While Nietzsche clearly admires the masters, he does not believe that we can go back to being them. The original masters were naïve, easy prey to the purveyors of the "slave morality" that inverted their values and turned them into guilt-ridden champions of the weak. Through this encounter with slave morals, terrible though it may have been, the human race emerged from its childhood and at least some of its members are now able to look without illusion upon the phenomenon of values as such, and to know the true sources from which values spring. These are, of course, the *Übermenschen* or overmen. Nietzsche bars us from going back, and exhorts us to go forward and to clear the way for the coming into being of humans who are actually, to use Benoist's term, superhumans.

So far as I can see, the only significant difference between Benoist's views and Nietzsche's is that Benoist chooses to call the overmen "the new pagans." But to designate them as such seems, at best, a half-truth. Nietzsche's overmen do have some characteristics in common with their pagan, "master" ancestors (such as a heroic attitude toward life). But in Nietzsche's dialectic, the overman represents a stage in human evolution *qualitatively different* from that of the masters. This qualitative difference centers around the overman's abandonment of illusions of any sort, including religious illusions (and Nietzsche takes all

---

[5] Friedrich Nietzsche, *Twilight of the Idols*, in *The Portable Nietzsche*, ed. and trans. Walter Kaufmann (New York: Penguin Books, 1982), 546. Later in the passage, Nietzsche states, "Nothing avails: one *must* go forward — step by step further into decadence (that is *my* definition of modern progress). One can *check* this development and thus dam up degeneration, gather it and make it more vehement and *sudden*: one can do no more."

religion to be illusory). If Benoist's "pagans" are essentially identical to Nietzsche's overmen then what Benoist offers us is a non-religious paganism, a paganism without gods. And this invites the obvious question, why does Benoist use the term "paganism" at all? Essentially, what Benoist presents us with is an atheistic humanism which reappropriates some of the attitudes and values of ancient pagans, but eschews their religion. In expounding this humanism, Benoist makes many points which are genuinely brilliant. But I cannot call this paganism.

3. THE GODS & THE GOOD

Let us take a closer look at Benoist's treatment of the religious aspects of paganism, specifically his treatment of the gods. Incidentally, I feel odd using such a term as the "religious aspect" of paganism because for pagans there was no "secular" realm: their orientation toward the divine structured all aspects of their lives. One of the difficulties with Benoist's account of paganism—perhaps the major difficulty—is his tacit claim that we can have the virtues and the "ideology" of paganism without the gods.

Benoist writes at one point that "while there is a difference of level between gods and men, there is no radical difference of nature. Gods are made in the image of men."[6] Now, it is certainly true to say that, as a general rule, people imagine their gods in human form, with human emotions, but it is not so clear that this means they *make* their gods. The experience of gods in polytheism was universally concretized in the form of human or animal characteristics, which made the gods accessible to all. But there are levels within any religion, and reaching the higher levels usually involves a realization that the iconography of the gods and descriptions of their actions are not always meant to be taken literally. That we have anthropomorphized our gods does not mean that we have invented them.

One might be justified in thinking that I may have read Benoist too literally, but elsewhere he makes it very clear that he believes the gods to be human inventions: "'Creator' of nature,

---

[6] Benoist, *On Being a Pagan*, 33.

man is also the creator of the gods. He shares in God every time he surpasses himself, every time he attains the boundaries of his best and strongest aspects."[7] This is "paganism" by way of the idealism of Fichte, Hegel, or Feuerbach, take your pick: there is no divine independent of man; man "actualizes" the divine in the world each time he overcomes himself.

Just as Hegelians insisted (rather unconvincingly) that their master did not mean to make man God, Benoist insists that "it is not a question in paganism of putting man 'in God's place.'... Man is not God, but he can share in God, just as God can share in him."[8] But given that in Benoist's philosophy "God" has the status of a kind of regulative ideal, not an objective reality, such language is misleading. Much earlier in the book, he writes:

> there is no need to "believe" in Jupiter or Wotan—something that is no more ridiculous than believing in Yahweh however—to be a pagan. Contemporary paganism does not consist in erecting altars to Apollo or reviving the worship of Odin. Instead it implies looking behind religion and, according to a now classic itinerary, seeking for the "mental equipment" that produced it, the *inner world* it reflects, and how the world it depicts is apprehended. In short it consists of viewing the gods as "centers of values" (H. Richard Niebuhr) and the beliefs they generate as value systems: gods and beliefs may pass away, but the *values* remain.[9]

What Benoist seems to be saying here is that the gods represent fundamental values: to believe in the gods is to "enshrine" those values. Benoist seeks to revive these pagan values, but their embodiment as "gods" is not something we need necessarily believe in.

Setting aside the issue of whether this is a correct understand-

---

[7] Benoist, *On Being a Pagan*, 156.
[8] Benoist, *On Being a Pagan*, 177–78.
[9] Benoist, *On Being a Pagan*, 15–16.

ing of the pagan divinities, Benoist's discussion of pagan values is problematic given his Nietzschean treatment of values as such. Benoist several times sets forth the typically Nietzschean opposition to the idea of "objective" value. He writes, "Ethics is a fundamental given in paganism, but there is no universal moralization. This amounts to saying that there are no values in the world other than those resulting from our initiatives and interpretations." He then immediately follows this up with a line from Nietzsche: "There are no moral phenomena; there are only moral interpretations of phenomena."[10]

But Benoist's assertion of moral relativism (or what appears to be moral relativism) is just as problematic as Nietzsche's. The idea that belief in objective moral truth necessarily commits one to believing in moral "objects" (such as Plato's forms) is a straw man. Granted that there are no moral things, only moral "interpretations" of things, might there be grounds to prefer some interpretations to others? Benoist certainly writes as if he thinks paganism is *objectively better* than monotheism. He presents some two-hundred pages of arguments in support of this value judgment in order (apparently) to convince us that it is true. Doesn't this constitute a kind of universal moralizing? One encounters the same difficulty in Nietzsche: he asserts a "perspectivist" position with respect to values, but then writes as if master morality *really is* superior to slave morality. Elsewhere, he establishes "will to power" as an absolute standard of value: all that which enhances will to power is good, etc.

Again, just as in Nietzsche, Benoist's commitment to moral relativism flows from his commitment to a general relativism about truth as such. At the end of the book he writes that reclaiming paganism "involves no longer seeking an objective 'truth' outside the world, but intentionally creating one out of a new system of values."[11] But what can this mean? I understand what it means to *discover* truth. For instance, reading Benoist, I discovered that the Greeks had set up a temple to the "Unknown God." I had no idea that this was true. Shortly after

---

[10] Benoist, *On Being a Pagan*, 186.
[11] Benoist, *On Being a Pagan*, 199–200.

reading that, I opened an email which appeared to be a personal communication, only to discover that, in truth, it was spam. I confess, however, that I have no idea at all what it means to *create* truth. Again, one encounters the same problem in Nietzsche. Do Benoist and Nietzsche mean that we get to simply "make up" the truth, and then decide to believe in it? I cannot quite believe that this is what is meant.

Both men are entirely right in rejecting the idea that there is a truth to be had "outside" the world. However, to infer from this that truth is entirely subjective, and left up to the whim of individuals or groups, is a huge *non sequitur*. Here is the key problem with Benoist's approach to truth and values: he has simply accepted monotheism's premise that the only standard of objectivity would have to lie outside the world. Rejecting the idea that there is such a transcendent standard, he leaps to the conclusion that objectivity is therefore impossible. This is a recurrent pattern among French intellectuals; one finds it, for example, in Jean-Paul Sartre.

Years ago I remember hearing a lecture by a distinguished historian, who spoke about the problem of interpretation in history. Specifically, he was speaking against the subjectivist claim that there is no truth in history, only interpretation, and that different interpretations are equally valid. He said, "Years from now historians will still be arguing about Germany's motivations in invading Poland. Conflicting interpretations will abound. But I know one that will never be offered: no one will ever say that Poland invaded Germany." There are limits to "interpretation." All theories and interpretations stand or fall on the basis of evidence, and on the basis of such considerations as consistency, comprehensiveness, and explanatory power. These standards are not the property of any particular culture or historical period; no transcendent deity has decreed them, nor has any man, but they bind us nonetheless. We know this because all attempts to dispute them wind up covertly appealing to them.

It will be objected, however, that the truth about who invaded whom is quite different from the truth about moral or religious values. The former can be evaluated on the basis of evidence, the latter cannot. But such an attitude again buys into one of the most pernicious products of monotheism: the idea that all standards of value lie outside the world, and that the knowledge we have of this world is therefore value-free. Since most modern, Western people no longer believe in sources of value outside the world, all value claims are therefore declared to be "unscientific" and subjective. But might there be sources of objective value within the world? And wouldn't *that* be a truly pagan way to approach the question of value?

In formulating his theory of pagan values, Benoist should have looked not to Nietzsche but to Aristotle, who was a real pagan. In Aristotle, the objective basis for values is human flourishing (*eudaimonia*). Aristotelian ethics makes the simple, unchallengeable assertion that over time we have found that certain behaviors and ways of life tend to be conducive to human survival and happiness, whereas others tend not to be. The basis for some of these claims can be purely biological and psychological, whereas the basis for others has to do with the dynamics of interpersonal relationships. For example, Aristotle suggests in Book I of the *Nicomachean Ethics* that it is a risky thing to center one's life on seeking the approbation of others, as it makes us too dependent upon them and too vulnerable to being hurt, should those others withdraw their approval. In short, independence is desirable. In general, Aristotle makes claims about what is good for human beings that are universally valid—but at no point does he appeal to the sort of transcendent standard that Benoist believes must be appealed to if value claims are to be rendered objective.

Benoist's relativism is not just a feature of his new, Nietzschean paganism: he argues that it was the standpoint of the ancient pagans as well. Benoist quotes Ernest Renan: "The Indo-European peoples, before their conversion to Semitic ideas, never regarded their religion as an absolute truth. Rather they viewed it as a kind of family or caste heritage, and for this reason intolerance and proselytizing remained foreign to them."[12]

Setting aside what is meant by "absolute truth," a discussion

---

[12] Quoted in Benoist, *On Being a Pagan*, 115.

of which could only bog us down uselessly, what does Benoist make of the phenomenon of syncretism as practiced by the Indo-Europeans? Caesar in his *Gallic Wars* identifies the German deities with his own Roman gods (e.g., Odin or Wotan is dubbed Mercury). The Greeks saw their gods in the Hindu pantheon when, led by Alexander the Great, they entered India in 327 B.C. Nor did the Indo-Europeans confine this procedure to their own peoples. In Egypt, the Greeks identified Thoth with Hermes, Imhotep with Asclepius, and Amon with Zeus.

What does this reveal about the attitude of the Indo-Europeans, and pagans in general, toward their religions, and the religions of others? I think it clearly shows that they believed all polytheistic religions to be drawing on a mysterious, common source. Different peoples have given different names to their divinities. They have also emphasized certain deities, and certain aspects of deities, over others. But underlying these surface differences is a fundamental identity. When pagans could not find an analogue for a god in their own pantheon, they would simply adopt it (e.g., the Roman worship of Mithras). This indicates an openness to the idea that other peoples had seen aspects of divinity that they had missed. Behind this is the root assumption that there is a common religious *truth*, that all people are seeking it, and that all have seen some aspects of it.

In sum, Benoist's relativism about truth and value seems to be quite un-pagan. Nor can he escape this problem by insisting that relativism, while not a feature of old paganism, is a desirable component of the new paganism. The philosophical difficulties with this position are very serious ones, and probably insuperable.

4. CONCLUDING REFLECTIONS

Having now written so much that is critical of Benoist's Nietzschean neo-paganism, I might surprise readers by saying that I sympathize with it in many ways. I have to agree with Benoist and Nietzsche that we cannot go back.

I am writing these words in a Starbucks Coffee. The front of the store consists in one large window, and through it I can take in, at a glance, a CVS Pharmacy, a Burger King, a Sizzler, a GNC, and a sea of cars parked in the lot, my own among them. In this setting, it seems absurd to think about such things as gods and dwarfs, land wights, giants, rainbow bridges, and rings of power. It also seems absurd to think about such things as heroes, and the virtues of honor, nobility, and purity of heart. When I am out in nature and away from modern civilization, all of this seems a lot less absurd, even rainbow bridges, and I feel as if I understand — if only a little — why my ancestors believed as they did. But like most people I am seldom out in nature, and I am thoroughly attached to the comforts of modern civilization.

I have begun to think, with Benoist, that if Christianity is to be replaced with something else, it cannot be a straightforward return to the old religion. In fact, I believe something stronger than this: I believe that there must be, in a way, a kind of break with the past. Both the polytheism and monotheism of our past are moribund, and have little to say to life in the present. And we can only live in the present. I am not saying that we should become ignorant of the past. I agree with Benoist that we must understand our historical situation, and I also derive a great deal of pleasure, and guidance, from studying what was believed in the past.

If something has indeed been lost through the Christian experience — some truth our ancestors possessed — I believe that the only way to recover it is to make ourselves open, in a very special way, to what might come forth to fill the religious void that is in us. We do not know what this will be, and it is better to have as few presuppositions about it as possible. For my part, I believe that the paganism of the past was founded on a genuine religious experience of a reality that exists "in the world," but is not of human invention. Call it the supernatural, call it the *numinous*, call it the gods, whatever. This is the fundamental difference between my idea of paganism and Benoist's. Benoist has said elsewhere, "I have not personally had any experience of the divine (I am the opposite of a mystic). . . . I have no connection to any religion nor do I feel the need to connect to one. . . . In the world of paganism I am not a believer but a guest. I find pleasure and comfort there, not revelation."[13] He believes, if I understand him, that there is nothing "out there" to encounter should we open ourselves, whereas I do believe there is something out there. His position is fundamentally atheistic; mine theistic.[14]

How do we achieve this openness? Let me answer this, initially, by indicating what thwarts openness or makes it impossible. The death of openness is the Promethean anthropocentrism that characterizes modern man — the very anthropocentrism that is the essence of Benoist's new paganism. To raise man up as the highest thing in the universe, to declare that man is the measure of all things, to maintain that the gods, the truth, the good, and indeed reality itself are his to invent, is to effectively close ourselves to the vast, non-human cosmos which gave birth to us, shelters us, and is there to instruct us if only we can swallow our pride and listen.

The position I am advocating involves a certain type of faith and expectation. Faith that there is something "out there" that corresponds, in some way, to what our ancestors called the experience of the gods, and expectation that should we succeed in altering our way of being this something will again enter our lives. But how do we alter our way of being? And what is the openness I referred to earlier? First, the alteration I speak of *does* consist in a going back to an earlier way. While I am skeptical that we can revive ancient traditions, I am hopeful that we can revive or recover the way of being that gave rise to them. Benoist is getting at this when he insists that contemporary paganism need not involve, for example, the worship of Odin, but does involve "looking behind religion and . . . seeking for the

---

[13] Alain de Benoist, "Thoughts on God," trans. Jon Graham, *TYR: Myth – Culture – Tradition*, vol. 2, 74–75.

[14] Given his essentially atheistic premises, one might ask why Benoist bothers with neo-paganism at all. I believe the answer is political. Paganism without gods is another form of European "identity politics," and Benoist is best known as the leading thinker of the French "New Right." As we shall see, however, Benoist's more recent approach to neo-paganism is genuinely religious and more than merely political.

'mental equipment' that produced it, the *inner world* it reflects, and how the world it depicts is apprehended."

In what I have said so far, some readers may have detected the influence of Heidegger. If the neo-pagan movement is to ally itself with any philosopher, I believe that it should be Heidegger, not Nietzsche. According to Heidegger, modern people essentially regard the earth and everything on it as raw material to be transformed in order to satisfy their desires and conform to their ideals. The result is that, "on the earth, all over it, a darkening of the world is happening. The essential happenings in this darkening are: the flight of the gods, the destruction of the earth, the reduction of human beings to a mass, the preeminence of the mediocre."[15]

To the modern attitude, Heidegger contrasts an older way of being: *Gelassenheit*. Translators of Heidegger usually render it "letting beings be." *Gelassenheit* is a term Heidegger appropriates from German mysticism, where it is used to convey an attitude of surrender to the world and to God, so that God can come into the soul. It is the negation of egoism, which involves an aggressive and manipulative attitude toward God and the world: insisting that they must serve our interests, conform to our desires, and in general be only what we make of them. In his ethics, Kant proclaims that we must "act so that we treat humanity, whether in ourselves or in another, always as an end-in-itself and never as a means only." *Gelassenheit* can be seen as extending this to all beings: in some sense we must regard all (natural) beings as ends-in-themselves, and never treat them *merely* as means.

The meaning of *Gelassenheit* is difficult to convey. Perhaps the best expression of what Heidegger means is the concept of "*wu*

---

[15] Martin Heidegger, *Introduction to Metaphysics,* trans. Gregory Fried and Richard Polt (New Haven: Yale University Press, 2000), 47. I am cheating a bit here, as this quote comes from the "early Heidegger," whereas the ideas I am discussing actually come from the "later" Heidegger of "The Question Concerning Technology." But I am skeptical about treatments of philosophers that neatly divide their ideas into "early" and "late" periods.

wei" in Lao-Tzu's *Tao Te Ching*.[16] *Wu wei* is often translated "non-action." Lao-Tzu writes, "the sage is devoted to non-action."[17] But this does not literally mean doing nothing. It means an approach to living in the world that is not grasping or controlling. It means learning the nature of things in order to use without destroying. It means going with the grain, rather than against it. It means openness to the things themselves, rather than seeing them merely in terms of our own wishes or theories. Consider the following two passages from the *Tao Te Ching*:

> Trying to control the world?
> I see you won't succeed.
>
> The world is a spiritual vessel
> And cannot be controlled.
>
> Those who control, fail.
> Those who grasp, lose.[18]

And:

> Act and you ruin it.
> Grasp and you lose it.
> Therefore the Sage
> > Does not act
> > [*Wu wei*]
> > And so does not ruin,
> > Does not grasp
> > And so does not lose.[19]

---

[16] Quite a bit has been written about the similarity between Heidegger's thought and Asian philosophy, and even about Asian influences on his thinking. See, for example, Reinhard May, *Heidegger's Hidden Sources*, trans. Graham Parks (London: Routledge, 1996). The author includes a chapter entitled "Dao: Way and Seeing."

[17] Lao-Tzu, *Tao Te Ching*, trans. Burton Watson (Indianapolis: Hackett Publishing, 1993), 3.

[18] *Tao Te Ching*, 29.

[19] *Tao Te Ching*, 64.

Benoist challenges the popular, Rousseauian conception of paganism, which sees a return to paganism as "getting back to nature." Benoist asserts, correctly, that human being is more than merely natural being, that man in some sense stands outside nature. Referring to historian Georges Dumézil's idea of the three Indo-European "functions," he remarks astutely that the "naturalistic" idea of paganism is, at best, a "third function" paganism seen through the lens of eighteenth- and nineteenth-century Romanticism. But when he attempts to formulate what the super-natural dimension of human being is, Benoist falls back on his Faustianism: man is the being who strives to impress his will on all of nature! He cites the ideas of Nietzsche and remarks, approvingly, that Nietzsche tells us that "man can only fully dominate the earth provided he can fully dominate himself."[20]

Heidegger too believed that man has one foot outside nature. He believed, however, that this consists not in our ability to *negate* nature and refashion it, but rather in our ability to let beings be, and let truth be. The truth, for Heidegger, is not something written down, but rather an event: a *disclosure* of how things are (not, *contra* Nietzsche and Benoist, a "creation"). Human nature consists in being this being that discloses the truth.

In an interview with Benoist published a decade after the appearance of the original French edition of *On Being a Pagan*, the interviewer, Charles Champetier, says "The tone of *On Being a Pagan* was rather Nietzschean. But since then, your writings on the sacred . . . appear to be more inspired by Heidegger."[21] In addressing this, Benoist acknowledges the influence of Heidegger on his thinking, and states "I think that paganism finds its own source in a sense of wonder, in the wondering gaze cast upon the world and [in] pondering the fundamental question: how is it that there is something, instead of nothing?"[22]

---

[20] *On Being a Pagan*, 200.

[21] Charles Champetier, "*On Being a Pagan*, Ten Years Later: An Interview with Alain de Benoist," trans. Elizabeth Griffin, *TYR*, vol. 2, p. 102.

[22] "*On Being a Pagan*, Ten Years Later," 103.

Earlier in the same interview Champetier remarks, "One sometimes has the impression that God is absent from neo-paganism," and points out that some have suggested that neo-paganism is a form of atheism. He then asks, "does paganism presuppose a faith or a belief?" In his answer, Benoist challenges (correctly) the idea that pagans "worshipped" their gods in the way that Christians worship God, but he appears to have moved away from asserting, as he does in *On Being a Pagan*, that the gods are simply a human invention. He goes on to say, "I believe . . . that paganism is incompatible with atheism, if we define the latter as the radical denial of any form of the divine or the absolute that cannot be boiled down to man. And I would add that paganism is not 'Promethean': on the contrary, it implies a rejection of this Titan's hubris which led him to rob the gods of their duties in the vain hope of taking them on himself."[23]

In another later work, Benoist says of the pagan gods, "It is not a question of believing in their existence but of awakening to their presence."[24] This is exactly right. The only way to truly revive pre-Christian paganism would be to revive the attitude toward the world that allowed "the gods" to become present to human beings in the first place. Minimally, we would have to come back to the earth and to the present and become *mortals* again, beings who recognize their limitations, and recognize that those limitations define them and mark out their good.

> Look at plain silk; hold uncarved wood.
> The self dwindles; desires fade.[25]

We must make a space within ourselves and within our world in which numinous and uncanny things may again show themselves.

I suppose that many readers will find these prescriptions extremely vague, hard to implement, and even, perhaps, "Romantic." Ultimately, from a Heideggerian perspective (and that is all

---

[23] Benoist, "*On Being a Pagan,* Ten Years Later." 93.
[24] Benoist, "Thoughts on God," 65.
[25] *Tao Te Ching*, 19.

I am attempting to lay out here), little more can be said. Indeed, some Heideggerians would object that I have already said too much. Heidegger makes it quite clear that there is nothing we can "do" to usher in a new age and cause the gods to return.[26] To assume that we can "do" something, that we can devise a plan or a method for returning to some pre-modern way of being *is itself a type of thinking that is wholly modern in nature.* The chief characteristic of modernity is the idea that everything—nature, human nature, history, consciousness, even the supernatural—is manipulable; we have only to find the right technique, and the world is ours to control.

For Heidegger, the most un-modern thing we can do, the only thing we can do to fight modernity, is to give up the idea that we can "do" anything. This type of thinking is typical of Taoism:

> Best to be like water,
> Which benefits the ten thousand things
> And does not contend.
> It pools where humans disdain to dwell,
> Close to the Tao.[27]

The most powerful thing one can do, sometimes, is to surrender the attempt to do anything at all. Perhaps it is in this surrender that that space I referred to earlier will open up, allowing the gods to re-enter the spiritual lives of Westerners. Then again, perhaps not.

---

[26] I should point out, lest I confuse readers unfamiliar with Heidegger, that Heidegger did not call himself a pagan and was not preoccupied with the idea of a return to the gods. Heidegger does use phrases like the "flight of the gods" to describe modernity, and he did famously state in an interview published after his death that "only a god can save us now." However, he seems to have used terms like "gods" and "God" in a largely figurative sense. My belief is that if we deliberately take such usages literally, then Heidegger can be read as saying something vitally relevant to neo-paganism. (However, even if he had never referred to "the gods," I would still argue for the relevance of his thought.)

[27] *Tao Te Ching*, 8.

WHAT GOD
DID ODIN WORSHIP?*

1. INTRODUCTION

In the *Poetic Edda*, Odin narrates his discovery of the runes:

I wot that I hung on the wind-tossed tree
All of nights nine,
Wounded by the spear, bespoken to Odin,
Bespoken myself to myself,
Upon that tree of which none telleth
From what roots it doth rise.

Neither horn they upheld nor handed me bread;
I looked below me—
Aloud I cried—
Caught up the runes, caught them up wailing,
Thence to the ground fell again.[1]

This is one of the most famous passages in the *Edda*, and one of the most mysterious. It seems to represent an act of self-sacrifice, through which Odin acquires the runes. But how can Odin sacrifice himself to himself? What can this mean? Of course, if Odin is the supreme God, the Alfather, then there is no greater god to whom he could sacrifice himself. But this hardly removes the mystery. If Odin is the supreme god, why does he need to do anything at all to acquire the runes? Why doesn't he already possess them, simply in virtue of being Odin? And yet he does do something: he sacrifices himself to

---

* First published at Counter-Currents/*North American New Right*, April 29, 2011, http://www.counter-currents.com/2011/04/what-god-did-odin-worship/.

[1] *The Poetic Edda*, trans. Lee M. Hollander (Austin: University of Texas Press, 1962), 36.

himself. This act (which gives the term "self-sacrifice" a whole new meaning) irresistibly suggests that there is a duality in Odin; that there are two "Odins": one who has the secret of the runes, and one who wants to acquire it. In this essay — which is a highly speculative exercise in the interpretation of myth — I will suggest that the Odin who speaks in this passage, and in general the Odin familiar to us, represents one half of a complex deity: the half that appears. Odin is the "face" of this god, who transcends appearances and never appears to us in his totality.

In making my argument, I will be drawing extensively upon the Indian tradition. It is a long-standing practice in the field of Indo-European studies to use one Indo-European tradition to shed light on another, and to help us fill in the blanks. This is always a speculative procedure, especially in the area of myth. No certainty is possible here. Further, my interest is not that of the detached scholar (though I certainly think that solid scholarship, and scholarly principles must guide us); my interest is that of someone who seeks to recover and reanimate aspects of his own tradition. In the absence of firm, historical confirmation it is permissible, therefore, to be guided by imagination, by intuition, by the "feel" of certain conceptual possibilities (and necessities), and by something that can only be described as "feeling for Tradition."

2. ODIN AS RUDRA/SHIVA

Rudra is the Vedic equivalent of Shiva, who was a pre-Aryan god: a god of the native peoples of India, worshiped prior to the Aryan invasion (second millennium B.C.). (In what follows, I will use the term "Aryan" to refer exclusively to those Caucasian peoples who invaded India, and their culture.) Shiva is, in fact, the oldest continually-worshiped divinity in the world, and the Indologist Alain Daniélou (himself a convert to the Shaivite religion) has argued for the identity of Shiva and Dionysus, and for Shaivism as a kind of *Ur*-religion which once dominated Mesopotamia, the Indus Valley, and Crete.[2] In time,

---

[2] See Alain Daniélou, *Gods of Love and Ecstasy: The Traditions of Shi-*

the Aryan tradition of the *Vedas* came to absorb the native Shaivite and Tantric traditions, so that Shiva eventually became one of the major gods of Hinduism.

There are two ways to understand this amalgamation of Aryan and non-Aryan elements. One is to see it as the result of social and political necessities. Just as the Aryan peoples intermarried over time and mingled their blood, so the two traditions intermarried, and the result is the Hinduism we know today. This account is undeniably true, but it misses the deeper, more interesting truth. The dominant Aryan tradition would not have absorbed—*could* not have absorbed—the pre-Aryan unless there were elements in that indigenous tradition that were not only compatible with the Aryan, but complemented it in important ways. My own view is that Shaivism and Tantra were amalgamated with the Aryan tradition because they were seen as keys that could unlock the deeper meaning of the Vedic religion. Further, within Shaivism and Tantra were beliefs and spiritual practices which promised mastery over the body and mind—and through them mastery over the world itself. This had to have been enormously appealing to the thumotic Aryans.

The name "Shiva" (meaning "auspicious one") originates in the Rig Veda as an epithet of Rudra. This epithet was eventually used more commonly than "Rudra," which came to be understood as another name for the god Shiva. However, this was no mere linguistic accident. The sages of India have long understood that the study of language is a means to discover great truths, and a complex philosophy arose from the identification of Shiva and Rudra. Daniélou writes: "In the later Hindu philosophy Shiva is the name given to the transcendent peaceful aspect of the disintegrating tendency, while Rudra represents the fierce, active, manifest personification of destruction."[3] Let us look at the contrast between these two gods—or, rather, two aspects of one god—in greater detail.

---

va and Dionysus (Rochester, Vt.: Inner Traditions, 1992).

[3] Alain Daniélou, *The Myths and Gods of India* (Rochester, Vt.: Inner Traditions, 1991), 192.

The etymology of "Rudra" is uncertain, but the translation of "howler" is widely accepted. Rudra is a terrible god – a god of violence and destruction. Daniélou writes that "Anyone who performs a function of destruction participates in the Rudra principle. Life, which can only exist by destroying life, is a manifestation of Rudra."[4] He is associated with storms, and with the hunt. Even the gods are frightened by his zeal for war, and the ferocity of his desire for destruction. He is lord of the animals, and can sometimes be encountered wandering the forests. He is also lord of ghosts, known to prowl about graveyards. Finally, Rudra is the father of the Maruts, "a restless, warlike troupe of flashy young men, transposition in space of the hordes of young warriors called the *marya* (mortals). They have been compared to a society of war-minded men with esoteric practices and formulae. They are the embodiment of moral and heroic deeds and of the exuberance of youth."[5]

The parallels to Odin/Wotan are fairly obvious. I should point out that many other authors have drawn the same comparison — one of the most notable being Kris Kershaw in his excellent book *The One-eyed God: Odin and the (Indo-) Germanic Männerbünde*. Odin is also a fierce, destructive god, associated with storms, war, and the "wild hunt." It is his role as the spiritual leader of the *Männerbünde* that Kershaw makes the primary basis for comparing him to Rudra, whose Maruts constitute just such a *Männerbund*, as the above quote from Daniélou nicely brings out.

Now, my suggestion is that the "other self" of Odin — the self to whom he sacrifices himself — is the Germanic equivalent of Shiva. But who is Shiva? To repeat, Rudra (Odin, I maintain) is "the fierce, active, manifest personification of destruction," while Shiva is the "transcendent peaceful aspect of the disintegrating tendency." Shiva is the dynamic source of all being — not "Brahman," a static one beyond all opposites (as in Vedanta), but an eternally self-generating, self-perpetuating *archē*; a horn of plenty. While Rudra might be represented as the sun,

---

[4] Daniélou, *The Myths and Gods of India*, 193.
[5] Daniélou, *The Myths and Gods of India*, 104.

the manifest source of life, Shiva is the black sun behind the sun. He is the deity Jung identified as Abraxas, "the eternal sucking gorge of the void." He is the personification of what Schopenhauer called *will*, and Nietzsche called *will to power*. He is the deity of life and death rolled into one, for life arises from death; creation from destruction. All that exists is an expression of Shiva's abundance. Shiva is the Absolute, comprising all aspects of existence, which unfold themselves in an eternal harmony of conflict, mutually supporting, and mutually canceling. The whole itself—Shiva himself—creates itself through a perpetual self-overcoming. Shiva has been represented through various sorts of images, but the most notorious is the *lingam* or phallus (another one-eyed god).

Now, an obvious objection will crop up at this point. Again, the Aryans absorbed Shiva, a non-Aryan god, into their religion. There is no reason, however, to believe that a religious evolution took place in northern Europe equivalent to that in India. There is no evidence that there was a "Germanic Shiva."

This objection is problematic, however. First, a similar process could actually have taken place in northern Europe. Many scholars have thought the Germanic myth of the "absorption" of the Vanir (including the phallic god Freyr) by the Aesir refers to the conquest of indigenous, non-Indo-European folk by the Germanic tribes, and the absorption of aspects of their religion. However, the most important response to the objection is purely philosophical. Again, the Aryans of India could absorb Shaivism because they saw that it revealed a deeper truth latent within their religion. The Vedic religion of the Aryans is closely related to that of the Germanic peoples—and the same deeper truths are latent within it as well; the same compatibility with Shaivism and Tantra (seen as perennial paths or teachings) is present in the northern tradition also. And even if there may have been no indigenous "Shaivism" or "Tantra" for it to absorb, within that northern tradition we may find, now and then, certain gropings in the direction of those philosophies; certain hints that may point us toward the same path the Vedic Aryans came to tread consciously and systematically, through a happy accident of history. The passage from the *Edda* quoted at the beginning of this essay is one such hint.

3. RÛNA

One of Shiva's many names is Maheshvara, the lord of knowledge. He is the possessor of a supreme wisdom: a knowledge of all things human and divine. As Daniélou notes, there are four main approaches to wisdom in the Indian tradition: through yoga, through philosophy (Vedanta), through the study of language, and through music (for the Western equivalent of this last, which may puzzle some readers, think of the Pythagoreans). Each is one avenue through which wisdom can be approached—but like any set of paths, each has its inherent limitations. The totality of the wisdom obtainable by these four can be gotten, however, from the *Maheshvara Sutra*: a strange formula that, quoting Daniélou once more, "contains all the possible articulate sounds arranged in a symbolic order said to be the key to the structure and significance of all language. It represents one of the esoteric word-formulae in which the ancient Shaiva wisdom was condensed and which are believed to constitute the earliest revelation." Daniélou continues with this tantalizing observation: "According to some strict followers of Shaivism, the transfer of symbolic value attributed to word-symbols to the magic incantations and poetic descriptions of the Vedic hymns could only be a new re-velation (i.e., unveiling) of the ancient wisdom following the Aryan conquest."[6]

The Germanic parallel to the *Maheshvara Sutra* is *Rûna*: the secret wisdom encoded within the formula that is the *futhark*, the "runic alphabet." It is to win the secret of *Rûna* that Odin hangs on that windy tree, all of nine nights. He wins that secret by sacrificing himself to himself: the manifest Odin must sacrifice himself, must "die" into the unmanifest mystery that is his "true self." He must die into the "Shiva" to his "Rudra," and "return" with the secret of *Rûna*, now made manifest in the world through the spoken and written sign.

Let us now look more closely at Odin's "sacrifice" – which can clearly also be described as a self-initiation into the runic

---

[6] Daniélou, *The Myths and Gods of India*, 200.

mysteries. In *The Hermetic Tradition: Symbols and Teachings of the Royal Art*, Julius Evola argues for the existence of a Traditional secret science of initiation, involving reintegration with a "primordial power." Evola argues for the essential identity of Kundalini yoga and alchemy; both, he believes, express the very same teaching. This "primordial power" is often rendered symbolically as a serpent. In Tantra, the serpent represents the Kundalini energy coiled up at the base of the spine. Initiation in the Tantric tradition involves raising this energy up the spine and, in a fashion, mastering it rather than being overcome by it. (A frightening example of what happens when one raises the energy prematurely, without having learned how to control and direct it, is to be found in the story of Gopi Krishna's struggles with Kundalini.)

This energy, this "primordial power" is really the power or energy of Shiva—and Evola tells us that it is also rendered symbolically as the "world tree."

In the Germanic tradition, both symbols occur. The world tree is, of course, Yggdrasil, which literally means "horse of Ygg." Ygg was another name for Odin, but why is the world tree his horse? The reason, so scholars believe, is that the gallows on which men were hanged were referred to as the "horse of the hanged." And as we have seen, Odin hangs himself on Yggdrasil in order to secure the secret of the runes. Hence, the very name of the world tree refers to the episode of Odin's runic initiation. Further, there is a serpent at the base of this tree: Nidhoggr, who gnaws at one of its roots. At the top of the tree is an eagle, with a hawk sitting between its eyes. A squirrel, Ratatoskr, scurries up and down the tree, conveying "words of abuse" between the eagle and the serpent. We find the serpent image elsewhere in Germanic mythology. Sigurd, of course, slays the dragon Fafnir and bathes in and drinks his blood, thus making himself invulnerable (in all but one spot) and able to understand "the language of birds."

According to Tradition, the trunk of the World Tree corresponds to the spinal column – a correspondence one finds even in the Jewish Kabbalah, where the diagram of the "tree of life" simultaneously represents the primordial man, Adam Kadmon. In Kundalini, the *chakra* system, stretching up the spinal column, is understood to correspond to the "world axis." We are thus faced with the tantalizing prospect that buried in the Germanic account of Yggdrasil and the story of Odin's self-sacrifice may be an esoteric philosophy equivalent to that of Kundalini/Alchemy, as treated by Evola. Does Nighoggr correspond to the Kundalini serpent? Is the hawk sitting between the eyes of the eagle at the top of the tree equivalent to the "third eye," the *Ajna chakra*? Does the squirrel Ratatoskr represent one of the "channels" running up and down the column of the *chakras*? Could Sigurd's slaying of the dragon, and acquisition of "dragon powers," represent the raising and conquest of the Kundalini/Shiva energy? (The "solar" hero's overcoming of a beast, representing mastery of a primordial power, is another Traditional theme — Mithras's slaying of the bull presents us with an excellent example of this.) These are all fascinating questions for those who find Evola's theory of a Traditional, initiatory "super-science" plausible. But how can any of this help us to understand Odin's sacrifice of himself to himself?

Suppose that Odin's hanging on the tree represents an act of magical asceticism, with the acquisition of occult power as its purpose. Suppose further that in this ritual one does not literally "hang" on the tree, one identifies with it. In literal terms, the central column of oneself becomes the central column of the world. This is an act of "self-sacrifice" in that one puts off one's personality, and identifies with the universal. Suppose further that the purpose of this act is the raising of a primordial energy in oneself, an energy that lies "at the base" of the world itself, as that from which everything flows. This energy is, again, identical to the Shiva principle described earlier. What we find in the *Poetic Edda* is the outward, manifest, "Rudra" aspect of Odin reintegrating with the unmanifest, "Shiva" aspect – which is the repository of all mysteries.

What is given in the *Edda*, it bears remembering, is a myth. It is not a report of an actual event. It is a mythic description of a magical act of initiation. One of the central tenets of Edred Thorsson's Odinism is the claim that Odin is an exemplar of the Left Hand Path – the path precisely of Evola's Kundalini/Alchemy (or Raja Yoga/Royal Art). One does not "worship" Odin, one identifies with him. What is described in the *Edda* is a path of initiation we ourselves may follow, into the runic mysteries. It is a path of asceticism, and of self-overcoming, in which we awaken within us a dormant power than can confer knowledge of mysteries.

One of the functions of the figure of Odin is thus to serve as a model for the seeker. In truth, we are all Odin, all the external expression of a transcendent power. To find the secret of *Rûna* we must re-integrate with that transcendent power, which is our innermost self. Just like Odin, we must sacrifice ourselves to ourselves. But how to do this? Again, Evola provides us with a few hints.

4. Chaos & Egg

Though it appears that Rudra/Odin is one god, and Shiva another, as I have argued they are actually a unity – two aspects of one god. In *The Hermetic Tradition*, Evola writes of two aspects of the supreme One: Chaos and Egg.[7] The One, the source of all, according to Evola is actually a *one-ing*. In other words, it is not a static "unity" beyond all opposites but a dynamic process of self-differentiation and integration. (In short, it is equivalent to the "Shiva principle.") The Egg is that aspect of the one that represents harmony, integratedness, and also fecundity. Chaos is the aspect of the one that represents dynamism, cancellation, overcoming. The One, the Whole of being itself, is a unity through opposites, or a unity through strife and overcoming. As Heraclitus said, "Changing, it rests." In the Shiva/Rudra complex Shiva, again, is "the transcendent peaceful aspect of the disintegrating tendency," and thus he is the "Egg principle." Rudra is "the fierce, active, manifest personification of destruction," and is thus the "Chaos principle." The One as Chaos and Egg is an image of the whole of reality –

---

[7] See Julius Evola, *The Hermetic Tradition: Symbols and Teachings of the Royal Art*, trans. E. E. Rehmus (Rochester, Vt.: Inner Traditions, 1995), 21.

and each thing in reality participates in the One as Chaos and Egg; each is an image of the whole. Each individual thing, in one fashion or another, maintains itself as individual through holding itself together, healing itself, reintegrating itself on a constant basis. Every individual, just insofar as it is individual, is a continual cancellation of multiplicity and the turning of multiplicity into one—whether this is a multiplicity of atoms, or organs, or moments in time. This deepest of all metaphysical truths is represented traditionally by the image of the *Ouroboros*: the serpent coiled around and devouring itself.

Following the path of Odin and replicating his self-sacrifice involves an identification with the primordial duality of the One. This involves, first of all, a process of "mortification" in which external, waking consciousness has been "reduced" (these are Evola's words). This stage is equivalent to the alchemical *nigredo*. It is one of the meanings of the "Hanged Man" Tarot card, and, of course, what is represented by Odin's hanging himself on the wind-swept tree. What must be achieved is a state of profound detachment from waking consciousness, and from desire.

In the UR material edited by Evola (and published as *Introduction to Magic*), "Abraxas" writes that

> the secret . . . consists in creating in yourself a dual being. You must generate—first by imagining and then by realizing it—a superior principle confronting everything you usually are (e.g., an instinctive life, thoughts, feelings). This principle must be able to contemplate, and measure what you are, in a clear knowledge, moment by moment. There will be two of you: yourself standing before "the other.". . . All in all, the work consists of a "reversal": you have to turn the "other" into "me" and the "me" into the "other.[8]

---

[8] Julius Evola and the UR Group, *Introduction to Magic: Rituals and Practical Techniques for the Magus*, trans. Guido Stucco (Rochester, Vt.: Inner Traditions, 2001), 48.

In other words, the first step of the work consists in bifurcating consciousness into an active, watching self, and a passive, experiencing self. The aim is to identify with this superior, detached, watching self. This is *much* more difficult than it sounds. The path to it consists in a complete emptying of self. It is the moment of complete self-abnegation (hanging on the tree, stuck by the spear, thirsty and hungry). This state, once achieved, becomes a dim reflection of the One, which, as we have seen, is itself and the overcoming of itself. The identification with the superior, watching self is the first step in the identification with the "Shiva principle": the Egg, the Serpent, the Bull. The greatest obstacle on this path is fear.

Evola writes: "But in this desert of death and darkness [of *nigredo*] a splendor announces itself. It is the beginning of the second kingdom, that of Jupiter who dethrones Black Saturn and is the prelude to the White Moon. . . . This is the 'White Opus,' the *albedo*."[9] Once the state of total self-abnegation and identification with the watching self is truly achieved, we begin to experience ourselves as an expression of the transcendent source. This occurs in the region of the *heart*. At this point, Evola tells us that we realize that all books, all philosophies, are no longer of any use to us.

In *rubedo*, the final stage, we no longer experience ourselves as a reflection of the transcendent source ("Shiva," or whatever it may be called), for in that experience there is still duality. Instead, we rise to a *complete* identification with that source. We *are it*. The watching self becomes the eternal self, the soul of the world. This is not the same experience as feeling "absorbed" into the source. That is what Evola calls the "wet way" or "mystical" path, which is fundamentally feminine and passive. This is, instead, an initiatory, magical path: the "dry way." Identification does not mean that the self disappears into the source. Instead, we realize we *are* the source, we are Shiva. What begins in *albedo* with self-abnegation ends in *rubedo* with self-elevation and radical self-assertion: the realization that we are the source of creation itself. In this state, mysteries—

---

[9] Evola, *Hermetic Tradition*, 114.

including the mysteries of the runes—unfold themselves before us, and we find ourselves endowed with unusual powers.

Rubedo is the attainment of gold, the achievement of the *Magnum Opus*. The alchemical symbol for gold is a circle with a dot at the center. This is also the symbol of the Monad, of the One: the dot in the center represents stability, the Egg, whereas the circle that surrounds it, looping round and round like the Ouroboros, represents the dynamism of Chaos. But there is more: this is also the symbol for the sun. And it can be understood as the *lingam* inserted into the *yoni*, seen from above. (The equivalent of *rubedo* in Tantra is the raising of the Kundalini to the crown of the head, the *Sahasrara Chakra*, in which the subject-object distinction is transcended.)

The above, of course, merely hints at the elements involved in the process of magical self-initiation into the mystery of *Rûna*. It is important to keep in mind that the runes are not physical marks or spoken sounds. The runes are objective ideas: aspects of the eternal *logos* of creation (see the next chapter "Philosophical Notes on the Runes"). This *logos* is grasped all at once when the objective of the *Magnum Opus* is obtained. In the traditional *futhark*, in the physical shapes that express the runes and their spoken names, clues to the aspects of this mystery are encoded. But the mystery may not be fully conveyed in language; it must be experienced. It is this mystery that Odin is initiated into. He "cried" and then "catches" the runes, "wailing." This is his experience of the final, transformative stage of the work—a stage that would overwhelm most. But Odin returns from this adventure, having made transcendent truth his own.

Philosophical Notes on the Runes[*]

1. Methodology

The purpose of the following notes is to treat the runes philosophically, as a system of ideas. To treat the runes philosophically means to discuss them as far as possible in abstract terms, without the use of images, symbolism, or stories. Let me say from the beginning that such an approach is inherently flawed. No abstract formula can fully capture the meaning of a rune. The runes are truths given in a non-conceptual, non-abstract form. To impose such a form on them is artificial, and would, if it were our exclusive approach, conceal more than it would reveal. Nevertheless, I am convinced that a philosophical approach can still be one useful tool in understanding the runes. Essentially, my approach is to do four things: (1) to interpret each rune as representing some aspect of the real, some real phenomenon or principle; (2) to invent some brief, abstract formula, which expresses the essence of the rune's "idea"; (3) to discuss the meaning of each rune in philosophical, non-imagistic terms; and (4) to arrange the runes in a system which makes philosophical sense.

Memory is of central importance in the Germanic tradition, where it is represented as the God Mimir. The wise God Hoenir proved to be literally empty-headed without Mimir (discovering this, the Vanir, who were given the two as hostages, cut off Mimir's head). The message is that intelligence is nothing without memory (or tradition) as a guide. True wisdom is informed by memory. This was Plato's belief as well. True philosophy was guided by a recollection of a truth to which humans have a mysterious, pre-reflective access. It is the Platonic conception of philosophy which has guided my abstract reflections on the meanings of the runes. In other words, in trying to

---

[*] This essay appeared in two parts in *Rûna*, no. 21 (pp. 4-9) and no. 22 (pp. 11-16).

give a philosophical account of the runes I have allowed my thinking to be guided by a recollection of certain perennial philosophical ideas, as well as a recollection of specific philosophical terms and concepts from out of intellectual history. I have studied the symbolism and myth surrounding the runes (the "mytho-poetic" and symbolic level), and attempted to grasp it conceptually through relating it to what I believe are the important truths revealed in the works of the great philosophers. If those works do indeed contain truth, then, if the runes are true as well, there should be a correspondence. The philosophers I have drawn inspiration from are chiefly the pre-Socratics (who I believe are the Western philosophers closest to the ancient Indo-European source), Plato, Aristotle, Jacob Boehme, Leibniz, Hegel, Nietzsche, and Heidegger.

Let me emphasize that this philosophical approach is not intended to replace a religious or "mystical" approach to the runes. In fact, my position is that a philosophical approach is dependent upon these others means of access to truth.

2. THE RUNES AS A SYSTEM

One way in which the runes elude our attempts to grasp them abstractly is in their relations to one another. The runes form an organic system of thought, and in such a system every part is related to every other (an idea which is, in fact, expressed in one rune: Hagalaz). New connections between the runes can always be discovered. I am speaking of connections between one rune and another, as well as groupings of more than two runes (for example, "triads" of runes, each of which, like Odin, Vili, and Ve, expresses one aspect or moment of a whole). These connections and groupings are infinite in number. Thus, the runes will always elude any attempt to fully understand the meaning they convey.

This should not surprise us. The runes are, in philosophical terms, a complete speech of the whole. The runes hold up a mirror to reality itself. Just as reality or the universe is too great and complex to ever be fully fathomed, so too are the runes. Certain philosophical texts have this same quality. Plato's *Republic* is also a complete speech of the whole. It attempts to present a complete world-view. It is a metaphysics, a theory of knowledge, a moral philosophy, a psychology, a political philosophy, a theory of history, and much more. The *Republic* is not a treatise, however, but a work of fiction in which the author's true meaning is never openly stated. Thus, the work involves multiple layers of meaning and invites different interpretations (sometimes differing radically). Its meaning seems never to be exhausted.

Hegel is another systematic philosopher whose works contain a similar unfathomable depth. Hegel's thought is, in many ways, the quintessence of Germanic philosophy, and of systematic philosophy as a whole. It is Hegel to whom I have looked for a model in terms of which to "systematize" the runes. Hegel divides his philosophy into three major parts. The first is what he calls "Logic" which is Hegel's metaphysics or ontology, his attempt to lay out the most fundamental categories of being. "Philosophy of Nature" delineates the fundamental categories of non-living and living matter. "Philosophy of Spirit" lays out what is fundamental to man. I take this tripartite division to be basic to any account of the whole. Thus, the runes as a system will give us an account of the fundamental categories of being-as-such, nature, and human being.

Hegel conceives his philosophy as an organic whole, and he imagines it as a circle. Each category of his philosophy is what he calls a "moment" of the whole. In other words, each category, while it is to a certain extent intelligible on its own, must be seen in its relation to the system as a whole. The full explanation of any one category shows how it "requires" supplementation by the other categories. This is obviously how the runes relate to each other. Each rune is a moment of an organic whole, and must be understood in its relation to the other runes.

Hegel is notorious for having organized his philosophy in terms of triads of concepts (e.g. "being," "nothing," and "becoming"). This is another thing that should recommend his philosophy to us as a model. Germanic myth is rife with triads (three norns, three wells, three roots, three brothers, etc.). Hegel's "dialectic" has a triadic structure: two antithetical concepts give rise to a third which reconciles them. This is very much like the Odinic mystery of the rune Dagaz, as I shall discuss shortly.

Finally, Hegel's philosophy "recapitulates" the entire history of philosophy. For example, it is possible to find the ideas of the pre-Socratics recapitulated in the first division of Hegel's Logic. Hegel "synthesizes" the ideas of his predecessors. In creating his own philosophy he "recollects" the truths of older philosophies. As I said earlier, this view of philosophy as recollective is essentially Platonic, and because of its emphasis on memory it is quite compatible with the Old Germanic worldview.

In *Futhark* and *Runelore*, Edred Thorsson discusses the Elder Futhark runes in their traditional order. I have found it necessary to depart from that order in "systematizing" the runes. Also, Thorsson presents two diagrams which attempt to show the relations between runes. The first diagram, "Diagram of the Futhark pattern of manifestation" seems to show the influence of Lurianic Kabbalah, with its depiction of the sephiroth in concentric circles. (This kabbalistic tradition influenced Jacob Boehme, and through him Hegel.) The second diagram, "The eightfold division of the futhark," divides the runes into eight groups of triads. My systematization of the runes does not follow either pattern, both of which are built on the traditional futhark order. Nevertheless, because every rune relates to every other, any combination of runes will yield some meaning. Thus, my ordering of the runes does not fundamentally contradict that presented by Thorsson.

The runes are a whole, they are given all at once. They are the *logos*, the order of things. But in order to understand them, we must articulate them into separate moments. As Jacob Boehme said of his seven "source spirits" (the moments of the being of God):

> These seven generatings in all are none of them the first, the second, or the third, or last, but they are all seven, every one of them, both the first, second, third, fourth, and last. Yet I must set them down one after another, according to a creaturely way and manner, otherwise you

could not understand it: For the Deity is as a wheel with seven wheels made one in another, wherein a man sees neither beginning nor end.

And Parmenides said: "It is all the same to me from what point I begin, for I shall return to this same point."

Here, then, is the system into which I have put the runes. They are divided into four groups of six, and each group represents a philosophical division. Further, I have given each rune a "philosophical title," a short, abstract formula which sums up what I take to be its meaning. All of this will be elaborated and explained shortly.

Ontology ("Logic")

Nadhiz ᚾ — Being Through Opposition
Ehwaz ᛖ — The One and the Dyad
Dagaz ᛞ — The Triad
Ingwaz ᛜ — Source of Being
Berkano ᛒ — Receptacle of Being
Tiwaz ᛏ — Transcendent Eternity

Philosophy of Nature: Mechanics and Physics

Fehu ᚠ — Expansive Force
Isa ᛁ — Contracting Force
Hagalaz ᚺ — The All in All
Eihwaz ᛇ — Immanent Eternity
Uruz ᚢ — Will to Form
Thurisaz ᚦ — Individuating Will

Philosophy of Nature: Organics

Sowilo ᛋ — Will to Power
Raidho ᚱ — Dynamic Order
Laguz ᛚ — Vital Force
Elhaz ᛉ — Will to Actualization
Gebo ᚷ — Complementarity

Wunjo ᛩ — Harmony in Diversity

Philosophy of Spirit

Jera ᛃ — Gift of Order
Kenaz ᚲ — Being in Dissolution
Othala ᛟ — Ancestral Being
Perdhro ᛈ — Horizon of Being
Ansuz ᚨ — Ecstasy
Mannaz ᛗ — Openness to the Divine

The discussion which follows presupposes that the reader is already thoroughly familiar with Edred Thorsson's discussions of the runes: their ideographic and phonetic value, their symbolism, their numerological significance. I will not repeat what Thorsson says here, except occasionally in passing. My philosophical interpretation of the runes builds on his discussions, which operate mainly on a mystical level.

3. Ontology

Nadhiz ᛏ — Being Through Opposition

I have given this rune as first because I regard it as the most fundamental category of being. Boehme said that "Nothing is revealed without opposition." For anything to be at all or to come into being, there must be an other which opposes. Things only are what they are (only have being) in *not* being other things. Thus, if only one was, then, paradoxically, it could not be anything. Thus, there cannot be only one. For anything to be, it must be opposed to an other.

We will see how this otherness or opposition develops itself throughout all being, and accounts for the coming into being and the individuation of all things, non-living and living, and human. Human consciousness, and self-consciousness, is only possible through opposition to another, or frustration by another. Life itself is a keeping-in-being in opposition to the other which frustrates or threatens.

This rune is the categorial basis or foundation for the next rune, Ehwaz, which is "twoness." We will see its principle recapitulated in the relation of Ingwaz and Berkano, and again in Thurisaz.

EHWAZ ᛖ – THE ONE AND THE DYAD

This rune represents the most fundamental duality in being. The language of the One and the (Indefinite) Dyad is borrowed from Aristotle's account of Plato's secret teachings. Plato conceived all being as a "mixture" of the One and the Indefinite Dyad. The one is the principle of definiteness, unity, order, harmony. It corresponds to the Chinese Yang, and to what Julius Evola calls the Uranic principle. The (Indefinite) Dyad is the principle of indefiniteness, lack of form, matter. It corresponds to Yin, and to what Evola calls the Chthonic principle. All of reality is a mixture of these two principles. To take a simple example, each man participates in the One insofar as he has a definite form. This form gives order and harmony to his body. Insofar as he does not perfectly realize this form (e.g., in so far as the proportions of his body are not ideal) he participates in the Dyad. The principle of indefiniteness is called the Dyad because it ranges between "greatness" and "smallness," or "excess" and "defect." It is that element of things that is not fully graspable, quantifiable, or intelligible. In human relations, the One and Dyad manifest themselves on a larger scale as the relation between the sexes: the male is the One (the Uranic), the female the Dyad (the Chthonic).

I have intepreted Ehwaz as the One and the Dyad because Ehwaz has to do with a relationship of complementary duality. Thorsson discusses how on one level the symbolism of Ehwaz points to the relationship of a man to his horse. He also says it represents the relation of husband to wife. (Another parallel would be the relation of the Aesir to the Vanir.) Clearly what we have in both cases is the relation of an ordering principle to something which must be "ridden" in order to be tamed or mastered. Uranos must rule Chthonos. In more abstract, philosophical terms, the One must rule, or govern, or inform the Dyad.

DAGAZ ᛞ — THE TRIAD

From the two comes a third, and this is the principle represented by Dagaz. Dagaz is dialectic of the Hegelian variety. Thorsson refers to this rune as the "Odhinnic paradox." In Dagaz, opposites are reconciled in a third thing. This reconciliation of duality is a fundamental principle of being, and is recognizable at all levels of reality. The most basic Germanic example of this dialectic is the "reconciliation" of fire and ice in a being informed by both but which is neither: Ymir. Dagaz governs all such reconciliations of polarity within the runic system.

It is important to understand that Dagaz does not express the mystic principle that sometimes goes by the name of *coincidentia oppositorum* (coincidence of opposites). The coincidence of opposites asserts that the world of duality we experience is unreal, and that everything is really "one." Hegel aptly parodied this doctrine as "the night in which all cows are black." The third to which Dagaz gives rise is not a transcendent "one" beyond opposites, but a concrete third thing which appears in the world, in some fashion.

INGWAZ ᛜ — SOURCE OF BEING

Whereas Ehwaz gives us the proper relationship of the One to the Dyad, of Uranos to Chthonos, of Male to Female, Ingwaz is the "male" rune itself, but only the male as fecundator. This rune is the complement of Berkano, and must be understood in conjunction with it. As I shall discuss shortly, Berkano is the Receptacle of Being, the "place" where being happens. In Heideggerian language, Berkano is the "clearing" in which being happens. It is a passive principle. Ingwaz is the catalyst or activator. It is what is released in order for there to be being. In order for anything to come to be, there must be a clearing in which it can come to be, and something which generates or catalyzes the being in that clearing. These twin principles are applicable to every kind of becoming, on all levels of reality. On the biological, human level, Ingwaz is the male genitalia and sperm, and Berkano is the womb.

Thorsson notes that Ingwaz may have been an old Germanic earth god. Another pictographic form of Ingwaz is ᛇ.

Thus, as Thorsson notes, the traditional futhark symbol (without the "tail") represents the castrated male. The most famous castrated earth-born god in myth is Uranus, child and consort of Gaea. What the myth of Uranus tells us is that if the male allows himself to become perpetually locked in the embrace of the female (perpetually enthralled to the wiles of the Chthonic) he cannot achieve consciousness. Kronos's castration of Uranus represents the separation of the male from the female, and the cancellation of the eternal non-consciousness of bliss by time. Paradoxically, the male, in order to achieve his true nature as knower, must be "castrated." In the act of copulation with the female, the supreme proof of physical virility, he sacrifices spiritual virility (to use Evola's term); he is spiritually castrated. Enthralled by the female, he loses himself. Thus, Ingwaz is the castrated male precisely because of his relationship to Berkano. (This is why Ingwaz is the rune of the "male" as fecundator, but not the rune of the properly-male Uranic principle. That is Tiwaz.)

This rune obviously has many levels of meaning.

BERKANO ᛒ — RECEPTACLE OF BEING

I have discussed this rune above. It must be understood in relation to Ingwaz. As I said, Berkano is the "clearing" where being happens. It is a passive principle; an opening, a receiving. Ingwaz is the catalyst or activator. Everything that comes to be happens through the intermarriage of these two principles. Berkano is the rune of containment, or concealing, while Ingwaz is the rune of revealing. In every act of revealing, there is a concomitant concealing. Berkano is the chthonic rune.

The title "Receptacle of Being" is an allusion to Plato's *Timaeus*. In this dialogue, Plato establishes that in order for things to come into being, there must exist a principle he calls the Receptacle (*hupodochē*), which he refers to as the "Nurse of Becoming," clearly characterizing it as feminine. The Receptacle has no character of its own, thus it is able to take on all characters. It is a "material principle."

TIWAZ ↑ — TRANSCENDENT ETERNITY

Tiwaz is Transcendent Eternity, whereas Eihwaz is Immanent Eternity, as I will discuss in a moment. These two must be understood in relation to each other. Eihwaz is the world column, the backbone, if you will, of the world. It is the central trunk of the world tree Yggdrasil. It and the branches of Yggdrasil form the "skeleton" of the universe: they hold the universe up by giving it an internal order and form and rigidity. We can discover the order (*logos*) of the universe in our experience of the universe itself. Precisely like Heraclitus's *logos* this is eternity in time: it is what stays constant through the ceaseless change of things. But this immanent eternity, since it transcends both time and the individual things that exemplify it, is simultaneously a transcendent eternity. Tiwaz and Eihwaz are dual aspects of the mystery of *logos*. Precisely through being in all things and in all times (immanence), order is outside any particular thing or time (transcendence).

As an ontological category, Tiwaz expresses the idea that whatever is is something. Each being is informed by order and by form. Tiwaz represents this order, which ultimately has a transcendent source. Tiwaz is, in fact, the Uranic principle alluded to in our discussion of Ehwaz. I said that Ingwaz is the "male" rune, but this is only in the sense of male as fecundator. Tiwaz is the male, Uranic principle of light (the Northstar) and order. (Berkano represents the chthonic principle whose identity, like Plato's receptacle, is to have no identity.)

The symbolism of Tiwaz is an arrow whose shaft is the world column (Eihwaz). We are being pointed up and through the world column, from immanent order to transcendent order.

4. TRANSITION FROM ONTOLOGY TO PHILOSOPHY OF NATURE

The preceding six runes give us the most basic abstract categories of being. In what follows, we see these principles expressed in the world (e.g., Eihwaz is the worldly expression of

Tiwaz). Hegel makes the transition from his Logic to Philosophy of Nature by saying that the Idea "freely releases itself." He is trying to explain the mystery of why there should be concrete, imperfect, physical being in addition to the perfection of the eternal principles. His language of "free release" calls to mind the Neo-Platonic doctrine of emanations from the One. Elsewhere, however, Hegel is clearer. He writes that the Logic shows us the Idea as being, whereas the "Idea that is, is nature." In some sense, the principles of being do not themselves have being. Because beings only have being by "expressing" or participating in these principles, the principles themselves are not beings. This is why Plato held that his form of the Good (which is a form of the One) was "beyond being."

However, as Boehme held, the nothing strives to be something. In itself, the principles of being are abstract and unrealized. They thus "strive" for realization in concrete reality. Another way to put this is that it is their natural end is to become embodied. The concept of *Geistleiblichkeit* or "spiritual embodiment" is a perennial idea in the Germanic mystical and philosophical traditions. It is the end of Idea to realize itself in nature. Thus, the realm of pure being is not to be understood as complete in itself or perfect, but as the abstracted nature of nature. To be sure, the categories of being are transcendent objects, which the mind can know. But their end is to become expressed in three-dimensional, spatio-temporal reality.

Thus, the realm of being "gives rise to" the realm of nature because it requires nature. This principle of not-being striving for being or realization is not one of the runes. It exists in the "fold" between the ontological runes and the others. It gets expressed to some degree in the Elhaz rune.

5. Philosophy of Nature

The first six runes dealing with what we may call the Philosophy of Nature have to do with what Hegel terms Mechanics and Physics (i.e., non-living nature). The second group of six deals with Organics (living nature).

Fehu ᚠ — Expansive Force

Fehu is fire essence. It is a dynamic force which is destructive and consuming, but at the same time it is a fire which ignites or catalyses. Fehu is destructive, yet creative.

Fehu is the opposite of Isa, Contracting Force. These are dynamic forces operating in things. They are similar to Empedocles's concepts of Love and Strife. The closest parallel, however, is again to be found in Boehme. Boehme's first two "source spirits" are Sour and Sweet. Sour (*Herb*) is a negative force, a "cold fire," the will of God to remain unmanifest, unrevealed. This corresponds to Isa and represents a contracting, inward-turning element. Opposed to Sour is Sweet, which is an expansive, outward-opening force. Boehme likely inherits these ideas from the Kabbalah, where contraction and expansion show up as the sephiroth Din and Hesed. Contraction and expansion as fundamental opposites appear widely in German philosophy and mysticism. Aside from Boehme, they figure, under different names, in the thought of Friedrich Christoph Oetinger, Goethe, Schelling, and Hegel.

Unlike the preceding six runes, Fehu is not an abstract category of being. Instead, it is a force active in things, manifesting itself in different ways.

Isa ᛁ — Contracting Force

As I have said, Isa is a contracting, inward-turning force equivalent to Boehme's Sour. It is the opposite of Fehu. Fehu and Isa represent the fire and ice which came together at the beginning of time in Ginnungagap to create the first being. Why is it that fire and ice are conceived of as the beginning of things? At the root of this conception is the idea that the coming into being of things involves a disruption, and release of energy. Boehme's term "cold fire" is very revealing, for it suggests that the cold is also a kind of energy. When these two antipodal forces interact there is an ignition of some kind.

The collision of Fehu and Isa functions on one level as a cosmogony. On a much smaller scale, these forces manifest themselves in the life of an organism (organic nature will be discussed in the next series of six runes). The organism opens outwards and takes in otherness (e.g., in devouring the other, or in perceiving it). But this opening outward is matched, and has to be matched, by a concomitant drawing inward. Having opened out, the organism draws in, taking what it has opened to and making it part of itself (i.e., in nutrition, or in learning). It is in this oscillation between opening and closing that living being happens.

Non-living being, with which we are primarily concerned in this section, is chiefly characterized by indrawing, by stillness, by holding together (a kind of will-to-cohesiveness). The advance of the living over the non-living is that the living can open outwards and respond to the other, and then, in drawing back into itself, adjust. Thus, the capacity of the living to oscillate between opening and closing, between expanding and contracting, equips it to survive more effectively than non-living matter, which only exhibits contraction.

HAGALAZ ᚺ — THE ALL IN ALL

This is the ninth rune in the Elder Futhark series. Nine, as Thorsson points out, is a number of completion in the Germanic world-view. An alternate form of Hagalaz is ✱. All of the runic forms may be derived from this pattern. Thus, Hagalaz is a whole which contains all the runes. Yet it is not simply the totality of the runes itself. It is an individual totality which contains the totality within itself.

Thorsson refers to Hagalaz as the "hail egg" and the "light crystal." It is the product of the interaction of the Fehu and Isa powers: it is a seed form, the most basic unit of worldly being. At the ultimate level of analysis all things are made up of these seed forms, each of which mirrors the universe as a whole. Each is the smallest unit of existence, and each contains the totality of being in itself. What we have here is a doctrine very much like that of Leibniz's *Monadology*.

The energy released by the interaction of Fehu and Isa gives rise to these tiny, non-living, many-faceted, crystalline monads.

Hagalaz is the residue left after the chemical reaction of Fehu and Isa in the alchemical retort that is Ginnungagap.

Eihwaz ᛇ – Immanent Eternity

I have already discussed Eihwaz extensively in the section on Tiwaz. As I said earlier, Tiwaz and Eihwaz are dual aspects of the mystery of order. Through being in all things and in all times (immanence), order is outside any particular thing or time (transcendence).

Eihwaz is the central trunk of Yggdrasil. It and the branches of Yggdrasil form the skeleton of the universe, holding the universe up by giving it an internal order and form. Eihwaz is eternal order in time.

Uruz ᚢ – Will to Form

Uruz is the "form-seeking" principle in all things. Unlike modern science, which posits that order came to be out of chaos or randomness, the Germanic view is that order and form are irreducible primaries. Things maintain themselves, in various ways, in their forms, or act (where possible) to preserve their structure or order. (Even inanimate objects "hold themselves" in their form unless some external agent acts to deprive them of form.) This is the "force" in nature represented by Uruz.

Uruz is a force within beings. It is a directedness toward pattern or form or order, coming from within each being. Uruz, as Thorsson puts it, is the "mother of manifestation" — Audhumla the primordial cow who licked the salted ice and created Buri, father of Odin. Uruz/Audhumla is thus, as Thorsson says, a "shaping power."

Thurisaz ᚦ – Individuating Will

Thurisaz is a primal form of "will" which is found in physical bodies. Hegel's discussion of electricity in his Philosophy of Nature is similar to the concept expressed by Thurisaz. Hegel conceives of electricity as a charge which exists in bodies and which establishes the individuality of a body by lashing out against other bodies. He refers to electricity as "the selfhood of the body" and as "the body's own anger."

Thurisaz is a repulsing, defensive will present in all things, in more or less sophisticated forms. In a certain way, it is the complement of Isa. Every body maintains itself as a body by contracting itself into itself, by holding itself together—but also by repulsing all else which is not it. These may be dual aspects of a single phenomenon, and they are reflected in two primal facts (1) the holding together of a body; and (2) the tendency of a body to maintain the same spatial location, or at least some spatial location. Insofar as a body resists the encroachment of other bodies—the tendency of other bodies to fill the same space it occupies—it possesses a repulsing power or will. Obviously, these two runes, Isa and Thurisaz, express the most fundamental conditions for physical integrity and individuality.

At a higher or more complex level of being, Thurisaz manifests itself in the tendency of the living organism to literally lash out and attack that which opposes or threatens it. Thurisaz is the power of the thurses, the unselfconscious, destructive giants who pre-exist the ordering of the world by Odin. It is also represents the defensive, reactive function of Thor.

The sign of Thurisaz depicts a thorn. Thurisaz, according to Thorsson, is the rune which represents male potency. As suggested by male anatomy, male sexuality is outward going, and inward going. It is no accident that the male organ is called a "prick." Thurisaz is the will which individuates, which strikes against the other and thus individuates self from other. The male "pricks" the female. This is the culminating physical expression of the male's protracted, lifelong individuation from, and yet fascination with, the female (an attracting/repulsing dialectic is basic to sexuality). However, this act of "individuation" climaxes in a moment when the sense of individuality is canceled and merged with that of the female. The male, however, overcomes this apparent defeat by utilizing the female's body to bring forth into the world another body in which he can directly confront his individuality: his child. It is through his child that he overcomes (seemingly) the threats to his individuation posed by the female and the world at large, for in his child his being achieves (potentially) a measure of immortality. In other words, in the procreative act he gives his being over into another vessel (or several vessels) who will carry it long after he is gone. He thus immortalizes himself at a physical level.

6. Transition from "Mechanics" and "Physics" to "Organics"

The first six runes in our "Philosophy of Nature" describe, in the abstract, physical being as such. They apply broadly to all spatio-temporal beings, not just to living beings (but they do apply to living things, as I have discussed). We now make a transition, however, to runes which deal more specifically with living or organic beings.

As I will discuss more fully under Laguz, modern thinkers tend to believe that we must understand the living in terms of the non-living, as derived from the non-living. This has things backwards: we must understand the non-living by looking toward, or back from, the living. It is the end or *telos* of abstract being to become embodied, and life is the *telos* of non-life. Life is the primary in terms of which non-life must be understood (recall how in the preceding six runes we have continually "looked forward" to how these principles manifest themselves in life). Thus, conceptually, the categories of non-life require the categories of life as the next set of necessary moments in the runic system.

Sowilo ᛋ — Will to Power

Thorsson describes Sowilo as the energy lashing out from Thurisaz. Thurisaz is an unconscious, repulsing will to individuation. Sowilo is a developed form of this will. It is a conscious, shaping will. A will to transform. Thus, it manifests itself only in organic, living being.

Thurisaz is an unconscious will which lashes out in defensive fashion. It is like the Akkadian god Apsu, an "unconscious" being who lashes out against his children because they disturb his slumber. Thurisaz is a will to repulse and be left alone. Sowilo, on the other hand, is a will to overcome the other and through it, to grow. It is a Will-to-Power, to borrow Nietzsche's phrase.

Thorsson suggests that Sowilo represents a magical, feminine will pervading nature. The identification of Sowilo as feminine has to do with the fact that it is one half of the sun wheel or Swastika: ᛋ. The sun is feminine in the Germanic *Weltanschauung* (e.g., *die Sonne*).

Certainly, what Sowilo represents is a shaping will which can take various forms. Inherent in all organic being is a consuming tendency toward the other. What is consumption except the cancellation of the being of the other and the making of it into oneself? Hegel discusses this idea extensively. In the human organism, this type of will can become destructive in an uncreative, nihilistic fashion. It can become a will to negate or to cancel all otherness, to destroy or transform all that which opposes, or all that which is merely other. This will is at the basis of the modern, Promethean project of the mastery and control of nature, which has led to the alienation of man from nature, from his own nature, from morality, and from the gods.

However, Sowilo can also be a positive force. It is Sowilo which can be used by the magician—in cooperation with the forces of nature—to bend things to his will.

Sowilo is also the rune of the Germanic code of honor, and the rune of victory. Thorsson suggests that this is because the Germanic *Männerbund* was a path to ecstatic experience (represented by Ansuz, as I shall discuss shortly). It is through the exercise of will, or Will-to-Power, that one can experience a powerful a sense of being transported outside oneself. One can experience *odhr* or *wut*.

RAIDHO ᚱ — DYNAMIC ORDER

This rune relates to Uruz. Uruz is Will to Order, in the sense of the form of a physical being. Raidho is the concept of order extended in time. Uruz + Raidho express the idea of the ordering of a living, organic being. A living being is one that maintains its order dynamically, as a kind of process. The living individual is a process involving acts which sustain it in existence. The "form" described under Uruz is close to the Platonic sense of form: an organizing principle or pattern, but one which is static or still. The order described by Raidho is closer to the Aristotelian sense of form as the function of a thing.

This account makes sense of the different qualities Thorsson predicates of Raidho. He describes it as involving cyclicalness, "right order," ritual, and rhythm. Raidho is the rune of order extended in time, across a life cycle (a rhythm is an order or proportion extended through time). Take human life as an example: to be human does not just mean to look like a human, or to have a human-shaped body; it means to function or to work as a human and to do "the human things." This doing as a part of order is what is represented by Raidho. Hence, Raidho can represent ritual as well.

LAGUZ ᛚ — VITAL FORCE

Laguz is one of the most mysterious of the runes. It represents a primal, vital substance which cannot be further analyzed. It is life itself. In my treatment of earlier runes, I have discussed what characterizes organic being (e.g., I discussed life as a conjunction of Uruz and Raidho). However, although we can see a certain continuity between living and non-living matter, there is a mysterious and unanalyzable qualitative shift between the non-living and the living. Many scientists and philosophers have sought — and still seek — to "derive" living from non-living matter (either conceptually or literally, in the laboratory). What Laguz represents is the idea that this cannot be done; that life is an irreducible primary.

We should not think of the non-living as primary, and the living as derived. Instead we should of life as primary, and as the natural "end" or *telos* of the non-living. The non-living should be understood in terms of, or in relationship to the living, not vice versa. Just as form or order is a primary, not to be derived from chaos, so life is a primary. Things are drawn to order, and matter is drawn to life.

Laguz is the animating presence in things, the life force, the *pneuma*, the *élan vital*. The fundamental reality of this vital fluid force was "intuited" in the perennial myth of the primordial waters.

ELHAZ ᛉ — WILL TO ACTUALIZATION

This rune represents the striving of the lower toward the higher. The "Will to Actualization" is the will present in all living things which strives for flourishing or excellence. Elhaz is related to Uruz, Will to Form, and to Raidho, Dynamic Form. It is, in a certain sense, the Will to Form as expressed in living beings. Uruz is a concept which applies to living and non-living matter. It says simply that things maintain themselves, in various ways, in their forms, and preserve their structure or order. In living things, this form-keeping becomes a dynamic process, and what it means to have a form is to function in a certain way: hence the Dynamic Form of Raidho. However, to each individual living thing there is a *telos* or end. This *telos* is not simply to function as a particular kind of thing, but to function well: to achieve excellence, flourishing, or perfection. This is the aspect of living being symbolized by Elhaz. Within each living thing there is a Will to Actualization.

Will to Form (Uruz) represents a directedness of all things toward a formal reality which transcends individual being — a directedness which can only be imperfectly realized in inanimate things. Elhaz represents a drive to, in a sense, overcome individuality itself and perfectly realize form: to achieve perfection. Human beings differ from all other animals in that we must choose to strive for perfection. Other beasts naturally seek to flourish. A wolf does not have to be persuaded to be the best possible wolf it can be. It will strive to be so, and will succeed to some degree or other, contingent upon its natural endowments. Humans find their perfection in a relationship to the divine, but this relationship can be avoided, cancelled, or perverted.

Thorsson states that Elhaz is "the power of human life and 'spirit' striving toward the world of the Aesir."[1] I have inter-

---

[1] Edred Thorsson, *Futhark: A Handbook of Rune Magic* (York Beach,

preted this rune more broadly and related it to living beings as such, not just human beings. Thorsson interprets the image of Elhaz to be a splayed hand offered as a sign of protection. I think it looks more like a man with arms stretched out towards the heavens, stretching toward the ideal. Thorsson also interprets Elhaz to be a symbol of the valkyrjur, who are semi-divine intermediaries between men and the gods. All of this supports my reading of Elhaz as signifying the relation of the individual to the ideal.

GEBO X — COMPLEMENTARITY

Gebo is the rune which signifies that the being of some things is actualized in their relationship to another. To a degree, this is exhibited on the level of non-living matter. For example, fire and ice are what they are in relation to each other. Day and night are what they are in relation to each other. But Gebo expresses a relationship which seems to be truly exhibited only in living things: a relationship whereby an individual is completed or made whole through another. The pre-eminent example of this would be the relationship of male and female. The individual may to a great extent actualize his or her being in isolation — but certain aspects of his or her being cannot be actualized except in relation to an opposite. Gebo expresses this idea of being-through-Complementarity — a concept which will appear again, in different guises, in Mannaz and Dagaz. In addition (as Thorsson points out) it relates to Ansuz.

Looking backward, this rune is prefigured in Nadhiz and Ehwaz (Nadhiz is the relation of Being Through Opposition; Ehwaz is the One and the Dyad, which is manifested in male and female — but Ehwaz tells us only of the "power relationship" between these two, and nothing of how they complete or complement each other). The overlap or close relationship between different runes should not confuse or disturb us: recall that each is simply a different aspect or expression of the whole.

Thorsson notes that "Gebo contains the secrets of psychical-

Maine: Samuel Weiser, 1984), 49.

ly joining two people (usually male/female), or several persons, in order that they may produce a creative power greater than their sum total. This is the rune of sex magic."[2] He also states that Gebo signifies "that which is exchanged between gods and men." The being of man is openness to the gods: this is what constitutes the essence of humanity, and what marks humanity off from all other beings. Thus, man is only completed or realized as man in relation to the gods. Gebo rules this aspect of man's nature, as well as the sexual. Aristotle observed that man is a "political animal"; i.e., that he is an animal of the *polis*, or city, who needs others to be fully human. There is thus another, non-sexual level of interpersonal need (involved with friendship, citizenship, comradeship, etc.) which involves the bringing into being of some side of the individual through relations to another.

WUNJO ᚹ — HARMONY IN DIVERSITY

Wunjo signifies the harmony that can be produced through the cooperation of different individuals. Again, this is a concept prefigured on the inorganic level, but only fully realized with living things. It refers to any association of living things where the association involves an awareness of and dedication to a common purpose which binds all together. This rune obviously is of great significance on the human level, where it has important implications for social and political philosophy. It is impossible to understand the functioning of the Germanic *Männerbund* except in the terms of Wunjo. Also, the unity of the traditional tripartite Indo-European society must be understood along these lines: as a harmony in diversity. The three tiers of society (ruling, fighting, and cultivating) are vastly different from each other, but they can work in harmony, for the good of all, if each does its part and does not encroach on the others. This is exactly what Plato tells us is the key to the well-being of his ideal city in the *Republic* — a city made up of exactly the three traditional Indo-European functions.

---

[2] Thorsson, *Futhark*, 32.

7. Transition from Philosophy of Nature to Philosophy of Spirit

The "Ontological" runes are an abstract description of being and not fully realized until embodied in three-dimensional nature. Thus, we understand those runes "forward": in terms of Philosophy of Nature. In the just the same way, we must understand non-living nature in terms of living nature. Life must be seen as primary; as the natural *telos* of the non-living. Recall how many times I have discussed a rune which applies to non-living nature as having its fullest or most genuine expression only in living nature. In just the same way, we can understand human nature as the highest, most developed, and most complex expression of all of the runes. In some sense, all that has gone before looks forward to "Spirit" (to use Hegel's term) or human nature. Thus, the final six runes, as categories of Spirit, complete our account. Each expresses some fundamental aspect of human nature.

8. Philosophy of Spirit

Jera ᛃ — Gift of Order

The title "Gift of Order" is an allusion to Raidho, Dynamic Order. Jera signifies the good harvest. As Thorsson notes, Jera symbolizes the yearly path of the sun, and Raidho the daily path. "Jera is the reward for honorable, right, and lawful (natural) past action," he writes.[3] The relation of Raidho to Jera is just this: the result of right daily action is a gift of nature over time. This could simply mean good health, or healthy offspring, or a good harvest.

To my knowledge, this is a concept which is not expressed by any philosopher. The idea of Jera is moving in the area of an ontology of man's relationship to nature. The closest thing we have to this concept in philosophy is the quasi-Aristotelian idea of Raidho: of Dynamic Order, of form as functioning. What Jera tells us, however, is that through right and natural action,

---

[3] Thorsson, *Futhark*, 42.

something else comes into being besides the action and the actor, as a kind of gift or reward. The key word in Thorsson's description is *natural* past action. Raidho refers to ordering action along natural paths. Jera refers to ordering according to nature on a larger timescale, and gives us a promise: that the natural ordering we do on the small scale will bear fruit.

Jera is the first rune of Spirit because it expresses one of the two most fundamental aspects of man's being: his role as steward of nature. (The other aspect is man's openness to the divine.) The truest expression of Jera is in the harvest. Man must choose to live according to nature. The harvest, the result of his deliberate choice of the natural, is literally the gift or reward of nature for this virtue.

KENAZ ᚲ — BEING IN DISSOLUTION

Thorsson describes Kenaz as dealing with the mystery of sacrifice — but Kenaz is an internalized sacrifice. The internalization of the sacrifice was one of the innovations of Indian mysticism which came about as a result of reflection on the Vedas. The Indians describe a kind of internal "ascetic heat" (*tapas*) produced by a yogi, which can have transformative and even magical powers. What Kenaz expresses is the mystery of how suffering, breaking down, or dissolution can give rise to growth within the human being. It is different from Fehu, which refers to a destructive force externally imposed, which obliterates and gives rise to something different. Kenaz is an internal fire, an internal dissolving energy which raises one up through breaking one down. This is why Thorsson refers to Kenaz as, among other things, "inflammation." It is something painful and pressing that comes up from within a being.

This is one of the key concepts of human nature, for human beings only excel (only reach actualization: see Elhaz) through growth, and growth only occurs through suffering. Kenaz is a rune of heroism, and a fundamental human rune insofar as the hero is one of the highest human types. Kenaz is the key to the psychology of the mystic G. I. Gurdjieff, who believed that human consciousness can be raised only through ordeals.

OTHALA ᛟ – ANCESTRAL BEING

Othala is the rune of inheritance. This rune expresses an aspect of being which, to my knowledge, is not treated by any philosopher: how the being of something consists in part in its relation backwards in time, through an organic connection with others. Part of one's being consists in a literal sharing of bodily being with others: one's kin. This is a relation backwards in time, but also horizontally through one's own time, to living relatives. Obviously, such relations exist in non-human organisms. But it is only in human beings that such relations become a conscious issue.

The being of things consists primarily in their relation to their form, and their functioning. Being in this sense is automatic. But in the case of human beings, what we are in part is what we have made ourselves, or what we take ourselves to be. For the human being, consciousness of blood relations is an important constituent in personal being. Again, this is something that I do not think has been discussed elsewhere: the relation of ancestry to being.

Consciousness of blood relations is (or can be) constitutive of being in the following ways. Aware of the deeds of one's ancestors, one may find one's entire life deriving meaning from a need to match or to surpass those ancestors (or, perhaps, to expunge what one's ancestors have done). Awareness of the proclivities or tendencies of one's ancestors affects one's own perception of what one is, or can be, or can do. This perception, in turn, places limits on one, and is thus constitutive of being (again, as I have said, the being of man is to some degree self-determined, self-demarcated).

In a broader sense, Kenaz as the rune of inheritance applies not just to blood ancestry but to heritage and tradition. This is constitutive of human being in exactly the same way. What we are, and think we may do, is to a large degree determined by our past. Blood relations, heritage, and tradition serve to bind together (as implied by the symbolism of the sign of Othala). They also serve to create a distinction between inner and outer, between those who belong and those who do not, between friends and enemies. Membership in this in-group, and distinction from the outgroup, is also constitutive of personal being. It is part of what we are.

Those who have no blood ties that they are aware of, no heritage, no traditions, and no in-group have only the automatic being I have said is bequeathed to us by nature: a human form, and biological function. Hence the mindless physical sensuality of modern man (particularly in America): all he has is his body. Hence his gnawing sense of needing something to "belong to." Aside from biological being, the only thing modern man really has is Kenaz: Being in Dissolution. The violence of modern man and the recklessness, the risk-taking, are desperate attempts to overcome the sense of beinglessness by pushing oneself to the limit.

PERDHRO ᛈ — HORIZON OF BEING

Perthro is the rune of *ørlög* and of the well of Urth. The *ørlög* is to be found in Urth's well because it is, in a sense, "in the past": it is the original, primordial pattern or law of the cosmos. All things eventually leave the present and enter the past (and at every moment the *acts* of all things are constantly going over from present to past). In the well of Urth we find all that has been, and the primordial forms that shaped all that has been and will be.

The language "Horizon of Being" is borrowed from Heidegger. As Heidegger's student Hans-Georg Gadamer puts it, "The horizon is the range of vision that includes everything that can be seen from a particular vantage point."[4] What cannot be seen from a particular vantage point is not on the horizon. In the Germanic *Weltanschauung*, the past serves as our "horizon of being": it is on the basis of the past that we project our future possibilities. And, of course, the present unfolding itself before us is a direct consequence of what is past.

We are the only creatures who live in a mindful connection

---

[4] Hans-Georg Gadamer, *Truth and Method*, trans. Joel Weinsheimer and Donald G. Marshall (New York: Crossroad, 1989), 302.

to the past. All living creatures, of course, strive to keep themselves alive and resist the going over into pastness (falling into the well of Urth). And all eventually fail, including man. However, traditional man rose above this fate by *choosing it*: by consciously choosing to live toward death; to create a glorious life for himself and a glorious death, which would be sung about and celebrated by future generations.

ANSUZ ᚫ — ECSTASY

This is the rune of Odin. The name Odin is derived from *odhr* which refers to an ecstatic state of consciousness. The Greek *ekstatis* literally means "standing outside," and an ecstatic state is one in which we are transported outside ourselves, in which we become more than what we are. Our capacity to experience *odhr* is one of the chief things that makes us human.

Odhr comes in three forms, corresponding to the three Indo-European "functions." (The following condenses information discussed much more fully in my essay "The Missing Man in Norse Cosmogony.") *Odhr* shows itself in religious ecstasy. *Odhr* also manifests itself in the fury of the warrior or berserker, in which one can easily lose one's self. Finally, *odhr* can show up in a "third function" form, as the ecstatic abandon sometimes felt, for example, in manual labor and in sexual intercourse. These forms of *odhr* exist in a hierarchy, with the highest being religious *odhr*.

Odhr corresponds to what Plato calls spirit (*thumos*). For Plato (and also for Hegel) having spirit is the most basic way in which we are distinct from animals. Animals do not yearn for or fight for an ideal, or transcendent principle, and do not "go outside" themselves. Thus, Odin, as the god of *odhr*, represents one of the things that is most human about us. Odin embodies those characteristics which make us human, but these are characteristics which we must strive to realize in ourselves. Our nature, in a sense, stands outside or above us as something which must be reached. (Recall my discussion of Elhaz.)

MANNAZ ᛗ — OPENNESS TO THE DIVINE

I have made Mannaz the final rune of Spirit, and the final rune, because it expresses the highest and most significant thing about human beings — indeed, the essence of being human — as well as the highest relationship in existence. Thorsson states that "*Mannaz* is the mystery of the divine (archetypal) structure in every individual and in mankind in general. . . . This is the rune that describes the Germanic peoples as being descended from their divine order and defines mankind as the progeny of the gods."[5]

In short, Mannaz concerns the human relationship to the divine. Our very nature is openness to being and, through that, openness to the gods. This openness is only possible, however, if there is a "space" or "clearing" in us through which the divine can make itself present. Such a space is to be found within us only if we still possess the capacity to be struck with wonder by the sheer being of things which we did not create and cannot control. What characterizes modern people is that they have lost this capacity for wonder, and thus lost openness to the gods. (I discuss these ideas at much greater length in "Knowing the Gods" and "Summoning the Gods.")

9. SOME REFLECTIONS ON THE COMPLETENESS OF THE SYSTEM

If one compares the runic system to say, the categories of Hegel's philosophy, one will be struck by the simplicity of the former and the complexity of the latter. Those trained in philosophy may be tempted to think that the runes should be supplemented by other concepts. The fact is that they can be: further distinctions can be made, using the runes as a basis. These would not constitute "new runes," but merely further specifications or refinements in our discussion of the basic runic system. The simplicity of the system is actually an advantage. Complexity is not a virtue. The ideal system is one in which everything can be explained using the smallest number of basic concepts. The test of the system is whether anything has been left out: is

---

[5] Thorsson, *Futhark*, 60.

there some fundamental fact of reality that has been left out of the system? I submit that there is not. Or, to put it another way: can the system explain everything that is basic to the world and to human experience? I submit that it can. Further refinements to these concepts are possible—indeed, infinite. But I believe I have demonstrated the philosophical power of the runes.

One way Hegel demonstrates the completeness of his system is by showing that it is circular: the end returns to the beginning. We can see that Mannaz in some sense is a return to Nadhiz. Nadhiz is the basic fact that being is determined through opposition. Mannaz is in one way the most basic opposition, and the highest or most exalted. Openness to the Divine implies the opposition of finite and infinite, human and divine, mortal and immortal. Furthermore, our openness to the transcendent and divine means, in part, knowledge of the runes. Thus, the entire system is "contained" within Mannaz. What Mannaz would mean—in part—is being open to and receiving and understanding the runic system as a whole.

It will be noted that throughout this essay I have omitted one crucial aspect of philosophical discussion: argument. At no point have I argued for the truth of each individual rune. The "proof" for the runes consists in the system of the runes itself. If the system is complete, if no crucial fact is left out, if it possesses explanatory power—the power of making sense out of the world for us—then what basis can there be for doubting its truth? As I have said, my procedure is recollective. I take the runes to be a mysterious, non-rational revelation of truth. Thus, they do not need to be supported by "argument." We know that they are true (if we are open) because studying them gives rise to a profound, and equally mysterious, intuition of their truth. This, plus the completeness of the runic system itself, is all that can be offered as "evidence."

Walpurgisnacht, 2001

THE MISSING MAN IN NORSE COSMOGONY*

1. INTRODUCTION

Comparing a variety of different Indo-European myths, and using linguistic clues, Bruce Lincoln has reconstructed what he takes to be the Proto-Indo-European creation myth. It involves two brothers, one a priest called *Manu (Man), the other a king called *Yemo (Twin), who travel together accompanied by an ox. For some reason, they decide to create the world. Manu offers up Yemo and the ox as sacrifices. He dismembers their bodies, and uses the pieces to create the different parts of the cosmos.[1]

There are certain obvious ways in which the Norse cosmogony expresses this proto-myth. Yemo, of course, is Ymir. The ox becomes Audumbla, the cosmic cow. It is Ymir's corpse which furnishes the parts of the world. But one important element is conspicuously absent from the Norse version. Where is Manu, the priest and brother of Ymir? I will argue that Manu is to be found, greatly transformed, in the Norse version.

2. THE NORSE COSMOGONY

First of all, it would be helpful to simply provide a short summary of the chief elements of the Germanic creation myth, culled from all the various sources.

In the beginning there was only an enormous abyss called Ginnungagap. In the north was a foggy, frozen region called Niflheimr, the land of the dead. Out of Niflheimr flowed a spring, which branched off into eleven rivers. In the south was Muspellsheimr, a burning region guarded by the black giant Surtr. Fire and ice flowed out from these regions, and met. The result was the creation of primal life. From out of this mixture

---

* First published in *Rûna*, no. 11.
[1] Bruce Lincoln, *Death, War, and Sacrifice* (Chicago: University of Chicago Press, 1991), 7.

was born Ymir, the first being.

From Ymir, the "rime-thurses" came into existence. From the sweat under Ymir's left arm two beings, male and female, were born. One of his feet mated with the other and produced a son. Out of the melting ice, still another being came forth, a cow called Audumbla. Ymir fed upon her milk. Audumbla licked the salty ice around her, until a man was shaped out of it. He was called Buri. Buri, in turn, generated a son called Borr, who married Bestla, the daughter of a giant called Bolthorn (evil thorn). Together, they had three children: Odin, Vili, and Ve.

For reasons which are not entirely clear, the brothers decide to kill Ymir. His blood drowns all the giants save one. The brothers take Ymir to the middle of Ginnungagap and dismember him. His skull becomes the heavens, at the four corners of which they set four dwarves: Nordhri, Austri, Sudhri, and Vestri. At the center the brothers build Midhgardr (Middle Yard) out of Ymir's brows. Near the ocean, in Midhgardr, Odin, Vili, and Ve find two trees: Askr (ash) and Embla (elm). They decide to turn these trees into the first human pair.

Note that there is no being equiprimordial with Ymir who initiates Ymir's murder, no priest-brother.

3. THE IDENTITY OF MANU

Manu is mentioned in the Rig Veda and Atharva Veda as the creator of mankind. In the Aitereya Upanishad, the cosmos is created out of the body of Purusa, who is dismembered by Atman, the "first self." Here, Atman clearly seems to be equivalent to Manu—or "Man"—at least in so far as man possesses a conscious self.

If we look for an equivalent of this "first self" in the Norse myth it would have to be the trio Odin, Vili, and Ve. Edred Thorsson has suggested that these three are in fact aspects of one being, and there is actually a very old tradition of interpretation which supports him in this.[2] Scholars have often noted

---

[2] Edred Thorsson, *Runelore* (York Beach, Maine: Samuel Weiser, 1987), 146. H. A. Guerber, *Myths of the Norsemen* (New York: Dover

that myths tend to repeat certain patterns, either to emphasize them or to articulate the different "moments" of a complex phenomenon. Repetitions in triplicate are quite common, especially in Germanic mythology.[3]

Thorsson tells us that the beings who came before the three brothers were not, strictly speaking, conscious. Or, perhaps, self-conscious would be a more accurate term. In other words, Odin-Vili-Ve is the first self. Odin-Vili-Ve are together Manu, or Man. But what of Manu's status as priest, and as brother of Ymir? As has been noted by Dumézil and his followers, Odin represents the "priestly function" in the tripartite Indo-European ideology. Notice also that Odin-Vili-Ve are brothers—just not brothers to Ymir. Their relation to each other, rather than to an unconscious other, is suggestive of the self-related or reflective nature of man's consciousness. In the Vedas, it is interesting to note, Manu is represented not as a single being but as multiple.[4]

4. ODIN, VILI, & VE

That the three brothers are the first self can be substantiated through an analysis of the identity of each. The three together represent an articulation of the different aspects of human selfhood.

Odin's name is derived from *odhr* which refers to an ecstatic state of consciousness. The Greek *ekstatis* literally means "standing outside," and an ecstatic state is one in which we are transported outside ourselves, in which we become more than what we are. In discussions of Germanic culture and myth, *odhr* sometimes is called *wut* or *wodh*, for the exact same linguistic reasons that Odin is also found under the names Wuotan and Woden or Wodhanaz.

Odhr comes in three forms, corresponding to the three

Publications, 1992), 37.

[3] Axel Olrik has written of a "law of three" in myth. See his *Epic Laws of Folk Narrative: The Study of Folklore*, ed. Alan Dundes (Englewood Cliffs, N.J.: Prentice Hall, 1965), 131–33.

[4] There are fourteen Manus, to be precise. Each rules over one *manvantaras*, or 4,320,000 years, which is one-fourteenth of a *kalpa*.

Dumézilian "functions." *Odhr* can manifest itself in religious ecstasy, a feeling of being transported out of oneself and directed toward the numinous. *Odhr* also manifests itself in the fury of the warrior or berserker, a rage or fighting frenzy in which one can lose oneself. Finally, *odhr* can show up in a "third function" form, as the ecstatic transport sometimes felt in manual labor, in agricultural festivals, in fertility rites, and in sexual intercourse. These forms of *odhr* exist, of course, in a hierarchy, with the highest and purest being religious *odhr*.

Odhr corresponds roughly to what Plato calls spirit (*thumos*). (There is also a somewhat similar notion in Hegel, called *Geist*, also usually translated as spirit.) Plato's spirit is one of the three parts of the soul discussed in the *Republic*. The other two are reason, and appetite or desire. Reason is the ruling part of the soul (or the part which should rule), and corresponds to Dumézil's first function. Appetite deals mainly with the satisfaction of physical drives, and thus corresponds to the third function. Spirit is what is manifested by the "guardians," the soldiers of Plato's city. Spirit involves fealty to an ideal. Spirited men take concepts like honor seriously, and are willing to die for them. In *The Phenomenology of Spirit*, Hegel shows how a concern with honor is the first and most basic type of spirit, and that there are higher and more refined modes of spirit in which the ideal we are directed toward is a religious or philosophical ideal.

For both Plato and Hegel, and for many other philosophers, having spirit is the most basic way in which we are distinct from the animals. Animals do not yearn for or fight for an ideal, or transcendent principle, and do not "go outside" themselves (for, indeed, they have no selves). Thus, Odin, as the god of *odhr*, represents what is most human about us. This is not to say that, properly understood, Odin is really just man, and that man is God. Odin (or, rather, Odin-Vili-Ve) is those characteristics which make us human, but these are characteristics which we must strive to realize in ourselves. Dogs do not have to strive to be dogs, they just are. But humans must strive to be human. Our nature, in some sense, stands outside us as something which must be reached. Do not forget that humans are created from Askr and Embla by having certain properties bestowed on them by Odin-Vili-Ve.

Vili means will, which is man's capacity to alter the given according to his aims and ideals; his capacity to impose himself on the world. Only human beings have this will. Ve means something like "sacred" or "holy." This is the third aspect of the human spirit which makes it uniquely human. Ve represents the openness of human beings toward the transcendent, or the Absolutely Other.[5] Only human beings possess this openness, and the sense of a divide running through nature and human existence — a divide between ideal and nature, God and man, sacred and profane, etc.

It can easily be seen that these three moments of the human spirit are bound up with each other. The divine openness, the sense of the Holy, provided by Ve is necessary before the higher forms of *odhr* can be experienced. It is also in *odhr* that we often become aware of our capacity for openness to the divine. Without openness to the divine, *odhr* would become a directionless frenzy of annihilation, or a drive for mindless sensualism. Will is the imposition of our ideals or plans onto nature. However, without openness to the transcendent, to an eternal order, will would become a purely personal affair, and potentially destructive (see chapter 1, "Knowing the Gods"). It is hard to see how openness to the transcendent needs to be "moderated" in any sense by either *odhr* or will, and thus the trio Odin-Vili-Ve emerges as roughly analogous to the Platonic triad Spirit-Desire-Reason, where Reason "measures" or orders the other two.

In Plato's scheme, Reason rules, but in the Germanic scheme it is Odin, not Ve. Does this mean that in the Germanic scheme Spirit rules? Yes and no. Spirit is *de facto* ruler, but Odin, as warrior chief, is also priest. He combines both functions. His is a spiritedness moderated by a transcendent wisdom gained from various sources (the runes, Mimir's well, the head of Mimir, Freyja, and the poetic mead). Thus, in a certain sense, it is

---

[5] Edred Thorsson, "The Holy," in *Green Rûna* (Smithville, Tex.: Rûna Raven Press, 1996), 41–43.

openness to the Holy, Ve, who actually "rules." The situation is precisely analogous to Plato's description in the *Republic* of the timarchy, which some believe was the society Plato truly advocated. In the timarchy, Spirit rules, or rather spirited men or warriors rule—but they are warriors trained and moderated by the philosophers, those who contemplate the eternal order of things. (The parallel is very precise, especially since the Germanic conception of wisdom is that it comes from memory, Mimir, and Plato believed that true wisdom was recollective.)

As I have interpreted the myth, Odin-Vili-Ve is an entity ontologically distinct from men, but which constitutes the characteristics which make us human. As I have said, the myth tells us that these characteristics stand outside us as something which we must strive to realize. The temptation, however, is to conclude that we are Odin-Vili-Ve; that we and the gods are one; that man is God. This conclusion has been irresistible for many. It shows up in the Vedantic identification of Atman and Brahman. Among the Germanic peoples, it shows up in mystics like Eckhart and philosophers like Hegel. But this interpretation cancels the separation between human and divine (or Holy) represented by Ve, and thus cancels openness to the transcendent, which is the essence of religion. It is, in fact, a radical humanism. (The practical, tangible results of this humanism in the lives of the Indian people needs no comment.) The ultimate result of the German version of this humanism was the philosophy of Karl Marx, Hegel's follower, which completely rejected the divine and, in essence, made of man a god. (The practical, tangible results of this humanism in the lives of the people of Europe, Asia, Cuba, and Central and South America also needs no comment.)

Interestingly, no element of this tendency seems to have been present in Greek religion, or in Greek philosophy. The Greek myths abound with warnings about the *hubris* of man: the tendency of men to think that they can be more than men. The stories of Icarus and Daedalus, and of Arachne, are perhaps the best examples. The Greek thinkers saw man as partway between beast and god. Man possesses physical drives and urges just like a beast, but unlike a beast he also possesses intellect, which he can use to contemplate the transcendent and eternal. It is a short step from this to the conclusion that there is a "divine spark" in man: that intellect is, in its nature, a divine thing.

In Aristotle we find a conception of the human-divine relationship which is not unlike the account I have given of the relation of men to Odin-Vili-Ve. For Aristotle, God, which he calls the Unmoved Mover, is a kind of pure self. He is pure self-related thought; thought which thinks itself. All creatures, including man, strive in various ways to "imitate" the Unmoved Mover: to be as independent, as self-sufficient, and as immortal as He. Most creatures, including most men, are unaware of this. But Aristotle says this schema explains why the world is the way it is: why creatures struggle to survive and endure; why they destroy or devour that which threatens their existence as independent entities; why they compete to produce offspring (an imperfect attempt at achieving immortality), etc.

Only humans can imitate the Unmoved Mover in the most adequate way. Humans possess intellect, and the Unmoved Mover is a pure intellect. Humans can engage in self-related thought through philosophy. Now, when human beings engage in such reflection, can they become identical to the Unmoved Mover? In theory, yes, but only when they are reflecting. Our imperfect, embodied nature always pulls us down from those heights. We never perfectly identify ourselves with God. I suggest that this may, in some ways, be a good model to use to understand the Germanic account.

5. FURTHER EVIDENCE

The idea that Odin-Vili-Ve is Manu, or the Atman of the Aitereya Upanishad, can be further supported through a comparison of the Norse and Greek cosmogonies. The Aitereya Upanishad gives us reason to believe that these seemingly very different accounts might be related. When Atman kills Purusa, Purusa's penis breaks off. Out of it comes semen, and out of semen the waters. What can this remind us of other than the castration of Uranus?

A brief account of Hesiod's creation story seems in order. In the beginning there was only Chaos (Abyss), from out of which arose Gaea (Earth) and Eros. Gaea bears a being who covers her, Uranus (Sky), and who she takes as a husband. From their union, the Titans are born, including Kronos (Time), as well as the Titanides, who include Themis (Order). Uranus hated his children. Getting wind of this, Gaea arranges for Kronos to kill his father. When Uranus next approaches Gaea, in a state of arousal, Kronos castrates him. The semen from Uranus's severed organ creates the foam of the ocean waves, and from this foam is born Aphrodite.

This myth raises many questions, but a crucial one is this: why exactly does Uranus hate his children? A clue may be found in a non-Indo-European source, the Akkadian creation myth, which is similar to Hesiod's account in a number of ways (similar enough to make one think that if there was no actual historical influence, then they are both probably expressing perennial themes).

According to the Akkadian story, Apsu and Tiamat were born from the primeval ocean. In turn, they produced Anu, the God of the Sky, and Ea. However, Apsu sets out to kill his children because they disturb his perpetual slumber. Luckily, Ea manages to use his magic powers to put Apsu back to sleep and then destroy him.

Both Apsu and Uranus represent unconsciousness ("sleep"). Uranus is continually, blissfully, locked in the embrace of Gaea. Both male gods seem to represent a timeless, unchanging, and unaware state of being. The products of Uranus and Apsu are randomly-produced, bizarre freaks and monsters—as are the products of Ymir: giants, androgynous beings like Buri, etc.

The sacrifice of Apsu, Uranus, and Ymir represents the death of unconsciousness, and of a chaotic, disordered fecundity. Time (Kronos) castrates the unconscious-timeless Uranus and thus puts an end to his unmeasured and monstrous procreation. Henceforth, all beings brought into the world will be brought in under the aegis of Themis (Order), Kronos's sister. In just the same way, with the ascension of Odin-Vili-Ve to supremacy, a rational, willed order or pattern is imposed on all coming-to-be. This order or pattern is not invented by the gods. It is the eternal runes. The beings who came before Odin-Vili-Ve were incapable of becoming aware of the runes, and thus incapable of being (or giving birth to) anything other than misshapen monsters. Thorsson writes that

> The triad of consciousness dissolves Ymir, and out of its matter reshapes the static cosmos into a dynamic, living, and conscious organization, according to the right (i.e., innate) patterns already contained in the matter itself (Ymir) and in the primal seed. . . . [T]hey shaped this primal substance according to the inherent runic structure.[6]

On this point—the creation of the world according to the runic patterns—we can find still more support for the identification of Odin-Vili-Ve with Manu, this time from the Vedic Indian doctrines. Alain Daniélou writes that

> Manu, the Lawgiver, is represented as having been the first being to perceive the thought-forms of objects and to have taught these thought forms to man and explained their relation with their objects, thus creating the first language. The thought-forms are envisaged as the subtle forms or subtle bodies of things and are permanent, indestructible formulas from which the impermanent physical forms can always be derived. The language that Manu taught was the primeval language, the eternal, true language made of root-words (i.e., meaningful basic monosyllables). Sanskrit is believed to be the language most directly derived from this original speech, while all other languages are its more or less corrupt forms.[7]

Thus, the Indian Manu plays a role exactly equivalent to

---

[6] Thorsson, *Runelore*, 146.

[7] Alain Danielou, *The Myths and Gods of India* (Rochester, Vt.: Inner Traditions, 1991), 334.

Odin's Hermes-like role as discoverer of the runes, and teacher of the runes to mankind.

Finally, it should be noted that Tacitus reports that in his time (first century C.E.) the Germans worshipped a God called Mannus: "In their ancient songs, their only way of remembering or recording the past, they celebrate an earth-born god, Tuisco, and his son Mannus, as the origin of their race, as their founders. To Mannus they assign three sons, from whose names, they say, the coast tribes are called Ingaevones; those of the interior, Herminones; all the rest Istaevones."[8]

Note that Mannus is here made progenitor of mankind, exactly like Vedic Manu, and like Odin-Vili-Ve. But there is much else here that is strange. Why is Mannus made the son of Tuisco? And who is Tuisco? Do the three sons of Mannus have a counterpart in the Norse account? There are at least two possible interpretations of the information Tacitus gives us.

(1) Tuisco is Ymir. Mannus is Odin-Vili-Ve, and certainly these three are descendents (if not "sons") of Ymir. The "three sons" of Mannus are actually the "three persons" of Mannus, called Odin, Vili, and Ve in the Norse account. Either there was an earlier separation of Mannus and three "sons" or perhaps Tacitus was simply getting the story wrong (this would be particularly likely if what he heard was a rather philosophical account of the "aspects" of Mannus). The main problem here is that the names Tuisco and Ymir bear no relationship to each other. But then there is no "Mannus" in the Norse account either, nor are the three names of Mannus' sons to be found.

H. R. Ellis Davidson supports the identification of Tuisco with Ymir, connecting Tuisco with Old Swedish *tvistra*, which means "separate" (a suggestion made by others).[9] This certainly suggests the meaning of Ymir's name, "twin," and his an-

---

[8] Tacitus, *Complete Works of Tacitus*, trans. Alfred John Church and William Jackson Brodribb (New York: The Modern Library, 1942), 709. The manuscripts of Tacitus give variant readings of the name Tuisco, including Tuisto.

[9] H. R. Ellis Davidson, *Gods and Myths of the Viking Age* (New York: Bell Publishing, 1964), 199. Old English "twist" meant "twine," the sense of two strands twisted together.

drogynous nature ("separate" in the sense of separated, or dual).

(2) Tuisco is Tyr. This suggests itself simply because of the similarity of the name Tyr (or Tiwaz or Tiu) to Tuisco. The first problem with this is that none of the other names match anything in the Norse account, so why should Tuisco? The deeper problem, however, is with the characterization of Tuisco as "earth-born." Tyr, as sky god, is hardly a chthonic deity! But recall Hesiod: Uranus, the sky-god, was born of Gaea, the earth.

In reasoning this way (and throughout all the preceding pages) I am assuming that there was some original Indo-European myth of which we can find different "pieces" in the Norse system, the Greek system, the Indian system, and in the religion reported by Tacitus. Perhaps Hesiod's account of the marriage of Uranus and Gaea was a later "corruption," an injection of non-Indo-European elements, or perhaps it was not. Perhaps it is something "forgotten" by the Norse.

The questions about Tuisco notwithstanding, what seems clear—especially when we bring in the evidence from the Indian and Greek traditions—is that Manu/Mannus has become Odin. Like Manu, Odin is the killer of Yemo (Ymir). Like both Indian Manu and Tacitus's Mannus, he is the progenitor of mankind. Like Indian Manu, Odin is also the discover and teacher of the eternal patterns of the real (i.e., he is the first "knower"). Like Tacitus's Mannus, furthermore, Odin is intimately associated with a trio, Odin-Vili-Ve.[10]

---

[10] I wish to thank Edred Thorsson for some suggestions related to the identity of Tuisco/Tuisto.

Karl Maria Wiligut's Commandments of Gôt*

Much has been written in the last four decades concerning "Nazi occultism," most of it nonsense. Incredibly, no one thought to publish a collection of original "occult" texts from the Third Reich—until Michael Moynihan and Stephen E. Flowers brought out *The Secret King: Karl Maria Wiligut, Himmler's Lord of the Runes* in 2001.[1] Called "Himmler's Rasputin" by some, Wiligut (1866–1946) came from a prominent Viennese family, and served honorably in the Great War. He delved deeply into the Germanic esoteric tradition, forming ties to Lanz von Liebenfels' Ordo Novi Templi, and joining a quasi-Masonic lodge, in which he was called "Lobesam" ("Praiseworthy"). In 1924, while sipping coffee at a Viennese café, Wiligut was forcibly hauled off to a mental hospital, where doctors noted his queer ideas, including his belief that he was descended from "Wodan."

After his release, Wiligut formed ties to the NSDAP, and began contributing articles to a *völkisch* journal called *Hagal*. Wiligut met Reichsführer-SS Heinrich Himmler in 1933, and subsequently joined the SS under the name "Weisthor." This was done with Himmler's knowledge and consent, in order to conceal Wiligut's embarrassing past. Within two months, "Weisthor" was made head of the Department for Pre- and Early History within the Rasse- und Siedlungshauptamt (Main Office for Race and Settlement). Himmler appears to have seen Wiligut as a guru, and in 1935 made him part of his personal staff. Wiligut

---

* First published in *TYR: Myth – Culture – Tradition*, vol. 1, ed. Joshua Buckley, Collin Cleary, and Michael Moynihan (Atlanta: Ultra, 2002), 191–205.

[1] *The Secret King: Karl Maria Wiligut, Himmler's Lord of the Runes*, trans. with introduction by Stephen E. Flowers, Ph.D., ed. Michael Moynihan (Waterbury Center, Vt. and Smithville, Tex.: Dominion and Rûna-Raven, 2001).

sent Himmler a regular stream of memos, purporting to unveil the secrets of Germanic esotericism. Wiligut was also highly influential in helping Himmler develop various aspects of SS ceremony and insignia. It was Wiligut who designed the famous SS ring. He developed a "name-giving rite" to be performed over the newborn children of SS men. Wiligut also contributed greatly to the conceptualization and renovation of the Wewelsburg castle, which Himmler intended as a worldwide headquarters for the "knights" of the SS.

Was Wiligut mad? This question is not relevant when examining the *ideas* of an author or a guru. Sanity is a relevant issue only when we must evaluate a *report* (such as eyewitness testimony in a trial) or a *promise*, in which case the reliability of the reporter or promiser must be assessed. Character and mental state thus become issues. But when ideas or theories are expressed, we must evaluate the ideas themselves, not the man who expresses them. Thus, when we read Wiligut we must ask such questions as: Are these ideas coherent (i.e., non-contradictory)? Do they seem to have some basis, or are they merely arbitrary assertions? And (most important of all in the case of ideas such as these): are they truly tied to Tradition? To dismiss a thinker's ideas by labeling him "mad" is simply *argumentum ad hominem*. (Besides, if the standard of sanity is being well-adjusted to the modern world, then sanity is hardly a desirable condition.)

It is my belief that the documents translated in *The Secret King* present a coherent mystical philosophy. Further, they give evidence of profound reflection upon the pagan Germanic religious tradition. Nevertheless, Wiligut's philosophy is deeply flawed. It is not a *fully* coherent and integrated system of ideas. Further, many of Wiligut's claims in his memos to Himmler do indeed seem like fanciful, arbitrary assertions, without any ties to authentic Tradition. And some elements of Wiligut's thought actually *clash* with authentic Germanic lore.

In the remainder of the essay, I will attempt to systematize Wiligut's ideas; to present his ideas *as far as possible* as a coherent body of thought. This is no easy task, as any reader of *The Secret King* will realize. I will structure my account around the very first text presented in the book, "The Nine Commandments of Gôt." It is my belief that these nine statements provide the framework of Wiligut's philosophy, in terms of which most of the other ideas can be understood. First, I will simply present this text in its entirety:

THE NINE COMMANDMENTS OF GÔT

1. Gôt is Al-Unity!
2. Gôt is "Spirit and Matter," the dyad. He brings duality, and is nevertheless, unity and purity . . .[2]
3. Gôt is a triad: Spirit, Energy and Matter. Gôt-Spirit, Gôt-Ur, Gôt-Being, or Sun-Light and Work [Werk], the dyad.
4. Gôt is eternal—as Time, Space, Energy and Matter in his circulation.
5. Gôt is cause and effect. Therefore, out of Gôt flows right, might, duty and happiness.
6. Gôt is eternal generation. Gôt's Spirit and Matter, Energy and Light are that which carry this along.
7. Gôt—beyond the concepts of good and evil—is that which carries the seven epochs of humanity.
8. Rulership in the circulation through cause and effect carries the highness: the secret eight.
9. Gôt is beginning without end—the Al. He is completion in Nothingness, and, nevertheless, Al in the three-times-three knowledge of all things. He closes the circle at N-yule, at Nothingness, out of the conscious into the unconscious, so that this may again become conscious.[3]

These "commandments" were apparently formulated by Wiligut in 1908, and communicated to Himmler in a memo, initialed and dated by Himmler "Sommer 1935." To the right of each commandment, Wiligut had drawn complex runic formu-

---

[2] Ellipsis in original German document. No text has been omitted.
[3] I have made a few minor changes to Flowers's translation of the "Nine Commandments," to make it more literal.

las. It is beyond the scope of this essay to attempt an analysis of these formulas.

The fact that there are *nine* commandments is, of course, significant, given the importance of the number nine in Germanic lore. In another text, Wiligut states: "In 'nine' the whole universal form is completed in a circle" (p. 74).

I will now comment on each of the Nine Commandments in turn.

1. GÔT IS AL-UNITY!

What is suggested here is the perennial mystic theology of *hen kai pan* (one and all). This Greek phrase achieved notoriety in the German-speaking world with the publication of Jacobi's *Über die Lehre des Spinoza in Briefen an der Herrn Moses Mendelssohn* (1785), in which Jacobi quotes Lessing as saying, "The orthodox concepts of the deity are no longer for me. *Hen kai pan*, I know no other." This quotation subsequently exercised a tremendous influence on German intellectuals, among them the young Hölderlin, Schelling, and Hegel, who adopted *hen kai pan* as their personal motto during their schooldays. *Hen kai pan* implies that God is beyond duality, hence "one," but not one in the since of being "simple," a bare unit. Instead, God is the unity of All. Ordinary experience displays to us not only duality, but a whole chaos of multiplicity. In truth, however, all the world is really one.

Wiligut later tells us (p. 54) that Gôt is Gibor-Othil-Tyr. This should remind us of another trinity of gods: Odin-Vili-Ve. Gibor, Wiligut says, is the sun rune (Sowilho) plus the ice rune (Isa) or "Sun-I." The significance of the sun and its relationship to I or ego will shortly become apparent. Othil is the "eternal manifestation of spiritual-material being." Tyr is the "victory of light over Matter [*Stoff*] in the action of Light (eternal cycle)." All this shall become clearer as we proceed.

It follows from the identification of Gôt with Gibor-Othil-Tyr that Gôt means (in Wiligut's words) "Hallowed All-Light of spiritual-material being in an eternal cycle in the circle of the creation in the All." On a cursory reading, this may seem like gibberish, but a careful reading will disclose that this is, in fact, a summary statement of the meaning of Gôt as Gibor-Othil-Tyr. As we shall see, Gôt for Wiligut is the eternal, dynamic realization of Spirit (*Geist*) in matter as part of the cyclical process which defines the whole of creation.

2. GÔT IS "SPIRIT AND MATTER," THE DYAD. HE BRINGS DUALITY, AND IS NEVERTHELESS, UNITY AND PURITY . . .

But Gôt, as we have seen, is Unity, so how can he bring duality? Wiligut is no Manichean: he does not oppose a positive unity-principle, to a negative "dual" principle (or principle of multiplicity or indefiniteness). Instead, duality comes from the One. This is a doctrine of emanation, such as we find in Plotinus. Wiligut gives the fullest statement of his cosmogony in a poem entitled "Number," published in *Hagal* in 1934:

N'ul-ni — the unconsious I, ul = Spirit,
    Ni = the non-spiritual essence.

In the beginning was a unity of two aspects: Spirit and non-Spiritual essence (proto-Matter). These are not two, but a unity which we must *understand* as two. Ni is the non-spiritual essence of Ul (spirit), *because it is the essence of spirit to become non-spiritual*. It is the end or aim of spirit to become *embodied*, and body is the opposite of spirit. If it is the end of the caterpillar to become a butterfly, then we may speak of the butterfly as the essence or being of the caterpillar. If it is the end of Spirit to become embodied, then the essence or being of Spirit is non-Spirit. Thus, Spirit (Ul) *is* Non-Spirit (Ni). They are not two but one. Furthermore, Non-Spirit only is what it is by participating in Spirit, thus the being (essence, end) of Non-Spirit is Spirit.

It stands beyond time and space,
    as "Nothing," which once had been . . .

Again, we are dealing with Gôt as beyond duality. It is, but is no-thing. ("which once had been" implies eternal cycles of creation and destruction). Wiligut represents this initial stage as a circle with a dot in the middle, which is also the astrological and alchemical symbol for the sun:

> It is "original-being, Ru" in Spirit and Matter,
>   which no force penetrated,
> Subdued by the Will of Gôt-har
>   as only a point in the Al—in being—
> There rest the commandments of Gôt—his I—
>   as a point in the circle . . .

The being of Gôt, which is Being-Nothing, One-All, Spirit-Non-Spirit, a unity of *polar tension*, is contracted into a point, and in this point is the incipient universe, from which will unfold the complete essence of Gôt (note "there rest the commandments of Gôt"—we are exploring precisely those commandments; Gôt's law or commandments are akin to the Platonic *eide*, the system of forms that is the Gôt-being).

> . . . it became the "world-egg,"
>   the Will toward solidification . . .

Wiligut posits that at the root of all being is a striving toward definiteness, concreteness, embodiment. What explains the overflow of existence from the dimensionless point that is the Gôt-being? It is simply the nature of Al to strive for full expression—concrete realization. This is a perennial theme in German mysticism, present in such authors as Schwenkfeld, Boehme, and Oetinger. It also carried over into philosophers like Schelling and Hegel. In Oetinger's terms, it is called *Geistleiblichkeit*, "spiritual corporeality." Oetinger sees God as coming to progressively greater concreteness or embodiment *through* the world. God is not some sort of wispy wraith. His true nature is to be the most concrete, specific, fully-realized individual being of all, while at the same time not existing merely as one being among others, but as *Being-as-such* (Aristotle's Unmoved Mover fits this description, although Aristotle does not see his God as developing or evolving through time and through the world).

And from this "egg" duality comes into being:

Duality: Spirit in Matter formed by Energy
>in order to complete,
It becomes the Eye of Gôt in a ring —
>"Drehauge" — to turn itself,
And from Two arises
>the "Three" we certainly all know
And which we call the Tri-unity as Gôtos' form...

Another piece by Wiligut, "The Creative Spiral of the 'World-Egg'!" (*Hagal* 11, 1934) seems to expand upon these ideas. It opens, "Primal law: 'Above as below, below as above!'" This is, of course, the famous maxim of Hermes Trismegistus, usually stated as "As above, so below." Wiligut reminds us in this text that "from *two* comes *one* (*ans*)." The unity of Gôt in His original state as unity of Spirit-Non-Spirit gives rise to the "World Egg": Spirit in its "striving" to be concrete (non-Spirit) and Non-Spirit in its "striving" to be in-formed (Spirit) exist in tension, and this tension, as an equilibrium of primordial forces, produces an excrescence on the "physical plane" (or, more properly speaking, this tension *creates* the physical plane). The "two" that is the Ur-Gôt gives birth to one (the "egg") which then must become two ("hatch" or "divide") and from this two comes other ones, and other twos until there is a proliferation of ultimate dualities within each of the primary "regions" of Being: definite/indefinite, one/multiple, positive/negative, straight/round, passive/active, rest/motion, systole/diastole, light/darkness, cold/hot, dry/moist, love/hate, sky/earth, male/female, good/evil, etc. Each pair is a pair of "ones" which only are what they in relation to another, and whose relation-connection "gives birth to" other *ones*, which then exist in further dual relationships.

Wiligut invokes the principle of "As above, so below" because of the replication of this pattern (the primordial creation process) on all levels of existence, high and low, above and below. Wiligut states (p. 80): "I recognize that in the 'spiral unity' the 'dyad' (duality) becomes a 'unity' in humanity through 'man and woman.' Man 'giving' and therefore 'Above,' woman taking him, therefore receiving and so 'Below.' And by means

of this 'unification to unity' (World-Egg) in generation..."
And (p. 81): "We are moreover Nordic, i.e., polarized from above. We — as Gôt-seed — impregnate 'Erda' [Earth] according to the Will of Gôt..."

3. GÔT IS A TRIAD: SPIRIT, ENERGY AND MATTER. GÔT-SPIRIT, GÔT-UR, GÔT-BEING, OR SUN-LIGHT AND WORK [WERK], THE DYAD.

"Energy" (*Kraft*) is now mentioned in addition to Spirit and Matter. Matter becomes inspirited (and spirit enmattered) through Energy. Energy is the Greek *energeia* which means function, act, or actualization. It is *matter doing*. All things are what they do, or how they function, act, or react to other things. This is Aristotle's conception of form: form = function. It is through having a characteristic function or doing (Energy, *energeia*) that Matter has a form or nature. Without *energeia*, matter is dead, dis-spirited. This is why Aristotle says that a severed hand is, in a real sense, no longer a hand at all (*Metaphysics* 1036b30).

Matter must do, act, *work* in order to have an essence or nature; in order to be inspirited (recall Wiligut's use of the sun symbol — circle with central dot — to represent the Ur-Gôt, Gôt-in-Himself). This is the primordial dyad: Spirit and Matter yearning for each other, joined through a middle which is Energy (the "Sun-Light"). The working of the thing (its Energy) is Spirit coming to be in it. All the acts of a being are directed toward the realization of Spirit (form), whether the actor is aware of it or not (this is, again, similar to Aristotle: all beings are, in all their acts or functions, "striving" to be like God). Through Energy, Spirit realizes itself in Matter, which is *its* ultimate aim.

Wiligut offers the following helpful diagram:

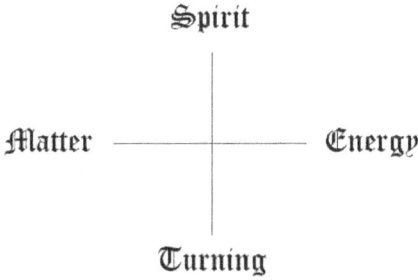

My interpretation of "Energy" is confirmed by other Wiligut texts. In "The Cosmos in the Conception of Our Ancestors" (*Hagal* 12, 1935), Wiligut disciple Gabriele Dechend offers several diagrams made up of combinations of triangles. She writes of one: "The upper triangle represents Spirit becoming conscious in Matter, and this actually by means of the current of Energy" (p. 119).

In the same text, Dechend writes: "When the Spirit, in eternal circulation, approaches the Energy-Matter Plane, which is set for release as a potential 'plan' — then the 'Will to Become' is awakened in this plane" (pp. 120–21). Incidentally, there is a "lower triangle" opposed to the "upper triangle" mentioned in the first quote. It contains a figure that is a combination of the Elhaz and Thurisaz runes:

ᛉ

This was apparently a very significant figure for Wiligut. In his Introduction, Flowers mentions that Wiligut disciple Richard Anders stated to an interviewer, "This is all I learned from Wiligut," and drew the following:

ᛉ + ᚦ = ᛉ

Of this figure (placed within the "lower triangle"), Dechend remarks, "The lower triangle becomes the image of the 'crucified,' or in the Wotan-cult that of 'Odhinn hanging on the world tree'" (p. 119). This is as good a place as any to mention one of the most puzzling and disappointing aspects of Wiligut: his belief in an "Irmin-Kristianity." Wiligut believed that this, and not "Wotanism," was the original religion of the Germanic people. Not only does this seem absurd (for all sorts of reasons, the least of them historical) but it is very difficult for us today to understand why Wiligut, and some other German *völkisch* thinkers, were so keen to save Christianity. (One is reminded, for example, of Chamberlain and Rosenberg's silly attempts to prove that Christ was really an Aryan.) Not able to imagine the complete dissolution of the faith in which they were raised, these men wanted to create (or rediscover) a virile, German Christianity—a Christianity with a K! This is reflected in Wiligut's bind rune depicting "the crucified." The Elhaz rune is commonly referred to as the "life rune": it is positive; life-affirming in Nietzsche's sense (and opposed, therefore, to a life-denying Christianity). The Thurisaz rune is (among other things) a symbol of virile male power. Its "thorn" is a clear phallic image (note how it can be inserted into Berkano, the rune of the "Great Mother"). Wiligut's Christ (Krist?) is a virile, life-affirming God. Christ as Dionysus.

4. GÔT IS ETERNAL—AS TIME, SPACE, ENERGY AND MATTER IN HIS CIRCULATION.

Matter awakens to Spirit as Energy (*energeia*) and produces Space and Time. Time can only be perceived if there is motion (e.g., the position of the sun overhead, the hands on the clock, the sand in the hour glass, etc.). Motion is *energeia*, and *energeia* exists only if there is Matter. (Aristotle wrote: "Time is just this: a measure of motion with respect to the before and the after," *Physics* 219b2.) Space only exists relative to material objects. Thus, Matter and Energy actualize Time and Space. "Gôt is eternal ... in his circulation" means: the cycle of matter "awakening" to Spirit through Energy is eternal. Spirit and Matter are *both* actual only in their relationship to each other (see above). Gôt is not Spirit, nor is He Matter or Energy. He is the dynamic interrelation of these three. Gôt *just is* the awakening.

5. GÔT IS CAUSE AND EFFECT. THEREFORE, OUT OF GÔT FLOWS RIGHT, MIGHT, DUTY AND HAPPINESS.

Might, right, duty, and happiness map onto the three Indo-European "functions" identified by Georges Dumézil:

1st Function (Priestly/Juridical): Right
2nd Function (War/Protection): Might (Power),
    & Duty (Control/Discipline)
3rd Function (Trade/Sustenance): Happiness (Pleasure)

This fourfold division appears to be Wiligut's description of the primary aspects of human life, and is reminiscent of the Hindu division of Virtue, Success, Pleasure, and Liberation. But why do right, might, duty, and happiness flow from Gôt *because* Gôt is "cause and effect"? We can answer this by looking, again, toward Hinduism: right, might, duty, and happiness flow from cause and effect, which means from *action* (*karma*). If this seems far removed from Wiligut's Germanic milieu, think again. In "Whispering of Gôtos—Rune Knowledge" (*Hagal* 11, 1934) Wiligut writes:

> As Spirit submerges to the depths
>   it is set free from the restraint of both!
> 'Life aware of Spirit,' mindful of Energy and Matter—
> Is awakened to its *Garma*—in a circular pattern . . .
> And becomes a child of Gôtos, a Spirit in the son of man . . .
> And thus Gôtos himself is able to recognize—
>   Gôt-Spirit on the throne . . .

In a footnote, Flowers reminds us that "Garma" was Guido von List's version of *karma*.

Incidentally, the above quote confirms my earlier claim that Gôt for Wiligut just is the "awakening" of Matter to Spirit in Energy, and takes it a step further. Wiligut is here speaking specifically of the awakening of Gôt/Gôtos *in man*, and he is saying that through man Gôt comes to consciousness of himself ("Gôtos himself is able to recognize—Gôt-Spirit on the throne . . ."). Recall Wiligut's decription of "N'ul-ni" as "the unconsious I," where ul = Spirit, and Ni = the non-spiritual essence. Gôt-in-Himself, as Al-Unity, before his unfolding in/as the world is "the unconscious I" (a union of Spirit and non-Spirit, Proto-Matter). Through His unfolding, Gôt becomes the Conscious I.

This is a perennial mystical teaching. Eckhart states that "The eye with which God sees me is the same eye by which I see Him, my eye and His eye are one and the same. In righteousness I am weighed in God and He in me. If God did not exist nor would I; if I did not exist nor would He." In the Kabbalah, *Ein-Sof*, the Infinite, is held to be identical to *Ayin*, Nothing. The end of *Ein-Sof/Ayin* is to develop into *Ani*, "I" (*Ayin le-Ani*, "Nothing becomes I"). This is also found in the "mainstream" philosophical tradition in the person of Hegel. The three primary divisions of Hegel's philosophy (*Logik, Natur, Geist*) are modeled on the Trinity: Father, Son, Holy Spirit. The reference to "Spirit in the son of man" and to "Gôt-Spirit on the throne" certainly call Hegel to mind. (Meister Eckhart, incidentally, also identified "the Son" with Nature.)

6. GÔT IS ETERNAL GENERATION. GÔT'S SPIRIT AND MATTER, ENERGY AND LIGHT ARE THAT WHICH CARRY THIS ALONG.

The awakening (Gôt) of Spirit in Matter through Energy is not a once-only process, or one which takes place outside space and time. It is perpetual, it is everywhere (even if, as suggested above, its *chief* or highest expression might be in man), it is without end. Gôt is the eternal fecundity of the world — or fecundity itself. Wiligut mentions Light here, making a quaternity of Spirit, Matter, Energy, and Light. What are we to make of this?

These are the primary categories introduced thus far in Wiligut's Commandments:

(Metaphysical Categories)
Al-Unity (N'ul-ni — the unconsious I) =
Spirit (ul) + Non-Spiritual essence (Proto-Matter) (Ni)
(tension gives rise to:)

(Natural Categories)
"World Egg"(in which are incipient:)
Energy
Matter
Space
Time
Light
"Turning"

("Human" Categories)
Right

Might
Duty
Happiness

(Note that while Wiligut clearly has a cosmogony and a doctrine of emanations, there is no explanation for why "the human" comes to be in nature—except, perhaps, that it *must* come to be so that Gôt can recognize Himself.)

The relation of Light to Energy is obvious: the display of energy frequently produces light (e.g., electrical phenomena), particularly when extreme heat is involved. Light is the apex of energy. It is the moment where matter becomes so energized that it gives rise to a phenomenon which *reveals* itself and others. It reveals itself to itself and/or to others, and/or reveals others to itself. In this Light, the Spirit, the Form of things is unveiled. Thus, when Wiligut links Energy and Light, he is linking Energy/Functioning with Manifestation or Revealing as such (Hegel held light to be "pure manifestation, and nothing but manifestation"). The natural or proper working or functioning of something leads, in the interaction of one thing with another, to the opening up and unveiling of the being of things. Being is "illuminated." In sum, Energy/Functioning, the actualization of Spirit in Matter, is the shining forth of Spirit in Matter, which in turn illuminates the Spirit in Matter elsewhere. (In truth, the revealing of a thing's being could not happen apart from the revealing of the being of others, since the being of something consists ultimately in its not being anything else.)

7. GÔT—BEYOND THE CONCEPTS OF GOOD AND EVIL—IS THAT WHICH CARRIES THE SEVEN EPOCHS OF HUMANITY.

The idea that Gôt—and higher consciousness—is beyond good and evil, is, of course, a perennial idea. What are "the seven epochs of humanity"? Wiligut describes them in an SS document written June 17, 1936 and marked read by "H. H." (Heinrich Himmler). Wiligut claims that an account of the seven epochs "was recorded on seven Runo-wooden tablets (of oak) in ancient Aryan linear script supplemented by images" (pp. 98–99). These were destroyed, he further claims, when his grandfather's house burned down in 1848. There is no point in going into an account of the seven epochs, for here we encounter Wiligut at his worst. The seven epochs are a fanciful, wholly invented account of prehistory. I make this claim for two reasons: (1) there are no independent (Traditional) sources that confirm Wiligut's account; and (2) there is no compelling reason to believe Wiligut's story about the "Runo-wooden tablets." Even mystics, or followers of mystics, cannot take things "on faith"; i.e, without either experiential evidence, or compelling reasons to believe. Wiligut tells us, among other things, that in the third epoch human beings "could fly and partly lived in the water, partly on land and had three eyes. The third one supposedly in the middle of their foreheads" (p. 100). The whole thing has the same ring of the arbitrary that we find in similar accounts in Theosophy.

Elsewhere, Wiligut has some rather more interesting things to say about human origins and history. He seems to endorse the belief in an original arctic homeland for the Aryans (p. 56). His "Runic Exhortation" (pp. 76–77) gives a poetic account of the dispersion of the Aryans and the gradual forgetting of runic wisdom.

8. RULERSHIP IN THE CIRCULATION THROUGH CAUSE AND EFFECT CARRIES THE HIGHNESS — THE SECRET EIGHT [*HEIMLICHE ACHT*].

I have little to say about this baffling statement. Does it refer to the characteristics of kingship? Is it claiming that rule (or true authority) consists in mastery of the "Gôt power"? And what (or who) is the "secret Eight"?

9. GÔT IS BEGINNING WITHOUT END — THE AL. HE IS COMPLETION IN NOTHINGNESS, AND, NEVERTHELESS, AL IN THE THREE-TIMES-THREE KNOWLEDGE OF ALL THINGS. HE CLOSES THE CIRCLE AT N-YULE, AT NOTHINGNESS, OUT OF THE CONSCIOUS INTO THE UNCONSCIOUS, SO THAT THIS MAY AGAIN BECOME CONSCIOUS.

The ninth "commandment" seems almost a kind of summation of the others. We are being told here, again, that God is an eternally generating cycle in which Matter is united with Spirit. "He is completion in Nothingness, and, nevertheless, Al..." God is All and Nothing is a perennial mystic doctrine (found, for example, in Boehme). God is nothing (no-thing; no-one-thing) precisely because he is All (or Al). But Wiligut says He is All "in the three-times-three knowledge of all things." 3 x 3 = 9. Nine commandments? Nine worlds? Is Wiligut saying that our nine-fold knowledge of Gôt in some sense completes or realizes Gôt as the Al-Nothing? Recall my remarks about the fifth commandment. Wiligut seems to be saying that originally Gôt is "unconscious I," who comes to consciousness through man. Recall these lines: "'Life aware of Spirit' ... becomes a child of Gôtos, a Spirit in the son of man ... And thus Gôtos himself is able to recognize—Gôt-Spirit on the throne..."

Note the final line of the ninth commandment: "He closes the circle at N-yule, at Nothingness, out of the conscious into the unconscious, so that this may again become conscious." Wiligut's use of "N-yule" is fascinating. "N-yule" is a play on German *Null*, zero, nothingness, and Yuletide, the end of the year, a time of winter and death. The year ends with *Null/Yule*. Life goes within itself: trees "die," animals hibernate, humans spend time huddled indoors, etc. This "within," is the implicit, the "in-itself" (to use the Hegelian term), which is the unconscious. But life arises out of this unconscious. It blooms and displays itself to itself: it becomes explicit, "conscious." The eternal cycle of generation is "unconscious," "dead" Matter *awakening* to "conscious," "living" Spirit through Energy. But Spirit in-itself, Idea, is only implicitly conscious. Spirit becomes *real* only when embodied in a reflective, material being who becomes conscious of its Spirit. Thus, Spirit goes over into Matter so that it may truly realize itself as Objective Spirit, or: "out of the conscious into the unconscious, so that this may again become conscious."

Gabriele Dechend also speaks of the "N-Yule": "Life as movement contains in itself a compelling drive, it comes to an 'eternal' generation, which is for its own part prevented, because 'without essence' Spirit, Energy and Matter tend to sink down into Nothing, into N-yule, into the Al. So here it becomes clear to us why the drive to reproduce is necessary! It turns the Need around: the sinking back into 'Nothing'" (p. 121). This passage does not seem to directly contradict the interpretation I have given above, but it is puzzling. What does "without essence" mean? Spirit, Energy, and Matter have a tendency to entropy, to sinking down into Nothing, into the darkness, death, and inwardness of winter: the winter of the year, and the winter of one's life. But living things resist this process—ultimately by reproducing themselves, and thereby achieving some measure of immortality. Always knowing that there will be a final winter, the winter of one's life, we pass on life (we reproduce) and thus the cycle continues.

Obviously, there is more to Wiligut than I have presented here, and my interpretations have been, of necessity, highly speculative. As I have said, Wiligut's philosophy is confused, often arbitrary, and frequently hard to reconcile with what we know of the Germanic tradition from other sources. Nevertheless, I hope this review has demonstrated that Wiligut's writings are highly thought-provoking, and worthy of study. Michael Moynihan and Stephen E. Flowers are to be commended for making these writings available to the public.

PATRICK MCGOOHAN'S
*THE PRISONER**

1. INTRODUCTION

A&E's DVD (and Blu-ray) release of *The Prisoner* bills this cult series as "television's first masterpiece." In truth, it is probably television's *only* masterpiece. *The Prisoner* is a triumph of acting, photography, design, writing, and thought. More generally, of course, it is a triumph of audacity and imagination. Like a great work of art, it is timeless. Very little about *The Prisoner* is dated — even though it went into production forty-five years ago. For the most part, the series looks as fresh as it did when first aired. And its message seems more relevant than ever.

Of course, the central problem with *The Prisoner* is what that message is exactly. Fans love to emphasize the "open-endedness" of the series: everyone has their own *Prisoner*. But when we interpret a text (even a cinematic text) our goal should not be to come up with a purely subjective, idiosyncratic interpretation. Interpretations of *The Prisoner* are often wildly speculative and subjective — and often completely ignore the public statements that Patrick McGoohan (the series' creator) made about it. Surely what we want is an interpretation which causes the text to open itself and reveal the meaning its creator put into it, if any. Serious-minded people don't treat texts as Rorschach blots. One begins the task of interpretation by carefully studying every detail of a text. One also studies the background of its author, and what its author has said about it.

Some interpretations work better than others. Some can explain the text as a whole, others only in part. The former is obviously preferable to the latter. For example, in the final episode of the series we at last discover the identity of the mysterious "Number One": he is the Prisoner himself. Can one interpret this

---

* First published in *TYR: Myth – Culture – Tradition*, vol. 1, ed. Joshua Buckley, Collin Cleary, and Michael Moynihan (Atlanta: Ultra, 2002), 167–90.

in an atheistic, or "secular humanist" vein? Does the final episode teach us that Number One is God, but that God is really us? One could indeed interpret things that way—but only if one ignored the fact that McGoohan was a devout Catholic.

What I have attempted to do in this essay is to present an overall interpretation of *The Prisoner*, situating it within the tradition of twentieth-century "anti-modernism." As an artist, McGoohan must be understood as belonging to the school of Pound, Yeats, Eliot, Joyce, Huxley, Lawrence, Kafka, and (to some extent) Orwell. It does not matter if McGoohan never read these authors; they would have recognized him as one of their own. It is my belief that such an interpretation is the most fruitful way to understand *The Prisoner*. But first, a little background information for the uninitiated . . .

At the time *The Prisoner* went into production, Patrick McGoohan was the highest-paid actor in British television. He was the star of *Danger Man* (shown in the United States as *Secret Agent*), in which he played a spy by the name of John Drake. But Drake was no James Bond knock-off. *Danger Man* premiered on September 11, 1960, almost two years before the release of the first Bond film, *Dr. No*. Incidentally, McGoohan was the first actor offered the part of Bond, but he turned it down. He felt that Bond's womanizing and killing were immoral. McGoohan made sure that Drake was never depicted in any amorous encounters with women, and that he never killed his enemies.[1] But *Danger Man* was plenty violent. Fisticuffs were a major feature of the series (and also of *The Prisoner*). McGoohan was physically imposing in the role of Drake. He was tall, tough, determined, and deadly serious. McGoohan's odd, sing-songy voice (a product of being born in New York, and later raised in Ireland and Sheffield) was also crisp and powerful. He radiated enormous inten-

---

[1] Since this essay was first published in 2002, I learned that McGoohan gave an interview a few years before his death, in which he stated that the *real* reason he turned down *Dr. No* was that he did not want to work with a certain individual on the crew, with whom he had worked before. Although he does not name that individual, it could only have been director Terrence Young, with whom McGoohan worked on *Zarak* (1956).

sity and intelligence.

In 1966, McGoohan's contract for *Danger Man* ran out, and he decided to quit (even though the first two episodes of the new season—the only ones in color—were already in the can; they were later edited together as a seldom-seen feature called *Koroshi*). Lew Grade, the head of ITC, the firm that produced *Danger Man*, wanted very much to keep McGoohan on. When the star put to him the idea for *The Prisoner*, Grade immediately agreed to it. He had no idea what he was getting into.

The germ of *The Prisoner* was provided by George Markstein, the script editor for *Danger Man*. Markstein had worked in British intelligence, and knew of the existence of a secret "rest home" called Inverlair Lodge, where old spies could live out their days without accidentally revealing their secrets when Alzheimer's set in. Somehow, Markstein, thought, this could be developed into an exciting series. This was basically the extent of Markstein's contribution to the series' format. *The Prisoner* was Patrick McGoohan's creation.

Here is the premise: A secret agent—whose name is never revealed in the entire series—angrily resigns his job and prepares to leave the U.K. on holiday. Unbeknownst to him, however, he is followed home by a man in a hearse, who knocks him unconscious using some kind of gas. When the secret agent awakens, he is in his own bedroom, but when he looks out the window, he finds that he is in a strange, cosmopolitan little town. He discovers that he is being held prisoner in this place, which is known only as "the Village." No one is referred to by name, only by number. The inhabitants wear colorful costumes, and spend a good deal of time parading and having fun, yet they are all curiously soulless. Underneath the Village is a complex of underground control rooms, from which a vast bureaucracy watches the Villagers' every move using sophisticated electronic surveillance equipment.

The highest ranking authority in the Village is called "Number Two," and the office is constantly changing hands. Number One remains in the background. The location of the Village is never revealed—nor is it ever revealed "which side" runs the place. The Villagers are cared for from cradle to grave. Some seem to work, whereas others do nothing. The masters of the Village have at their disposal the most advanced technology imaginable. They can invade one's dreams, brainwash one into believing anything, switch minds from one body to another, and bring a dead man back to life. Escape is impossible. The perimeter of the Village is guarded by a mysterious creature that looks like a balloon and is called only "Rover." It lives at the bottom of the sea and can suffocate escapees, or merely stun them. Is it alive? Is it a machine? "That would be telling," says Number Two in the first episode (see the Appendix to this essay).

The men behind the Village want to know why our hero—who they call "Number Six"—resigned his job. He refuses to tell them, or to conform. They try to break his will in various ways. They drug him. They hypnotize him. They trick him into thinking he has escaped, only to reveal that he has never left. They raise him to the exalted position of Number Two, then literally beat him and deposit him back in his bed. They turn his old friends against him. They make him doubt his own identity. They perform a mock lobotomy on him. They trick him into believing he is a gunfighter in the Old West. They regress him back to his childhood, then "bring him up" all over again. They even allow him to actually escape, and then lure him back. Finally, with no more tricks left up their sleeves, the Villagers admit defeat and beg the Prisoner to lead them.

Oh, and aside from McGoohan the only other regular is a dwarf.

This was—and is—quite simply, the most unusual thing ever made for television. Only David Lynch's *Twin Peaks* rivals it for sheer strangeness and originality.[2] McGoohan arranged with

---

[2] Since this essay was first published, I have seen two television series that remind me of *The Prisoner* in terms of their intelligence and imagination: the Sci-Fi Channel's *Battlestar Galactica* (the "reimagined" version of the original, god-awful '70s series), and the Fox Network's *Dollhouse*. Both are flawed, but have much to recommend them. The ABC series *Lost* has often been compared to *The Prisoner*. I was intrigued by this series at first, but ultimately disappointed by it. In 2009 AMC aired a six-episode remake of *The Prisoner* starring James Caviezel as No. 6 and Ian McKellen as No. 2. I made it about

Lew Grade to produce *The Prisoner* under the auspices of his company, Everyman Films, which he had set up in 1960. This gave him total control over every aspect of the production. ITC budgeted the series at £75,000 an episode, a huge amount in those days. Extensive location shooting was done at Portmeirion in Wales: an artificial village constructed over several decades by architect Clough Williams-Ellis. McGoohan planned out in detail the world of the Village. He contributed to the design of sets, props, and costumes. The Village even had its own font (based on Albertus), which was also used for the opening and closing titles of the series.

The production included many *Danger Man* alumni. Particularly striking were the sets designed by art director Jack Shampan. They included a large, circular chamber which could be re-dressed to serve as several settings: No. 2's office, the sinister "Monitor Station," and others. These sets are ultra-modern and ultra-simple. They look as impressive today as they did in 1966. The music was one aspect of the production that McGoohan was less happy with. The original theme, contributed by Wilfrid Josephs, was deemed too avant-garde (though it still appears in the background in several episodes). Ron Grainer, the composer of *Dr. Who*, contributed the theme that was finally used. Albert Elms contributed background music which works brilliantly in the series, but sounds thin and repetitive when heard apart from the visuals (a series of CDs was released a number of years ago).

The Prisoner is visually opulent and looks even more expensive than it was. The photography is crisp and provocative. Scenes call to mind Bergman, Fellini, and Hitchcock. The color is vivid. The editing is like that of a Bond film: fast-paced, each shot lingering only briefly, presenting only essentials. Indeed, every aspect of this series is polished and top-drawer. *The Prisoner* exhibits that same consummate professionalism that one finds in other British series of the time, like *The Avengers* and *The Saint*. Some of the best direction in the series came from McGoohan himself (he helmed five episodes, wrote three, and

---

twenty minutes into the first episode before shutting it off, and can honestly say I have no desire to return to it.

probably re-wrote all the rest).

The story goes that as production of the series went on, McGoohan began asserting more and more control over every aspect. He was a perfectionist, who delegated little. George Markstein quit and subsequently attacked McGoohan in interviews for his "megalomania." But one can hardly argue with the results, for *The Prisoner* is a brilliant creation. Nevertheless, after a year in production, only thirteen episodes were completed, and the stories were getting stranger and stranger. ITC decided to pull out and told McGoohan to wrap things up with a final four episodes. When the last episode was broadcast, viewer reaction in Britain was so hostile that it is said McGoohan and his family felt they had to leave the country.

Originally McGoohan had only wanted to do seven episodes. Indeed, roughly ten of the episodes are fairly routine adventures, lacking much intellectual substance. The seven "primary episodes" are:

"Arrival"
"Dance of the Dead"
"Free for All"
"The Chimes of Big Ben"
"Checkmate"
"Once Upon a Time"
"Fall Out"

Like many television series, the episodes were not broadcast in the order in which they were filmed.

2. INTERPRETING *THE PRISONER*

So, to quote No. 6 in "Arrival," what's it all about? *The Prisoner*, like many texts, has different levels. The exoteric *Prisoner* is an adventure series with lots of action, gee-whiz technology, and a dashing, intransigent hero. Even at this level, the series makes the viewer ask certain questions. Chief among these are:

(1) What is the hero's name?
(2) Who runs the Village?
(3) Where is the Village?

(4) Why did our hero resign?
(5) Who is No. 1?

The first three questions are insignificant and will lead one astray. Anyone who thinks that these are important questions probably also thinks that the central question of *The Trial* is what the K in Joseph K stands for.

The Prisoner is not John Drake. He is Patrick McGoohan, if Patrick McGoohan had been a secret agent. The Prisoner's birthday is March 19 — the same as McGoohan's (this is mentioned *twice* in the series). In the final episode, he credits each of his stars — Leo McKern, Alexis Kanner, and Angelo Muscat — at the bottom of the screen, but bills himself as "Prisoner." Furthermore, the Prisoner shares other biographical details in common with McGoohan: he boxed in school and had a talent for mathematics ("Once Upon a Time").

But there is much else to the character that is *not* McGoohan. In fact, at times it seems No. 6 is *everything*. He can build a boat and navigate it, he can fly a helicopter, he can fence and shoot, he can speak several languages, he can water-ski, he is a gymnast, he can ride a horse, he knows the sciences, he knows literature, etc. In truth, he is Everyman. He is all of us. (In Biblical terms, six is the number of man, for man was made on the sixth day.) What is he trying to say about all of us? I will address that in section four, below. As to the location of the Village and who runs it, I will deal with those issues in passing.

Of the above questions, only those concerning the Prisoner's resignation and the identity of No. 1 have any real significance.

It is made clear that the Prisoner resigned his job for matters of principle. ("The Chimes of Big Ben" has the Prisoner revealing that his resignation was "a matter of conscience"; in "Once Upon a Time" he says that he resigned for "peace of mind.") Part of McGoohan's message must surely be to convey that principle.

In "Living in Harmony" the story of *The Prisoner* is played out in an Old West setting. The Prisoner resigns his job as sheriff, then is kidnapped and taken to another town where he is forced to become the new sheriff. He refuses to wear guns, however. Naturally, this calls to mind John Drake. So, did our hero resign his job because he could no longer stomach killing? This cannot be the case, for in the same episode he does put on his guns briefly in order to kill the homicidal "Kid." This shows that he is willing to kill, if he thinks it justified (he also kills with abandon in "Fall Out"). No, our hero did not resign because he thought it never right to kill; he resigned because he could no longer, in good conscience, kill for, and in the name of, his society. His act of resignation is a rejection of his society, and its regime (in "Once Upon a Time," when Leo McKern says "You resigned," McGoohan replies "I rejected").

One of the mysteries of *The Prisoner* is why the Villagers cannot see that this is all there is to it. But this is what one should expect: modern people find nonconformists to be thoroughly inexplicable creatures. How could anyone reject this wonderful world in which, to quote Ned Beatty in *Network*, "all necessities [are] provided; all anxieties, tranquilized; all boredom, amused." There *must*, they think, be another reason why he resigned!

Nevertheless, the Prisoner clearly has some vestigial loyalty to Her Majesty. In "Arrival" he insists that his loyalties don't change. In "A, B and C" he condemns B for working on the "wrong side." Almost every episode opens with No. 6 demanding of his captors "Whose side are you on?!" This is one of the two ways in which No. 6 is portrayed as being *misguided*. He is portrayed as a hero, and as an extremely virtuous individual, but he has failings nonetheless. In "The Chimes of Big Ben," No. 2 tries to set him straight on the issue of "whose side" they are on:

> *No. 2*: It doesn't matter which side runs the Village. Both sides are becoming identical. What in fact has been created [here] is an international community. When the sides facing each other suddenly realize that they are looking into a mirror, they will see that this is the pattern for the future.
> *No. 6*: The whole earth, as the Village is?
> *No. 2*: That is my hope.

"A, B and C" informs us that the Prisoner believes in "absolute truth." But he needs to realize that neither side (democratic-capitalist or communist) embodies his ideals, and that neither side is salvageable. He tries to escape the Village to get back to "my world" (as he puts it in "Dance of the Dead"), thinking that it's "different" ("The Chimes of Big Ben"). But, in essence, they are the same. The Village is the essence of modernity laid bare. But No. 6 does not see it.

What he needs to see is that, as Heidegger claimed, the two sides are *metaphysically identical*. Both capitalism and communism are based on the supremacy of materialism, and on the rejection of man's higher nature. In "Arrival," No. 2 says "We have everything here." But there is one thing conspicuously absent from the Village: a church. The Villagers are devoid of any spiritual dimension. They are happy, healthy, well-fed humanoids, with an army of psychologists at the ready to drug away their every doubt and blue mood.

The Village is a microcosm of modern society. (In fact, No. 6 calls it that in "Many Happy Returns.") First of all, it has no cultural or ethnic identity. ("Are you English?" the Prisoner asks No. 2 in "Dance of the Dead"; she does not answer.) Physically, the place is a mix of international architectural styles. ("It's very international," says a girl in the first episode.)

The authorities know everything about you—but no one cares, because it makes everyone feel "safe." Don't worry about car accidents, you aren't allowed to drive yourself anywhere (too dangerous). And don't forget to be in by curfew at 10:00 pm.

The Villagers pride themselves on their democracy, even though the whole process is rigged ("Free for All"). "Of the people, by the people, for the people," a sign proclaims. They think themselves free, even though their "freedoms" are things like the freedom to walk on the grass ("Arrival"). "You do what you want. . . . As long as it's what the majority wants," No. 2 tells us in "Dance of the Dead." Run for office by all means, but don't try and change anything if you win. ("You want to spoil things!" No. 6 is told in "Dance of the Dead.") Don't make the mistake, however, of thinking that the Villagers have no ideals. "Progress! Progress! Progress!" they scream in

"Free for All." (McGoohan has said that the "penny-farthing bicycle," seen in the series as the Village's emblem, represents the ideal of progress.)

A cheery radio announcer makes sure that a light, informal tone is maintained at all times. To "simplify" things, everyone goes by number, rather than by name. Those who claim not to be numbers are laughed at ("Free for All") — and resented. The Villagers wear silly costumes — colorful capes, straw hats, striped sailor shirts. Dignity is, of course, a terribly old-fashioned idea, and, again, likely to stir resentment.

Everything is automated. The houses have radios and TVs which can't be shut off because, after all, why would anyone want to shut them off? Leaving for the Village store to buy processed food? Don't forget your credit card and identity card.

Got troubles? Go to the Citizen's Advice Bureau ("A Change of Mind"). Need work? Queue up at the Labour Exchange, where you will be given an aptitude test ("Arrival"). Suffering existential *Angst*, or anti-social tendencies? "There are treatments for people like you!" ("Dance of the Dead"). Do you wonder "Who am I? Why am I here?" ("Schizoid Man"). Sign up for Group Therapy at the hospital. It "counteracts obsessional guilt complexes producing neurosis" ("Arrival"). And remember: "Questions are a burden to others; answers a prison for oneself" ("Arrival" and "Dance of the Dead"). In fact, "if you get [an] attack of egotism, don't wait. Go . . . to the hospital immediately" (No. 2 to the Rook in "Checkmate"). The Village treats men as soulless pieces of meat to be manipulated by science ("We mustn't damage the tissue," No. 2 cautions in "Free for All"). Pavlovian methods of conditioning are employed (methods first perfected — as No. 6 points out *twice* in "Checkmate" — on dogs).

When your mind is completely gone and you can no longer shop for yourself, you are retired to the Old People's Home, where you are encouraged to enjoy a second childhood.

3. *THE PRISONER* AS ANTI-MODERN MANIFESTO

In short, *The Prisoner* attacks modernity on the following grounds:

1. Modernity rests upon a materialistic metaphysics (all is matter), and champions materialism as a way of life (the focus on material comfort and satisfaction).
2. Modernity is spiritually empty (again, no church in the Village); it must deny or destroy what is higher in man.
3. Modernity destroys culture, tradition, and ethnic and national identity in the name of "progress" (called "multiculturalism" and "globalization" today). It is significant that we do not know where the Village is, for modern people are really "nowhere." As Nietzsche's "Madman" said, "Where are we headed? Are we not endlessly plunging—backwards, sideways, forwards, in all directions? Is there an up and a down anymore? Do we not wander as if through an endless nothingness? Do we not feel the breath of empty space? Hasn't it grown colder?" (*The Gay Science*).
4. Modernity promises only trivial freedoms (e.g., the freedom to shop) while suppressing freedom of thought, freedom of religion, freedom of association.
5. Modernity involves the belief that nature (including human nature) is infinitely malleable, open to the endless manipulation and "improvement" of science. In a 1977 interview with Canadian journalist Warner Troyer, McGoohan said, "I think we're progressing too fast. I think that we should pull back and consolidate the things that we've discovered."
6. Modernity systematically suppresses ideals that rise above material concerns: ideals like honor, and dignity, and loyalty (the Village is filled with traitors).
7. Modernity preaches a contradictory ethos of collectivism, and "looking out for No. 1."
8. Modernity banishes the sacred, and profanes all through oppressive levity, irony, and irreverence (masking cynicism).
9. Modernity places physical security and comfort above the freedom to be self-determining, to be let alone, and

to take risks.
10. Modernity fills the emptiness in people's lives with *noise* (the TV and radio you can't turn off). Silence might start people thinking, which could make them unhappy.

In addition to the hostility to religion, the Village also seems to be hostile to marriage, sex, and procreation. It is not clear whether there are any married couples in the Village. Sex is probably forbidden. No children are seen until "The Girl Who Was Death," and those children are depicted as living in a kind of barracks. There is a touch of Plato's *Republic* in *The Prisoner*.

The Villagers are Nietzsche's "Last Men." In *Thus Spoke Zarathustra*, Nietzsche has his prophet proclaim:

"Alas the time of the most despicable man is coming, he that is no longer able to despise himself. Behold, I show you the *last man*.

"'What is love? What is creation? What is longing? What is a star?' thus asks the last man, and he blinks. . . .

"'We have invented happiness,' say the last men, and they blink. They have left the regions where it was hard to live, for one needs warmth. One still loves one's neighbor and rubs against him, for one needs warmth. . . .

"One still works, for work is a form of entertainment. But one is careful lest the entertainment be too harrowing. One no longer becomes poor or rich: both require too much exertion. Who still wants to rule? Who obey? Both require too much exertion.

"No shepherd and one herd! Everybody wants the same, everybody is the same: whoever feels different goes voluntarily into a madhouse.

"'Formerly, all the world was mad,' say the most refined, and they blink.

"One is clever and knows everything that has ever happened: so there is no end of derision. One still quarrels, but one is soon reconciled—else it might spoil the digestion.

"One has one's little pleasure for the day and one's little pleasure for the night: but one has a regard for health."

Zarathustra's audience is not horrified by this vision of man at the end of history. When he finishes speaking, he is interrupted "by the clamor and delight of the crowd. 'Give us this last man, O Zarathustra,' they shouted. 'Turn us into these last men!'"[3]

To borrow from Eliot, the Villagers are "hollow men." Or to borrow from C. S. Lewis, they are "men without chests." They have no soul and no spirit. They are concerned only with comfort, safety, and satisfaction. They have no ideals, and consider nothing to be worth fighting for. In "Free for All," No. 6 tells the Villagers, "I am not a number, I am a person." They laugh at him. Then, when he continues to address them, briefly expounding views which No. 2 characterizes as "individualistic," their faces are blank, uncomprehending. Later in the same episode, No. 6 addresses the Town Council: "Look at them. Brainwashed imbeciles. Can you laugh? Can you cry? Can you think? . . . In your heads must still be a brain. In your hearts must still be the desire to be a human being again." McGoohan's portrayal of modern man might have seemed an exaggeration in 1967, but not today. Contemporary man—forty-five years on—does not even rise to the level of a Babbitt or a Willy Loman. He is Dilbert. He is Homer Simpson.

All right, we have seen what McGoohan is against, but what is he for? I will offer the following guesses—with apologies to the late Mr. McGoohan if I happen to misread him.

First and foremost, based on what we know of McGoohan himself, as well as clues internal to the series, I think we can say that he was a theist who believed that man is a creature of God, with an immortal soul, subject to divine law. (Obviously, McGoohan was against materialism in metaphysics and in culture—in "Fall Out" the President states that No. 6 has triumphed "despite materialistic efforts.") He believed that when

---

[3] Friedrich Nietzsche, *Thus Spoke Zarathustra*, trans. Walter Kaufmann (New York: Viking Press, 1986), 17–18.

men no longer turn their souls toward God, they stop being men. He believed that societies have souls too, and that the soul of a society is its spirituality. Again, the most significant fact about the Village is the total lack of any religious or spiritual institutions.

McGoohan also seemed to place importance on cultural and ethnic identity. We cannot simply be "citizens of the world." We are English, or Irish, or French, or Estonian, or Japanese. He was against the modern homogenization of the globe (physically embodied in the "internationalism" of the Village) which is rapidly making every place look pretty much like every other.

McGoohan seems also to have advocated minimal government and self-reliance. He opposed government intrusion into our lives, as well as "cradle to grave" socialism. This is the "libertarian" aspect to *The Prisoner* (the least interesting aspect and, of course, the one that gets the most attention). McGoohan also would seem to have favored somehow limiting what science and technology can meddle with. One supposes that he was a conservationist, who in particular regarded human life as sacred and inviolable.

If McGoohan wanted us to identify him with his character, then, based on what we learn about No. 6 in the course of seventeen episodes, we can conclude that McGoohan believed in honor, in dignity, in fighting for what one holds dear, in discipline, in self-denial, and in absolute truth. He believed in self-sacrifice and service to others (note how he buys the candy for the old lady in "It's Your Funeral"), not out of duty to "the majority" or to the state, but out of benevolence (note the use of the Beatles' tune "All You Need Is Love" in "Fall Out"). Quite simply, he was a Christian. Not a mushy "Jesus Freak" sort of Christian, but a tough, muscular C. S. Lewis sort of Christian.

Finally, McGoohan believed in a life that makes room for silence, for thought, for contemplation. He believed in taking life seriously. Was McGoohan a liberal or a conservative? His emphasis on freedom of thought and freedom of expression, and his belief in minimal government seem to make him a classical liberal. But his spirituality, his emphasis on place and culture, his skepticism about "rule by the majority," and his old-fashioned ideals make him look like a conservative (in "A Change of Mind" one Villager accuses him of being "reactionary"). In truth, it is really unimportant where we locate McGoohan on the political spectrum. If we had asked him, we can be fairly sure he would have eschewed all our ready-made labels.

So what did McGoohan propose doing about our plight? Here the answer is simple: he advocated a revolution. In "Dance of the Dead," "Bo Peep" states: "It is the duty of all of us to care for each other, and to see that the rules are obeyed. Without their discipline we should exist in a state of anarchy." No. 6 replies "Hear! Hear!" In the same episode, he finds a transistor radio on a dead body. When he switches it on, we hear the following: "I have a message for you. . . . The appointment cannot be fulfilled. Other things must be done tonight. If our torment is to end, if liberty is to be restored, we must grasp the nettle even though it makes our hands bleed. Only through pain can tomorrow be assured."

Furthermore, in interviews McGoohan has actually said that he had hoped the protest movement of the 1960s would lead to a revolution. He referred to the action of the final episode of *The Prisoner* as "revolution time." But who are to be the revolutionaries, other than McGoohan? He probably wondered the same thing. In the world of the Last Man, what can one do except cultivate one's own garden? McGoohan made his impassioned, seventeen-hour speech on behalf of revolution. He spent his last years writing poetry that may never be published, and acting only occasionally.

4. Patrick McGoohan's Anti-Individualism

Earlier, I said that although No. 6 is clearly portrayed as a hero, he is not perfect. He is misguided in two significant ways. The first I have already discussed: he does not seem to realize that in essential terms his own society and the Village are identical. There is no *physical* escape from them. The second way he is misguided is that he is an individualist. This statement will surely shock many fans of the series.

Several episodes (such as "Free for All") explicitly refer to his individualism. No. 6 continually asserts his individuality. In "Arrival" he tells us that he will not be "pushed, filed, stamped, indexed, briefed, debriefed or numbered! My life is my own." Fourteen episodes open with his proclaiming "I am not a number! I am a free man!" In "Dance of the Dead," No. 6's costume for Carnival is his own tuxedo, specially delivered for the occasion. "What does that mean?" asks his maid. "That I'm still . . . myself," he answers, dramatically. In the same episode, No. 2 tells him, "If you insist on living a dream you may be taken for mad." "I like my dream," he says. "Then you are mad," she replies.

But the attitude of the series toward individualism is, contrary to appearances, ambivalent. Up to the final episode, one could perhaps be excused for thinking that *The Prisoner* is an unqualifiedly positive portrayal of an individualist hero. But in "Fall Out," when No. 6 addresses the assembly, he begins his first sentence with "I" and the assemblymen drown him out chanting "I! I! I! I! I! I!" The President states that No. 6 has "gloriously vindicated the right of the individual to be individual" — but his unctuous manner suggests that these are merely empty platitudes. When the Prisoner enters No. 1's chamber, he sees himself on a TV screen saying "I will not be pushed, filed, stamped," et cetera, as quoted earlier. Then we hear his voice speeded up, hysterically chanting "I! I! I! I! I! I!" And we see the image that closes almost every episode: iron bars slamming shut over McGoohan's face, this time over and over again. Are we being told here that the ego is a prison?

No. 1 wears a mask like that of the assemblymen: half-black, half-white. When No. 6 rips it off, underneath is a *monkey mask*. The monkey face gibbers "I! I! I!"along with the soundtrack. When No. 6 rips that mask off we see that No. 1 is McGoohan. He laughs maniacally and disappears through a hatch in the ceiling. The Prisoner had wanted to discover the identity of No. 1, and now he finds out that he has been No. 1 all along. Understanding the meaning of this is the key to understanding the entire series. In the 1977 Troyer interview, the following exchange occurs:

McGoohan: [The audience] thought they'd been cheated. Because it wasn't, you know, a "James Bond" No. 1 guy.
Troyer: It was themselves.
McGoohan: Yes, well, we'll get into that later, I think. (Knowing laughter from Troyer) Come back to that one, that's a very important one.

That the Prisoner is No. 1 is hinted at throughout the entire series. McGoohan has said that he did not know in advance that things would work out the way they did. However, given his description of how "Fall Out" essentially "wrote itself," we have some grounds for supposing that McGoohan knew the identity of No. 1 all along, subconsciously. The number on the Prisoner's house in London is "1" (the actual address is 1 Buckingham Place). The dwarf butler always bows to him. The large red phone No. 2 uses to speak with No. 1 in "A, B and C" (and seen again in other episodes) is shaped suspiciously like the number 6. Finally, at times it seems that the Village exists just in order to break No. 6; as if he is at the center of the whole thing.

No. 1 represents man's ego in the bad sense. In an interview that predates *The Prisoner*, McGoohan was quoted as saying, "But what is the greatest evil? If you're going to epitomize evil, what is it? Is it the [atomic] bomb? The greatest evil that one has to fight constantly, every minute of the day until one dies, is the worst part of oneself." In the Troyer interview, we read the following:

Audience member: No. 1 is the evil side of man's nature?
McGoohan: The greatest enemy that we have. No. 1 was depicted as an evil, governing force in this Village. So, who is this No. 1? We just see the No. 2's, the sidekicks. Now this overriding, evil force is at its most powerful within ourselves and we have constantly to fight it, I think, and that is why I made No. 1 an image of No. 6. His other half, his alter ego.

No. 1 is the embodiment of what I call "Will" (see chapter 1, "Knowing the Gods," for a fuller discussion of this concept).

Will is that dark impulse inside all of us which desires to close itself to what is other (including the transcendent, divine other) and to raise oneself above all else. No. 1's monkey mask represents this primal, brutish aspect in all of us. (Significantly, the first task No. 2 sets for himself in "Once Upon a Time" is to find the Prisoner's "missing link.") When Warner Troyer asked McGoohan about the monkey mask, McGoohan said:

> Yeah, well, we're supposed to come from these things, you know. It's the same with the penny-farthing bicycle symbol thing. Progress. I don't think we've [truly] progressed much. But the monkey thing was, according to various theories extant today, that we all come from the original ape, so I just used that as a symbol, you know. The bestial thing and then the other bestial face behind it which was laughing, jeering and jabbering like a monkey.

Will manifests itself in more or less sophisticated forms. In "Knowing the Gods" I write:

> In its higher forms, Will manifests itself... in (1) the transformation of the given world according to human designs, and (2) the yearning to penetrate and master the world through the instrument of the human mind—through exploration, analysis, dissection, categorization, observation, and theory. In its most refined form, Will becomes what might be called a "Titanic Humanism": a seeking to make man the measure, to exalt man as the be-all and end-all of existence, to bend all things to human desires.

Modernity is the Age of Will, the age of this Titanic Humanism. It is this which *The Prisoner* so brilliantly lays bare and parodies as "the Village."

Why is Will, as "No. 1," the head of the Village? Or: why is Will the true master of modernity? I write, further, in the same essay:

> It is no accident that all the grand schemes and contriv-

ances of modernity (the technological mastery of nature, the global marketplace, socialism, universal health care, etc.) have as their end exactly what [Will in its infantile form] seeks: the satisfaction of desires, and the maintenance of comfort and security.

East and West, Communism and Capitalism are metaphysically identical because both are run by Will; both are run by an exclusive concern with the values of the Last Man: comfort, security, and satisfaction of (physical) desire. McGoohan has said, "I think progress is the biggest enemy on earth, apart from oneself, and that goes with oneself, a two-handed pair with oneself and progress."

But why does McGoohan confront us with this hard truth by having our hero discover that No. 1 is himself? Isn't he the exception? Isn't he the man who has rejected Will and the world it has created? No. 6 has indeed rejected modernity, but he himself exhibits Will in one of its more subtle forms. He does not turn from modernity to anything higher than it, or higher than himself. He turns inwards and wills himself as, in effect, an atomic individual. As I have said, the most significant thing about the Village is that it has no church. But perhaps the most significant thing about No. 6 is that he doesn't ask about this. Again, we see him fly a helicopter, build two escape rafts, mix it up with thugs (countless times), box, fence, shoot, play chess, demonstrate his psychic powers, display his knowledge of Shakespeare, do gymnastics, and much else, but we never see him pray. No. 6 is, in effect, a secular humanist who believes that he can stand alone, needing no one, not even God. (In this respect, of course, he is *not* McGoohan, but "Everyman"—or, perhaps, McGoohan in those moments of doubt that all of us have.)

The series presents us with numerous examples of No. 6's *hubris*. In "Free for All" he shouts "I'm afraid of nothing!" In the same episode, after he is elected the new No. 2, he gets on the Village loudspeaker and cries "I am in command! Obey me and be free!" A psychologist in "Checkmate" expresses the desire to learn No. 6's "breaking point." "You might make that your life's ambition," he says to her. In "Once Upon a Time," the silent butler obeys No. 6. "He thinks you're the boss!" Leo McKern exclaims. "I am," McGoohan replies. When he sits down on the throne in "Fall Out" he seems quite pleased with himself. No. 6 is a strong man, but he is not introspective. He is a man of action. He lacks self-criticism.

"Many Happy Returns" is an episode that many take to be a straightforward thriller: No. 6 wakes up to find the Village deserted, sails away on a raft, but, predictably, winds up back in the Village by the end of the hour. There is more here than meets the eye, however. Consider what No. 6's behavior in this episode reveals. Finally left alone—a lone wolf, a true individual, an atom in the void at last—he does not look inside himself and take stock. Instead, he promptly goes in search of the world that, in the beginning of the series, he rejected and sought to escape from. *Then*, once back there, he goes in search of the Village! No. 6 is the proverbial rebel without a pause. He is constantly *reacting* against the world. He needs others, he needs the world, in order to reject them, for he can do nothing else. He is sheer negativity—sheer rejection and cancellation of otherness. His constant activity—pacing around his apartment, walking around the Village, working out—as well as his acts of violence, are expressions of this.

Now, this life of rebellion and negativity is not a truly human life. It is a kind of Purgatory. It is no accident that there are continual references in the series to No. 6's being *dead*. An undertaker in a top hat, driving an old hearse, is the man who kidnaps him and takes him to the Village. (This lends itself to the irresistible, but wrong-headed speculation that in the beginning McGoohan really dies, and that the Village is Hell, or Purgatory!) In "Dance of the Dead" No. 6 asks No. 2 why he doesn't have a costume for Carnival. "Perhaps because you don't exist," she says. In the same episode, after the Villagers try and kill the Prisoner, No. 2 tells him, "They don't know you're already dead." She tells him that the body he found on the beach will be "amended" to look like him, so that to the outside world No. 6 will be dead. "A small confirmation of a known fact," she says. There are suggestions that the Village is populated by the living dead. Once again, in "Dance of the Dead" (note the title itself!)

No. 6 finds the key to the morgue hanging on a hook outside the door. What can this mean, except that the door is locked not to keep people from getting in, but to keep them from getting out? In "Once Upon a Time," No. 2 cries "I'll kill you!" "I'll die," whispers our hero. "You're dead," No. 2 replies. Then there is No. 6's dalliance with "The Girl Who Was Death." And finally, there is the fact that No. 6 almost always appears in black.

The best literary parallel I can think of for No. 6 is the character of Hazel Motes in Flannery O'Connor's *Wise Blood*. Motes is also an atomic individualist who despises society and modern people. Raised in a religious home, he rejects the God that society believes in and founds an atheist "religion": "the Church Without Christ." He buys a disastrous used car (an old Essex), but no matter how many times it breaks down and reveals its frailty, he insists that it's a fine car and will get him wherever he needs to go. "Nobody with a good car needs to be justified," he says. The car represents man's mortal coil, and the Catholic O'Connor is telling us that man cannot stand totally alone; he must turn his soul to something higher.

McGoohan is telling us something similar. He is saying, "Fine. Reject society. Reject materialism and the modern world. But if you reject them in the name of your own ego you are buying into that primal, Biblical sin that is at the root of modernity itself: the placing of ego and its interests, narrowly conceived, above all else." Without preaching to us, without ever mentioning religion, McGoohan invites us to rise above our No. 1, and turn our souls toward the Real Boss. One need not be a Christian, let alone a Catholic, to understand and sympathize with this message. Indeed, the idea that it is our ego that holds us back from enlightenment or true liberation is a perennial idea. (One of the ironies of the series is that *resignation* is a trait No. 6 is singularly lacking!)

Christian themes are to be found throughout *The Prisoner*. In several episodes we hear a march-version of the hymn "How Great Thou Art." This occurs first in "The General," in which No. 6 destroys a supercomputer with the question "Why?" (One is reminded of the old story—probably apocryphal—of President Eisenhower asking Univac if there is a God; "Now there is," the computer is said to have shot back.) In "Once Upon a Time" we hear this theme played on a church organ. In "Fall Out" we are repeatedly bombarded with the old spiritual "Dry Bones." "Them bones, them bones, them dry bones! Now hear the Word of the Lord!"

"Dry Bones" is an old Negro spiritual inspired by the Book of Ezekiel, which is one of the prophetic books of the Old Testament. In Chapter 37, the prophet relates his "vision of the dry bones":

> The hand of the Lord came upon me, and he led me out in the spirit of the Lord and set me in the center of the plain, which was now filled with bones. . . . How dry they were! He asked me: Son of man, can these bones come to life? "Lord God," I answered, "you alone know that." Then he said to me: Prophesy over these bones, and say to them: Dry bones, hear the word of the Lord! Thus says the Lord God to these bones: See! I will bring spirit into you, that you may come to life.

In the Bible, the bones represent the Israelites who have lost hope and faith. In "Fall Out," the dry bones are modern men, who have lost their souls. When the young rebel No. 48 sings "Dry Bones," the members of the assembly (who bear such titles as "Welfare," "Identification," "Therapy," and "Education") go mad: "Them bones, them bones gonna walk around!" They are the dry bones of our world. "The bones is yours, dad!" says No. 48. "They came from you, my daddy."

No. 48 and No. 2 are fastened to metal poles, in a manner that suggests crucifixion. When No. 6 speaks some soothing words to No. 48, the young man says "I'm born all over," suggesting the Christian theme of the second birth. No. 6 also undergoes a Christlike temptation at the hands of the President, who offers him "ultimate power." Then there is the small matter of Leo McKern's "resurrection."

Does No. 6 get the message in the end? Not at all. In the Troyer interview, McGoohan states that his character is "essentially the same" at the end of the series. The final shot of the series is the same as the very first: there is a thunderclap, and the Prisoner comes speeding towards us in his hand-built Lotus. He is caught in the circle: an eternal cycle of rebellion, leading nowhere, and certainly not upwards. He is still a prisoner—not of the Village or of society, but of his own ego.

Appendix: What About Rover?

The one thing everyone seems to remember about *The Prisoner* is Rover. Mention the series to people over 40, and they are likely to say "Is that the one where he's chased around by the big white balloon?" Indeed, Rover is one of the most curious, frightening, and unforgettable aspects of the series. Despite his claim (in "Free for All") that he is afraid of nothing, No. 6 is *clearly* frightened by Rover. Here are some of the odd facts about this strange beast/machine:

1. It is first seen in "Arrival" as a tiny white ball, bobbing on a jet of water at the top of a fountain. It then expands into the size of a weather balloon (which is apparently what the prop man used).
2. It roars.
3. It can stun (several episodes) or kill ("Schizoid Man"). How it does this is not clear, but it involves covering the victim's face.
4. It can understand language ("Schizoid Man").
5. It can divide into small balls in order to move unconscious victims ("Chimes of Big Ben" and "Free for All").
6. It has some connection with the "lava" inside the lava lamps seen throughout the Village.
7. It seems to "live" on the ocean floor, where it is apparently part of a larger body of "goop." When "activated" (by a flick of a switch on No. 2's desk) it separates itself from this goop and rises to the surface.
8. It can move at high speeds.

Now, some of the above suggests that Rover is a living thing—but other things suggest that it is a machine (in "Schizoid Man" No. 2 commands, "Deactivate Rover immediately!"). That it has a mind of its own was implied in the original "Arrival" script, in which Rover is a sort of windowless hovercraft with a police light on top. "Who drives it?" No. 6 was to have said. "*Drives* it?" No. 2 was to have replied, incredulous.

What does Rover mean, if anything? Here there is a danger, for making Rover a balloon was a last-minute inspiration. The original Rover machine—just described—sank in the ocean during filming. But over time, the new form of Rover must have acquired some significance in the minds of McGoohan and the other writers, and so we can ask about its "meaning" nonetheless.

My suggestion is that Rover is supposed to be a hybrid animal-machine. It represents the mysterious, amorphous, chthonic, primal, uncanny element in nature, which modern man tries to factor out, to deny, or to control. It is what Sartre calls "the viscous." But man cannot fully tame the chthonic. Rover's imprisonment in the lava lamp represents man's attempt to do this. Rover's killing "Curtis" in "Schizoid Man" represents man's failure to do so. Even the masters of the Village are afraid of their "machine." No. 6's fear-reaction when confronted by Rover has a special quality: he is reacting to the terrible, the uncanny. When not doing man's bidding, Rover sinks to the bottom of the ocean, where it reunites with a much vaster "viscous," the parameters of which we do not see—suggesting our inability to *comprehend* the chthonic. It is our confrontation with the uncanny that is often our first confrontation with something that transcends human knowledge and power. Thoughtful people reflect on this, and eventually turn their gaze upwards.[4]

---

[4] After writing the above, I purchased a lava lamp to celebrate the completion of this essay. The lamp came with a card from the manufacturer, which concluded with the following statement: "The Lava brand is a philosophy. It stems from the primordial ooze that once ruled our world [and] has now been captured in perpetual motion in our Lava brand wax. . . . The Lava motion lamp is pre-historic and post-modern."

THE SPIRITUAL JOURNEY OF ALEJANDRO JODOROWSKY*

1. INTRODUCTION

Alejandro Jodorowsky is known to English-speaking audiences as the director and star of the cult film *El Topo* (1970). His other films (of which there are only a few) are lesser known, and his work outside of film is hardly known at all in America. But Jodorowsky is also a stage director, composer, psychotherapist, mime, and author. His books deal with the tarot and other matters mystical, and he has also published some thirty graphic novels.

Born in Chile, to parents of Jewish extraction, he lived and worked for many years in Mexico where he studied under a Japanese Zen master. He now makes his home in France, where he stages elaborate psychodramas and offers free tarot readings. In short, Jodorowsky seems impossible to categorize.

But there is a common thread running throughout his life and work, and that thread is a spiritual quest. Jodorowsky might, therefore, plausibly be described as a lover of wisdom, less plausibly as a "mystic." All that Jodorowsky does—even the comic books and the mime—can be understood as playing a role in this quest. This is a man seeking enlightenment not through religion or philosophy, but primarily through art. As anyone knows who has met him or seen him interviewed, this is also a man who is wonderfully, hilariously strange—and wise.

The Spiritual Journey of Alejandro Jodorowsky (a translation of *Mu: Le maître et les magiciennes*)[1] is an autobiography of sorts, though of a strangely impersonal sort. Details about Jodo-

---

*This essay was originally written for *TYR: Myth—Culture—Tradition*, vol. 4, ed. Joshua Buckley and Michael Moynihan, but it has not yet appeared in print.

[1] Alejandro Jodorowsky, *The Spiritual Journey of Alejandro Jodorowsky* (Rochester Vt.: Inner Traditions, 2008)

rowsky's work and personal life (his wife and many children are scarcely mentioned at all) are included only insofar as they are relevant to explaining a further step in the quest. These steps are a series of alliances with strong, charismatic women. (What the wife thought of this is not recorded.) However, the most powerful influence—and the catalyst for these alliances—is a man: the Zen master Ejo Takata.

Jodorowsky frankly admits that his spiritual quest is motivated, at some level, by a search for a father figure. His description of his childhood is pitiful: unloved by a mother who never wanted him, and tormented by a brutal father. Jodorowsky's search for wisdom is a search for love, and for benevolent, order-giving authority; for the feminine and the masculine. When Jodorowsky reflects on this, he emphasizes the search for the father figure: but this search continually leads him back to the mother. In fact, early on in the book the father figure Ejo literally "rejects" him and hands him off to a woman, the surrealist painter Leonora Carrington. This is providence at work, for Jodorowsky's root problem is not so much with the father as it is with the mother: his strongest desire is to be loved and accepted. This is not the sort of love and acceptance sought by the people one finds on Craigslist, however. What Jodorowsky seeks is the love and acceptance of the universe: to know that he *belongs to the universe* and that, in a sense, the universe belongs to him.

Now, all of the above seems as if it constitutes the makings of a psychoanalytical interpretation of Jodorowsky's quest—and, indeed, the makings of a psychoanalytical interpretation of mystical questing itself. And all such interpretations are deflationary. In other words, they all tend to wind up claiming that "The mystical quest is *nothing more than* . . ." The idea is to debunk, to demystify. But such a move is a *non-sequitur*. Jodorowsky's spiritual quest is *not* the search for a father or mother figure: instead, the search for the father or mother figure is what catalyzed his spiritual quest.

Jodorowsky did not seek, as others with similar backgrounds almost always do, to heal himself through sex or serial love relationships. Instead, he was launched on a spiritual quest. Why? Because he has an exceptional, brilliant, and strange mind. No other explanation is possible. Had Jodorowsky been born with a conventional mind, to a conventional family — had he received an abundance of love and acceptance and attention, he would not have embarked on his spiritual journey. It is very often the case that what pushes us on to great things is precisely some lack or absence in us or in our lives. But this does not mean that all our achievements are *nothing other* than a reaction to that lack. Parsifal left home on what eventually became the Grail Quest no doubt partly out of a desire to get away from his mother. That does not mean, however, that the Grail Quest can plausibly be understood as matricide.

2. Ejo Takata

In the Prologue to the book, Jodorowsky naïvely tells Ejo that he has achieved the state of "empty mind, empty heart." Ejo bursts into laughter at this and tells him "Empty mind, *full* heart: that is how it should be." Jodorowsky comes to accept this correction, realizing its wisdom. And it effectively summarizes exactly what he seeks, and finds by book's end. Ejo is saying that he must silence his mind, which acts as an obstruction to Jodorowsky's efforts to understand himself and the world. The intellect abstracts from life in forming its theories, and we come to live, for all intents and purposes, within theories rather than within the world. In other words, the intellect abstracts from experience — and the result is that *we* wind up becoming abstracted ourselves: removed from life and from the present. To combat this, we must "empty our minds."

To a rationalist (and virtually everyone in the modern world is a rationalist) this sounds like a prescription for stupidity and, if accepted on a mass scale, chaos. The assumption here is that there is nothing else in us that can provide guidance other than the intellect. (This is the personal, psychological equivalent of the hubristic modern view of history: before modern scientific rationalism came on the scene there was nothing to guide humanity other than woolly superstition.) The root assumption of Zen (which derives, in fact, from Taoism) is that when the mind is silent, the voice of the heart speaks: the voice of the sentiments and instincts. Pre-rational, pre-scientific human beings did not appear on the earth bereft of any means to guide their actions. Like every other animal we came equipped with innate drives and instincts which, if heeded, promote survival and flourishing. There is, in short, a "wisdom of the body." And much of Jodorowsky's spiritual journey is an attempt to silence the mind so that the body may speak.

Jodorowsky's spiritual quest consists essentially of two aspects. With Ejo, he attempts to break down the intellect; to tame it or silence it. With the women, he attempts to break down "emotional armor" in order get in touch with the body's wisdom. This latter part of the journey is fundamentally Tantric in character. A great deal of the book is devoted to Jodorowsky's relationship with Ejo, and while this makes a touching and sometimes profound "buddy story" it is also often tedious.

Ejo uses the Rinzai Zen method of the *koan* to try and help the intellectual Jodorowsky "learn to die." A *koan* is a question to which no rational answer can be given. The most famous *koan* is "What is the sound of one hand clapping?" In Rinzai monasteries, students would be given *koans* by their masters, and would try to answer them. Any attempt to answer them in straightforward, logical terms would be rejected (for, indeed, such an answer is really impossible).

The point of the exercise is to get students to let go of the intellect entirely and to open to an experience of the world itself, free of the entanglements of theory and language. Such an experience is called *satori*. The masters would look for some genuine sign that a student has advanced to this stage — and often it might consist in a completely illogical, but strangely "appropriate" response to the logically insoluble *koan*.

It is obvious that Jodorowsky delights in *koans*, and much of the book is taken up with them. It is this material that becomes, after awhile, tedious and may seem largely pointless to the reader. For how is the *koan* technique supposed to work if one already knows the "trick"? I may very well be missing something here, but if one already knows that the point of the *koan* is to push us beyond intellectual understanding, what is the point in trying to "answer" a *koan*? If it is impossible to give a *logical* answer to a *koan*, then won't just about any answer do? Nevertheless, Jodorowsky and Ejo proceed as if they believe there are "correct answers" to *koans* (we also are told about the existence of a book which contains the "correct answers" to all the classic *koans*). The following exchange is typical:

> "It never begins and it never ends. What is it?"
> "I am what I am!"
> "How does the intellectual learn to die?"
> "He changes all his words into a black dog that follows him around!"
> "Do the shadows of the pines depend on the moonlight?"
> "Pine roots have no shadow!"
> "Is the Buddha old?"
> "As old as I am!"
> "What do you do when it cannot be done?"
> "I let it be done!"
> "Where will you go after death?"
> "The stones of the road neither come nor go!"
> "If a woman advances on the path, is she your older or younger sister?"
> "She is a woman walking!"
> "When the path is covered with snow, is it white?"
> "When it is white, it is white. When it is not white, it is not white."

Reading this, I was reminded of the following exchange between Batman and Robin from the old, 1960s *Batman* series. The Dynamic Duo are attempting to solve some conundrums left for them by the sinister Riddler:

> *Batman*: Robin, listen to these riddles. Tell me if you interpret them as I do. One: What has yellow skin and writes?
> *Robin*: A ballpoint banana!

> *Batman*: Right! Two: What people are always in a hurry?
> *Robin*: Rushing people? . . . Russians!
> *Batman*: Right again. Now, what would you say they mean?
> *Robin*: Banana . . . Russian? I've got! Someone Russian is going to slip on a banana peel and break their neck!
> *Batman*: Precisely, Robin. The only possible meaning.[2]

Robin's "solutions" to the Riddler's riddles are about as arbitrary as Jodorowsky's "solutions" to Ejo's *koans*. This leaves us with a problem: if we are wise to the Zen trick, how then do we kill the intellect? I myself studied briefly with a Zen master and gave up precisely because of this problem. When my American Zen master was first given a *koan* by his Japanese master, he told me he responded with a fully-worked out speech about silencing the intellect and listening to the heart, etc. His master responded (in broken English): "Your idea perfect. *But is only idea.*" In other words, you've got the "Zen theory" but you have not *realized* its truth in your life. How do we go about doing that? There can be no single answer here, applicable to everyone. The *koan* gimmick worked for Jodorowsky, and that is fine. It may, however, leave the reader cold.

Ejo Takata was born in Kobe, Japan in 1928 and began his study of Zen at the age of nine in the monastery at Horyuji. In 1967 he emigrated to the United States and wound up in California, where he was quickly adopted as a guru by some hippies. It took Ejo only a couple of days to peg these people as narcissistic phonies—and soon he had hitchhiked his way to Mexico. Some time later he met Jodorowsky, also a stranger in a strange land, who promptly involved him in his all-nude stage production of Nietzsche's *Zarathustra*. (Ejo appeared on stage—fully clothed—meditating throughout the entire production.) As mentioned already, early on in the tale Ejo "expels" Jodorowsky, telling him, "You think that you can only

---

[2] Actually, this is from the *Batman* movie (Twentieth Century Fox, 1966), written by Lorenzo Semple, Jr., directed by Leslie H. Martinson, and starring Adam West and Burt Ward as Batman and Robin.

learn from men. The archetype of the cosmic father dominates your actions." And he sends him to "study" with Leonora Carrington, saying "Let her give you the inner woman who is so lacking in you."

3. LEONORA & THE TIGRESS

On Jodorowsky's first meeting with Leonora she greets him with the words, "Are you the mime that the Japanese sent to us?" And she rechristens him "Sebastian." Jodorowsky's apprenticeship consists largely in being under foot in Leonora's household, where he becomes absorbed in the affairs of her strange family (her husband Chiki wears a beret that he never removes). Surrealist hilarity ensues as Leonora paints and utters her own *koans*, to the bafflement of Jodorowsky:

> Everything lives because of my vital fluid. I wake up when you sleep. If I stand up, they bury you. Who am I? ... We shall transform ourselves suddenly into two dark, dashing Venezuelan men drinking tea in an aquarium. Why? ... A red owl looks at me. In my belly, a drop of mercury forms. What does it mean? ... A transparent egg that emits rays like the great constellations is a body, but it is also a box. Of what? ... Only bitter laments will enable us to cry a tear. Is this tear an ant?

Jodorowsky achieves an epiphany when Leonora unveils her portrait of the Mexican film actress Maria Felix, at a party held at the actress's home. Felix stares transfixed at her own image then scans the room. All eyes are upon her, worshipping her, including those of her dog, Eldra. "Even the dog desires me!" she cries in a moment of supreme self-affirmation. Jodorowsky realizes that he has never truly felt desired — by anyone or anything. "I had always lived with the feeling that nothing really belonged to me; in order for the world to belong to us, we must believe that the world desires us. Only that which desires us can be ours." He begins to work on himself: to try to arrive — somehow — at the realization that the world desires his existence.

Jodorowsky soon discovers that he is desired by one Irma Serrano, a cabaret actress popularly known as "The Tigress." Rumored to be the mistress of Mexico's president, Jodorowsky portrays the Tigress as the ball-busting female she-devil from hell. She has had multiple plastic surgeries to reshape her breasts, buttocks, cheeks, chin, lips, and other parts. Her body is cold and hard to the touch. The surgical filling in her calves alone weighs four pounds. Jodorowsky witnesses her lathering black dye onto the long hairs on her legs: "I want them to see that I'm not another Indian but the descendent of Spaniards!"

On their first meeting, the Tigress and Jodorowsky imbibe vast quantities of mescal. Through an alcoholic haze, Jodorowsky fires off a *koan*: "Which is the way?" Refreshingly, she responds, "I'm not a railroad track." Eventually they wind up in bed, where the Tigress orders Jodorowsky to enter her. The mescal and the Tigress's castrating, she-devil persona have shriveled Jodorowsky's penis down to the size of a cashew. And to top it off she declares, "If you don't get it up, I'll tell the journalists, and all of Mexico will know that you are impotent." Nevertheless, after "a short but agonizing moment," Jodorowsky succeeds in getting hard. ("I am very virile," he has confessed in interviews.) But the sexless, marble-bodied Tigress doesn't desire an orgasm. The act of penetration is enough: Jodorowsky has passed the test.

The Tigress declares that the two of them will stage a sensational new production of *Lucrezia Borgia* in which she, naturally, will play the title role—and they hatch an elaborate plan to generate publicity. Together, the Tigress and Jodorowsky attend a convocation of Mexico's journalists, in the middle of which, by prearrangement, Jodorowsky's wife Valerie bursts in wearing a phony plaster cast on her leg. She accuses Jodorowsky of having an affair with the Tigress—an accusation Jodorowsky appears to confirm by his behavior towards both women. (This is, by the way, about the only time Jodorowsky's wife is mentioned in the book.)

The event generates a scandal and tremendous advance publicity for *Lucrezia Borgia*. But on the eve of the premiere it is apparent that the Tigress has still not learned her lines. Jodorowsky and the other performers are furious, and they walk out and abandon her. The Tigress is hardly fazed by this at all, however. She simply stages her own production of *Lucrezia Borgia* across town, in which she appears nude, stalking around on the stage repeating lines fed to her by an off-stage prompter. This production runs successfully for two years. Meanwhile, Jodorowsky remounts his own production of *Lucrezia Borgia* with a different, better, fully-clothed actress. It runs for four months.

The episode with the Tigress is fascinating—but it is hard to discern what, if anything, he learns from her, and how she represents a stage on Jodorowsky's spiritual journey.

4. Doña Magdalena & the End of Zen

Jodorowsky's next "spiritual bride" is Doña Magdalena, who rescues him from a gang of street urchins bent on raping him in an alley. "Leave him alone! He belongs to me!" she cries, and they pull their pants up and scatter. Then, addressing herself to the terrified Jodorowsky she advises, "Don't give so much importance to being penetrated." Magdalena takes Jodorowsky back to her home, where she strips and then goes to work on his body—spending hours scraping it with a blunt knife and massaging his organs. Strangely enough, this turns out to be one of the most profound and interesting parts of the book. She tells Jodorowsky:

> If bones are beings, then joints are bridges across which time must pass. Every one of your ages continues to live in you. Infancy is hidden in your feet. If you leave your baby stuck there, he will impede your walk, dragging you into a memory that is both cradle and prison, cutting you off from the future and trapping you in a demand that cannot give or act.

Jodorowsky comes to realize the ways in which painful memories—memories, for example, of abuse by his parents—have become locked in his body, especially his muscles. Magdalena's work, like that of a Reichian therapist, is to help his body to free itself of this "armoring."

The theories that guide Magdalena's practice are an eclectic combination of ideas borrowed from here and there. Discussing the spinal column she states that it culminates in the cranium, "in ten thousand petals opening to the luminous energy pouring down from the cosmos." Magdalena's theories are, in essence, a wedding of Reich and Kundalini. They are the sacralization of the Reichian body. Liberation will consist in a freeing of the body—but this is a sacred path; a path to *feeling* (not thinking) one's unity with the source.

At one point, Magdalena tells Jodorowsky that the contractions of the muscles "give you the sense of existing." This is an important and profound idea. I had always thought that one of the benefits of yoga was to help us "get in touch with the body." But after two years of practicing it, it occurred to me that the point of yoga was actually to eliminate the feeling of *having* a body at all.

We speak, of course, of "having a body" partly due to the way our language works, but also because we are often so uncomfortable in our skin that it does indeed feel like the body is an other. We tense our muscles, grind our teeth, walk and sit hunched over, feel tension in the pit of the stomach, or in the form of a headache. Babies are born without any of this. These problems develop as a result of negative life experiences—and are particularly acute in modern people. Hatha yoga is a technique that leads to bodily mastery, and involves the development of flexibility and control. It helps us to overcome the patterns of physical "armoring" that have become fixed in us. And the net result is that one gradually overcomes the sense of opposition between the self and the body. Or, to put it a different way, *one becomes one's body*.

Predictably, the highlight of Jodorowsky's encounter with Magdalena is when she goes to work on his genitals. As I have said before, Jodorowsky's spiritual journey is a Tantric one. Magdalena introduces this portion of her "therapy" with the following observations about the difference between the male and female sex organs: "For us women, our internal sex is visceral. But for you men, this viscera has become an organ. We feel our vulva as a creative center, whereas you feel your phallus as a sort of companion, a pleasurable tool, and you separate it from your emotional center. Now lie down, I am going to show you the roots of your sex."

I will not attempt to describe what happens next. Suffice it to say that as Magdalena manipulates Jodorowsky's organs, she discourses on the nature of the sexual center and its relationship to the rest of the body, and to the body's subtle centers, and to the cosmos. Again, her remarks betray the influence of Kundalini, mixed together with elements of Taoist theory about the circulation of *chi*.

Throughout this section, one wonders just how much Jodorowsky is embellishing the words of Magdalena. At one point, for example, he says that "She awakened my vital energy by causing my navel (which she called Eden) to sprout four intangible rivers branching into thirteen centers in my body, which she called temples." Indeed, one wonders throughout the book about the words Jodorowsky attributes to others, and the degree to which he has exercised a certain license in setting forth his recollections. But ultimately this is a completely unimportant issue. What matters here are the ideas themselves — whatever their source may be — and their relevance to our own lives.

The final stage of Magdalena's therapy consists in her getting down on her hands and knees and washing Jodorowsky's shadow — cast on the floor behind him — with lavender-scented soap and water. At this point I laughed out loud. I don't feel, however, that this reaction in any way diminishes my fundamental conviction that this is a book of great profundity. It just also happens to be extremely funny (in the same way that Jodorowsky's films are both profound and funny). I am even prepared to believe that there may be something to shadow washing. Furthermore, that these people were able to do all of this apparently without being drunk or stoned should be an inspiration to us all.

In any case, the experience with Magdalena lasts forty days. At its conclusion, Jodorowsky walks down the street: "I no longer felt that the weight of my body was a burden. Instead, it was a link of union with this mirage I called reality. Every step was a caress, every breath of air was a blessing. These sensations were so surprising that I felt as if I were living in a new body and a new mind." His transformed state is an expression precisely of that which I was trying to get at earlier with my remarks about overcoming the feeling of "having" a body, or of becoming one's body.

There follows a new episode with Ejo, which constitutes the climax of Jodorowsky's dalliance with Zen. Realizing that Jodorowsky is going through a spiritual crisis, Ejo decides on a rather dangerous measure: *rohatsu*. This is the Zen Buddhist equivalent of the U.S. Marine "Hell Week": constant meditation for seven days, with only very short breaks for sleep and eating. It is a practice regularly carried out in Japanese Zen monasteries. One can easily imagine, however, that in some individuals it could precipitate a psychotic break. The point does, in fact, seem to be to bring about a crisis of sorts — and this is exactly what occurs in the case of Jodorowsky.

At one point, unable to take it anymore Jodorowsky leaps up and leaves Ejo sitting *zazen*. He rushes out into the night, wanting to be around ordinary people (not monks), wanting to be humdrum (not mystical). He dives into a nightclub, only to find himself feeling "like an extraterrestrial who, after a long interstellar voyage, arrives in a prison. The dancers seemed like galley slaves, going through their motions; smoking their tobacco and marijuana; ingesting their alcohol, cocaine, and pills; aware of only this tiny sliver of time and space."

Jodorowsky is in the uncomfortable position of all lovers of wisdom who have advanced quite a way down the path. He feels utterly alienated from ordinary people, almost seeing them as if they were a different species. Yet in a way, oddly, he yearns to be one of them again — to be "ordinary" and uncomplicated. Many intellectuals live in this tension — feeling that they have somehow transcended ordinary life, yet halfway yearning to be ignorant again. They may even envy ordinary people, seeing them as more connected to the world.

The truth, however, is that most ordinary people are just as disconnected from the world, in their own way, as the intellectuals are. The meagerness of their knowledge, and the narrow range of options of which they are aware impoverishes their experience. Their ability to truly appreciate life is roughly commensurate with their understanding of it. The tension the intellectual experiences between enlightenment and life is actually a dialectic which ought to resolve itself in the following realization: that enlightenment is not an abandonment of ordinary life but actually an indescribably intense experience of it. The wise man is not otherworldly but profoundly this-worldly. And one reaches this state—I believe—through a radical acceptance of the *facticity* of the world, acceptance of that which is irreducibly other and unchosen. (This is what it means to "annihilate the ego.") True mastery of life is possible only in one who has recognized the impossibility of mastery.

Jodorowsky returns to the makeshift *zendo*. He has had his moment of clarity:

> I realized that I was alive for a duration of time that was infinitesimal within the eternity of the cosmos, and what a privilege, a gift, and a miracle this life was. This instant of my existence was the same instant in which the stars were dancing, in which the infinite and finite were united, in which were united the here and the beyond, the perfume of the air and the memory within all matter, the gods of imagination and unimaginable energy, lights and abysses, colors and blindness, the humble sensitivity of my skin and the ferocity of my fists—but also the miserable peasants, the soldiers, the imbecilic fat man, the passengers in the train chattering like monkeys, the cloud of dust following the bus: all of this was a remedy if I accepted it as such so that it was transformed by my vision. The world is what it is: a remedy instead of the poison I had believed it to be.

5. Reyna the Robot

Enter Reyna D'Assia, the daughter of the mystic G. I. Gurdjieff. Jodorowsky's chapter on Reyna is, in many ways, the highpoint of the book. It is certainly the Tantric highpoint and comes quite close in many places to being pornographic. It is also probably the best brief account — and critique — of the ideas of Gurdjieff that I have ever come across. Jodorowsky meets Reyna in Mexico City after a screening of El Topo. She introduces herself to him as the daughter of Gurdjieff. Jodorowsky is dressed as the character he plays in the film — in a black leather cowboy outfit. Together, they take a taxi to her hotel, necking the entire way. In her room, she asks him to penetrate her, still dressed as El Topo (the Mole). Jodorowsky does so, but before he can start thrusting, Reyna's vagina begins vibrating and convulsing around his penis. "A few seconds later, my semen flooded her. I had three successive ejaculations."

Reyna takes full advantage of the refractory period to teach Jodorowsky a few things. (In fact, she never stops talking.) She explains that she learned these sexual techniques from her mother, who was taught them by Gurdjieff. "Gurdjieff taught my mother to awaken and develop her soul by developing a living vagina." Since Reyna claims to have been the product of a brief encounter between Gurdjieff and her mother, one wonders just how quickly such sexual skills can be imparted. Credulity is strained further when Jodorowsky describes Reyna squatting down and absorbing several olives, which she then fires from her vagina with such force that they ricochet off the ceiling. Reyna blows out a candle using her vagina — which seems a bit anticlimactic after the olives. But she manages to top that by inserting a thread into her vagina and — what else? — knotting it.

Finally, Reyna's vagina sings with a voice Jodorowsky likens to "the song of whales," and to the sirens of Homer's *Odyssey*. This reduces him to tears. Reyna comments: "In the most ancient times, women chanted lullabies with their vulvas to make their babies sleep, but as this art became lost and forgotten, children ceased to feel they were loved. An unconscious anxiety settled in the souls of human beings. That whimpering of yours expresses the pain of having a mother with a mute vagina, but we are going to resolve that."

Central to Gurdjieff's mysticism is the idea that for much of our lives we live under the control of "the robot," by which he means that we are fundamentally unconscious. We spend most of our waking lives unconscious — acting automatically. A simple example would be driving. How often have we driven someplace we frequently go, and literally been unable to remember driving there? Clearly, we had to have been "conscious" in some fashion, else we could not have negotiated the traffic. Yet, we acted robotically. Our minds, our self-awareness were, in a more important way, shut off. The trouble is that most people go through their entire lives like this. The robot even takes over in sex. The goal of Gurdjieff's system is to "remember the self," and to put the robot out of commission. In this there is, however, a great irony — as anyone knows who has ever had contact with Gurdjieffians. These people are *extremely* robotic. Everyone I have ever known who was into Gurdjieff seemed tightly controlled, humorless, obtuse, and utterly lacking in spontaneity.

What happens next in Jodorowsky's account is a concrete illustration of this irony: machine-like, Reyna proceeds to perform a number of physical and mental "tricks":

> Standing on her left leg, Reyna D'Assia traced a figure eight in the air continuously with her right leg. Meanwhile, her left hand continuously traced a square and her right hand a triangle. All the while, she recited a seemingly chaotic succession of numbers.... "Listen carefully: $2 \times 8 = 16$. If I add the 1 and 6, I get 7, you understand? No? Another example: $8 \times 12 = 96$ and $9 + 6 = 15$ and $1 + 5 = 6$. Therefore $8 \times 12 = 6$."

And on and on and on. Further tricks are performed until she begins to seem to Jodorowsky like a "sinister machine." Finally he grabs Reyna and essentially tells her this. In true Gurdjieffian fashion, she dismisses him as a poor fool who, if only he could advance a little further on the evolutionary scale, would be able to understand the serious purpose of these exercises. They quarrel over this until Jodorowsky puts an end to it like a true Tantrika: "Shut up and let's fuck again!"

Reyna's philosophy, like Gurdjieff's, is a mixture of sense

and nonsense. At one point she tells Jodorowsky, "you have been trying to transcend the body, whereas you should be submerging yourself within it to become so small that you arrive finally at that inner offering that is your birthright—that indefinable diamond that we call 'soul' but which is beyond words." This is sound advice and makes Reyna seem like a Tantrika herself. But she is deeply confused. In spite of this assertion about submerging oneself within the body, and in spite of her remarkable sexual skills, Reyna is witheringly cerebral. As D. H. Lawrence might say, she's got her sex—and her Tantra—in her head. Jodorowsky confronts her with this:

> The pain you have undergone in order to live in accord with what you believe to be your realization is enormous. Yet how can you really live in peace while making such strenuous efforts? Where is everyday tranquility in all this? The simple pleasure of eating a piece of bread next to a river, of doing nothing, or walking in the street, smelling the wet asphalt after a rain, watching a flock of sparrows fly without wondering where they're going? What about simple weeping in grief as we scatter the ashes of a loved one in a beautiful landscape, or speaking of ordinary, unimportant things with a child, an old woman, or a madman . . . ?

"What bad taste!" Reyna responds, and then—predictably—she suggests that he is suffering from herd mentality. The goal of the spiritual quest is evolution to *a higher form of consciousness*—and the universe itself is evolving toward a state of "pure thinking." In short, the Gurdjieffian philosophy is yet another progressivist ideology promising some future state of perfection as the only thing which can make the here and now meaningful. The adherents of such ideologies—whether they are Marxists, Christians, Ken Wilburites, Aurobindonians, Gurdjieffians, Liberal Democrats, Neoconservatives, or whatever—have one thing in common: a disconnection from the present, from the body, and from nature. The present state of the culture and of humanity is undeniably rotten, and it is perfectly natural to hope that the future may bring something better. But these ideologies, in one way or another, denigrate the pursuit of happiness in the here-and-now, on earth — and in the process denigrate pleasure and beauty. Furthermore, because they insist on the perfectibility of man they must deny any version of biological determinism, no matter how mild. Hence the disconnection from, and often outright hatred of, the body.

Jodorowsky isn't buying any of this. Nevertheless, he agrees to travel with Reyna to Monte Alban, a six-thousand-foot mountain flattened by the Zapotecs for ritual purposes. On the way, in the back seat of their chauffeur-driven car, Reyna shows Jodorowsky "how the larynx can perform astonishing movements if it is vibrated simultaneously with the aid of certain Tibetan mantras." At the Zapotec pyramid, Reyna attempts to free a stone in order to cause the pyramid to "produce life." Jodorowsky has now had enough. He finds a flower growing between the stones and cries out to her: "You see, the pyramid doesn't need your help in order to produce life.... Reyna, I remain convinced that you give too much importance to effort. Stop carrying so many heavy stones! Allow something to be born in you that is not a product of your will..." She is livid with anger and throws the stone at Jodorowsky's head, narrowly missing him. Then, incredibly, Reyna undergoes a transformation. She concedes Jodorowsky's point, wholly and completely. "I must find another way," she says.

The other way consists in visiting a sorcerer named Don Prudencio Garza, who lives several miles away, in the desert. Reyna and Jodorowsky go on foot to find Don Prudencio. When they do, the grizzled old man feeds Reyna mushrooms which are said to produce "real, physical death." If one is lucky, however, one can return transformed — having come back from a profound vision quest. Jodorowsky — who does not partake of the mushrooms — is ordered to remain absolutely silent, lest Reyna wake up as a demon and drink his blood. Don Prudencio feeds Jodorowsky some goat's milk laced with what turns out to be a sleeping potion. When Jodorowsky awakens, Reyna has returned from her inward journey. "I am the same yet not the same," she says. "The process unfolded in me as the sorcerer said it would: At first the mushrooms made me lose all sensation of my flesh and bones. I realized then that I had always lived in my body as if it were a prison. As I began to lose it, I felt an intense love and compassion for it." (It would have been safer to have taken Reyna to Doña Magdalena, who produced a similar effect in Jodorowsky, but Magdalena disappeared shortly after finishing her work on him.) Jodorowsky also learns that when Reyna returned to consciousness she found Don Prudencio raping her (no doubt this was the reason he gave Jodorowsky the sleeping draught).

A few years later, Jodorowsky receives a letter from Reyna D'Assia with a photograph of herself and her daughter. "I don't know whether her father is you or Don Prudencio," she writes.

6. Conclusion

The final episode of the book takes place a decade later. Jodorowsky has returned to Mexico to give a lecture at the University. Jodorowsky's visit occurs just two weeks after the death of his young son Teo in an accident. He is struggling to deal with this loss, in the midst of fulfilling his numerous commitments. And now he must lecture on "enlightenment" to a crowd of college students. To his surprise and joy, Jodorowsky finds Ejo in the audience, and they are now reunited. Later, Ejo consoles him with a single Spanish word: *duele* (it hurts). What more can be said?

The two men, however, are now greatly changed. Both are, in fact, ready to leave Zen behind. Ejo has realized that much of Zen practice is too rigid and formal, and has its origin in historical developments that are anything but spiritually motivated. Jodorowsky has filmed *The Holy Mountain* which ends with the realization that there are no "spiritual masters" and that the quest for them is folly. This abandonment of Zen may seem disappointing to some, but it should not be. After all, as they say, once one has reached the opposite shore it would be silly to pick up one's raft and continue to carry it around.

Has Jodorowsky (never mind Ejo) reached the other shore? Has he achieved Enlightenment? In order to answer this question, we have to have some idea of what Enlightenment is. In a 1994 interview Jodorowsky states, "All this Chinese, Japanese, and Tibetan stuff, it's all bollocks. Enlightenment doesn't exist. We are all enlightened, we just don't realize it. The great mystery is to be alive now. Nothing else is as important and incredible as being alive. It's an incredible mystery. What more do we need to look for?"[3]

As we have learned from Jodorowsky, Enlightenment (for lack of a better term) is certainly not a leaving behind of the body. And if we are embodied, and if we accept that, then we are finite and vulnerable. Hence Enlightenment, if it involves acceptance of the body, cannot be a state of invulnerability. Nor could Enlightenment be a state of all-seeing, all-knowing. The acceptance of the body and of finitude goes hand in hand with the acceptance of the state of not-knowing: an openness to the mystery of being. *And this is the basis of paganism, and of radical Traditionalism.*

Modernity is essentially a war against finitude or limitation of any kind. Modern people — openly or tacitly — reject the idea that there should be any limits on the mind's ability to understand or to improve upon nature, or themselves. They regard the cycles of nature and the cycles of life as something to be overcome. Why shouldn't youth last forever? Why can't we overcome death? Why can't we have babies in our seventies? Why can't we engineer better tomatoes? Why can't we spend more than we earn? Why can't both parents have careers? Why can't we have stable marriages and sleep with whomever we like? Why can't money buy happiness? (It might not have in the past, but things have changed, haven't they?) Why can't we enjoy all our consumer goods, and still be "green"? Why can't we have a cohesive society made up of people who share neither culture nor language? Why can't women be as masculine as men and men be feminine? Why can't Heather have two mommies?

We reject any suggestion that there may be necessities in life, meaning things that can only be one way, and not another. And

---

[3] From the 1994 documentary *The Jodorowsky Constellation*.

we especially deplore the idea of biological necessity—i.e., the idea that the body may limit us. Radical Traditionalism is, at root, a call to return to our ancestors' acceptance of finitude: their recognition that certain things are unchangeable, and that all attempts to change them lead to disaster. Paganism has the same root. "The gods" show themselves precisely in that which resists us. The gods are the mysterious facticities of life which stop us in our tracks because they are bigger than we are, and we are powerless against them. They are terrible, or beautiful, or both.

But how to return to the gods, or to get them to return to us? This is the question that nags radical Traditionalists and neo-pagans. How can we do this when all cultural forces are arrayed against us, and when we are all—if truth be told—children of modernity? Traditionalism teaches that we are living in the Kali Yuga, the Iron Age, the age of decline. In this time, the old ways seem to have lost their power. We are free to consult the runes and call to Odin. No Christians will burn us. But we do so fourteen floors up, as the air conditioner hums, and the Olestra gurgles in our innards. The earth, the water, the air, and our bodies have been developed, explored, cultivated, irradiated, and, generally, trashed.

In this age, the only honest path open to us is the *left hand path*: taking that which debases and corrupts lesser mortals and using it as a means to self-transformation. This is Tantra, and this is what Jodorowsky's book is about. What does it accomplish, exactly? *Empty mind, full heart.* The way back is not through mimicking the outer forms of the culture of our ancestors. It is through transforming our consciousness into some semblance of theirs. In other words, through taming the intellect and its tendency to fall into hubris; through silencing the mind and letting the wisdom of the body speak. As I said earlier, we did not spring upon this earth without any means to guide us, until modern rationalism came along. We came equipped with natural sentiments, instincts, and intuitions.[4] It

---

[4] Incidentally, there is nothing "sentimental" about natural sentiments. They include love of one's own—*not* universal love (which is

is these that must be recovered, for this is what it means to have a "full heart." It is from such "empty" minds and full hearts that Traditional culture sprang. Once we have achieved this—if, indeed, we can achieve it—will we reconstitute those same cultural forms? In outline yes, for they are perennial and natural; in detail, no.[5]

This is a path to be followed by individuals, without any assurances at all that they may be laying the ground for a new world, beyond the Kali Yuga. To achieve what I have described is to make of oneself an alien in this world, but a native of the next, or of the one that has passed away. It has nothing to do with "fighting for the future," for the future focus is one of the traps of modernity: believing that a future ideal state may confer meaning upon life in the present. No, the Tantric path is a leap of faith and a leap into the abyss: a radical embrace of uncertainty, mystery, and finitude—with no guarantees.

---

impossible)—and the sentiment of "us *vs.* them."

[5] The foregoing is not a rejection of neo-paganism. Our quest to return to the spiritual standpoint of our ancestors may include studying their beliefs and, in some cases, doing as they did. I merely mean that without a radical, internal transformation of consciousness, neo-paganism is a conceit. Of all the theorists involved with neo-paganism, it is Edred Thorsson who takes the most promising and philosophically sophisticated approach. Thorsson openly declares himself to be a practitioner of the left hand path, while at the same time attempting to reconstitute and revivify the pagan ways of his ancestors. Such a synthesis is possible in Thorsson's case because he takes Odin himself to have been a devotee of the left hand path. Thorsson's "Odinism," therefore, is not worship of Odin, but rather an attempt to achieve an "Odinic consciousness." The left hand path, obviously, cannot be practiced in the abstract, and must take concrete form as a specific *practice*. Thorsson draws his practice from the pagan Germanic tradition, augmented by elements drawn from modern left hand path teachings.

INDEX

A
Abraxas, 85
Adam Kadmon, 87–88
Alexander the Great, 73
Amon, 73
Anders, Richard, 140
Anu, 128
Aphrodite, 128
Apollo, 69
Apsu, 108, 128
Aquinas, St. Thomas, 12, 32
Arachne, 126
Aristotle, 49, 54 n45, 56, 72, 94, 99, 113, 127, 137, 139, 141
Asclepius, 73
Askr, 122, 125
Atman, 122, 126, 127
Audhumla, 106, 121–22
Austri, 122

B
Babbitt, George, 160
Batman, 176–77
Beatty, Ned, 155
Benoist, Alain de, vii–viii, 62–80
Bergman, Ingmar, 152
Bestla, 122
Boehme, Jacob, 94, 96, 98, 103, 104, 137, 146
Bolthorn, 122
Bond, James, 149, 152, 164
Borr, 122
Brahman, 84, 126
Buckley, Joshua, iii
Buri, 122

C
Caesar, Julius, 73
Campbell, Joseph, 60 n53
Carrington, Leonora, 173, 178
Cassirer, Ernst, vii, 40–44
Caviezel, James, 151 n2
Chamberlain, Houston Stewart, 140
Champetier, Charles, 78–79
Chaos, 128
Christ (Jesus), 66, 141, 168

D
Daedalus, 126
Danielou, Alain, iii, 82–84, 86, 129
D'Assia, Reyna, 184–89
Davidson, H. R. Ellis, 130
Dechend, Gabriele, 140, 146
Dilbert, 160
Dionysus, 82, 141
Diotima, 50
Drake, John, 149, 154
Dumézil, Georges, 78, 123, 124, 141

E
Ea, 128
Eckhart, Meister, 126, 142–43

Eisenhower, Dwight, 168
Eliade, Mircea, 45–46
Eliot, T. S., 149, 160
Elizabeth II, Queen of England, 53, 155
Elms, Albert, 152
Embla, 122, 125
Empedocles, 104
Erda, 139
Eros, 128
Evola, Baron Julius, iii, vii, ix, 1, 14, 87, 88, 89, 90, 91, 99, 101

F
Fafnir, 87
Felix, Maria, 178
Fellini, Federico, 152
Feuerbach, Ludwig, 2, 69
Fichte, J. G., 69
Flowers, Stephen E., 132, 134 n3, 140, 147
Flynt, Larry, 30 n9
Franklin, Benjamin, 25
Freud, Sigmund, 10, 64
Freya (Freyja), 3, 125
Freyr, 85

G
Gadamer, Hans-Georg, 117
Gaea, 101, 128, 131
Ganesha, 37
Garza, Don Prudencio, 188–89
Gibor, 135–36
Ginnungagap, 104, 106, 121
Goethe, J. W., 104
Gofann, 35 n12

Goibniu, 35 n12
Grade, Baron Lew, 150, 152
Grainer, Ron, 152
Guénon, René, iii, vii
Gurdjieff, G. I., 115, 184–86

H
Hatab, Lawrence J., 21 n1, 29, 48
Hegel, G. W. F., iii, 2, 9, 15, 69, 94, 95–96, 100, 103, 104, 106–107, 109, 114, 118, 119, 120, 124, 126, 135, 137, 143, 144
Heidegger, Martin, iii, v, vii, 4, 10, 22, 23, 26, 27, 52, 76, 77 n16, 80, 94, 117, 156
Hephaistos, 35 n12
Heraclitus, 23, 26, 89, 102
Hermes, 35 n12, 73
Hermes Trismegistus, 138
Hesiod, 22 n1, 128, 131
Himmler, Heinrich, viii, 132–34, 144
Hitchcock, Alfred, 152
Hobbes, Thomas, 13 n10
Hoenir, 93
Hölderlin, Friedrich, 135
Homer, 16, 185
Husserl, Edmund, 31 n10
Huxley, Aldous, 149

I
Icarus, 126
Imhotep, 73
Indra, 2

J

Jacobi, Friedrich Heinrich, 135
Jesus, 66, 141, 168
Jodorowsky, Alejandro, iv, ix, 172–92
Josephs, Wilfrid, 152
Jove, *see* Zeus
Joyce, James, 149
Julius Caesar, 73
Jung, C. G., 37, 85
Jupiter, *see* Zeus

K

Kafka, Franz, 149
Kanner, Alexis, 154
Kant, Immanuel, 22, 40, 56, 76
Kershaw, Kris, 84
Krishna, Gopi, 87
Kronos, 101, 128

L

Lao-Tzu, iii, 77
Lawrence, D. H., iii, 1, 25, 58, 149, 187
Leibniz, G. W., 94, 105
Lessing, Gotthold Ephraim, 135
Lewis, C. S., 160
Liebenfels, Lanz von, 132
Lincoln, Bruce, 121
List, Guido von, 142
Locke, John, 12
Loman, Willy, 160
London, Jack, 1
Lynch, David, 151

M

Magdalena, Doña, 180–83, 189
Maheshvara, *see* Shiva
Mannus, 130, 131
Manu, 121, 123, 127, 129, 131
Markstein, George, 150, 153
Martinson, Leslie H., 177 n2
Marx, Karl, 2, 12, 126
McGoohan, Patrick, 148–71
McKellen, Sir Ian, 151 n2
McKern, Leo, 154, 155, 167, 169
Mercury, 73
Midhgardr, 122
Mimir, 93, 125
Mithras, 73, 88
Motes, Hazel, 168
Moynihan, Michael, iii, 132, 147
Muscat, Angelo, 154
Muspellsheimr, 121

N

Ni, 136, 142
Nidhoggr, 87, 88
Niebuhr, H. Richard, 69
Nietzsche, Friedrich, 9, 10, 13 n9, 55, 57, 64–68, 70–72, 73, 78, 85, 94, 109, 141, 158, 159, 177
Niflheimr, 121
Nordhri, 122

O

Occator, 42
O'Connor, Flannery, 168

Odin (Óðinn, Wotan, etc.),
vi, viii–ix, 48, 69, 73, 75,
81–92, 94, 106, 107, 118,
122–31, 135, 140, 192 n5
Oetinger, F. C., 104, 137
Othil, 135–36
Otto, Rudolf, vi, 46 n27

P
Parmenides, 51, 52, 97
Parsifal, 174
Plato, vii, 10, 13, 47, 49–56,
70, 93, 94, 99, 101, 102,
103, 113, 118, 124, 125,
159
Plotinus, 136
Pound, Ezra, 149
Purusa, 122, 127

Q
Queen, the (Elizabeth II),
53, 155

R
Rand, Ayn, 8
Ratatoskr, 87, 88
Reich, Wilhelm, 181
Renan, Ernst, 72
Riddler, the, 176–77
Robin, 176–77
Rosenberg, Alfred, 140
Ru, 137
Rudra, ix, 82–86, 88, 89
Russell, Bertrand, 58

S
Sarasvati, 37–38
Sartre, Jean-Paul, 71

Savitri Devi, x
Schelling, F. W. J., 104, 135,
137
Schopenhauer, Arthur, 85
Schwenkfeld, Caspar, 137
Semple, Jr., Lorenzo, 177 n2
Serrano, Irma, 179–80
Shakespeare, William, 166
Shampan, Jack, 152
Shang Ti, see Ti
Shiva, ix, 82–91
Sigurd, 87–88
Simpson, Homer, 160
Socrates, 50–52, 54, 55 n47,
48, 56 n49
Sudhri, 122
Surtr, 121

T
Tacitus, 130–31
Takata, Ejo, 173, 174–78,
183–84, 189
Themis, 128
Thor, iv, 107
Thorsson, Edred, iii, viii,
46–49, 88, 96, 98, 100,
101, 105, 106, 109, 111,
112, 113, 114, 115, 122–
23, 125 n5, 129, 131 n10,
192 n5
Thoth, 73
Ti, 45
Tiamat, 128
Tiu, see Tyr
Tiwaz, see Tyr
Trotsky, Leon, 12
Troyer, Warner, 158, 163,
164, 165

Tuisco, 130–31
Tvástr, 35 n12
Tyr, 46, 131, 135–36

U

Ul, 136, 142
Uranus, 101, 127–28, 131
Urth, 117–18
Usener, Hermann, vii, 40–44

V

Vâyu, 36
Vé, 48, 94, 122–31, 135
Vestri, 122
Vico, Giambattista, 34
Vili, 48, 94, 122–31, 135
Visvakaram, 35 n12
Vulcan, 35 n12

W

Ward, Burt, 177 n2
Watts, Alan W., 24 n3, 31
Weisthor, see Wiligut, Karl Maria
West, Adam, 177 n2
Wiligut, Karl Maria, viii, 132–47
Williams-Ellis, Clough, 152
Woden, see Odin
Wodhanaz, see Odin
Wotan, see Odin
Wuotan, see Odin

Y

Yahweh, 69
Yeats, W. B., 149
Yggdrasil, 87–88, 102, 106
Yemo, see Ymir
Ymir, 100, 121–22, 123, 128–29, 130, 131
Young, Terrence, 149 n1

Z

Zarathustra, 57, 160
Zeus, 34, 69, 73

ABOUT THE AUTHOR

COLLIN CLEARY, Ph.D. is an independent scholar living in Sandpoint, Idaho. He is one of the founders of *TYR: Myth – Culture – Tradition*, the first volume of which he co-edited. A fellow of the Rune-Gild, his writings have appeared in *TYR* and *Rûna*. This is his first book.

www.ingramcontent.com/pod-product-compliance
Lightning Source LLC
Chambersburg PA
CBHW031317160426
43196CB00007B/575